OXFORD THEOLOGICAL MONOGRAPHS

OXFORD THEOLOGICAL MONOGRAPHS

Right Practical Reason

Aristotle, Action, and Prudence in Aquinas

DANIEL WESTBERG

CLARENDON PRESS · OXFORD

OXFORD

UNIVERSITY PRESS

Great Clarendon Street, Oxford OX2 6DP

Oxford University Press is a department of the University of Oxford
It furthers the University's objective of excellence in research, scholarship,
and education by publishing worldwide in

Oxford New York

Athens Auckland Bangkok Bogotá Buenos Aires Calcutta
Cape Town Chennai Dar es Salaam Delhi Florence Hong Kong Istanbul
Karachi Kuala Lumpur Madrid Melbourne Mexico City Mumbai
Nairobi Paris São Paulo Singapore Taipei Tokyo Toronto Warsaw

with associated companies in Berlin Ibadan

Oxford is a registered trade mark of Oxford University Press
in the UK and in certain other countries

Published in the United States
by Oxford University Press Inc., New York

ISBN 0-19-826731-2

Printed in Great Britain
on acid-free paper by
Biddles Short Run Books
King's Lynn

In loving memory of
Lynne Newbery
1950–1984

PREFACE

The part of this work which may lay some claim to originality, or at least to offer a solution of a stubborn difficulty in Thomist studies, is Part III, on the process of action. An interpretation is presented which is both faithful to the *Summa Theologiae* treatment, and avoids the cumbersome scheme of alternating actions of intellect and will, helping to clarify the account of practical reason. The necessary foundations and the implications for a revised view of prudence complete the structure of the book.

This study began as a thesis for the Faculty of Theology at Oxford University, for which I received a D.Phil. in 1989. I am indebted to the Rev Dr Oliver O'Donovan, Regius Professor of Moral Theology, for suggesting the topic of prudence and encouraging me to see its importance.

I am thankful to my supervisor, Fr Herbert McCabe, OP, for his wisdom, patience, hospitality, and grasp of St Thomas; and to my examiners, Professor John Mahoney, who made suggestions for revision, and Dr Antony Kenny, who also assisted in arrangements for publication.

Professors James Reilly of the Pontifical Institute of Mediaeval Studies, Toronto, and Russell Hittinger, of the Catholic University in America, and an anonymous reader of OUP, read the entire typescript (at different stages), and offered helpful suggestions for improvement. I am indebted to the careful copy-editing of Mr R. M. Ritter for avoiding a number of errors and ambiguities.

Others have encountered smaller portions of the work. Chapter 8 (in shortened form) was read and favourably received at the International Conference on Medieval Philosophy in Ottawa, August, 1992. Other chapters were read by Frs Joseph Owens and Walter Principe of the Pontifical Institute in Toronto; and Fr Lawrence Dewan, of the Collège Dominicain de philosophie et théologie, Ottawa, kindly helped me with the chapter on metaphysics. None of those named are responsible, of course, for remaining errors or infelicities.

In addition to what may be described as these 'formal causes', the production of the book involved many others in efficient and instrumental causality. For financial support I am grateful to the

Anglican Church of Canada and the Diocese of Toronto for study grants, and especially to a number of interested friends, mainly at the Church of the Messiah, Toronto, and in the villages of Beaverton and Cannington, Ontario. I will always be grateful to Jack and Irena Tippett who organized this group to support our move to England after the death of my wife Lynne.

At the stage of producing and revising, thanks are due to Diana Fong for her assistance in typing, and to Little Trinity Church, Toronto, for computer facilities. For assistance in the preparation of the index, their most direct involvement in the book, I am pleased to acknowledge the help of my children, Stephen, Mark, Timothy, and Elisabeth. My wife, Lisa, who listened and supported me from the very first insights to the completed book, deserves thanks greater than can be expressed here.

D.W.

Charlottesville, Virginia
Feast of St Thomas Aquinas
28 January 1993

CONTENTS

ABBREVIATIONS

WORKS OF AQUINAS

De anima	*Quaestiones disputatae de anima*
De caritate	*Quaestio disputata de caritate*
De malo	*Quaestiones disputatae de malo*
De veritate	*Quaestiones disputatae de veritate*
De virt. in comm.	*Quaestio disputata de virtutibus in communi*
De virt. card.	*Quaestio disputata de virtutibus cardinalibus*
In Boeth. de Trin.	*Expositio super librum Boethii De Trinitate*
In De Anima	*Sententia super De Anima*
In De div. nom.	*Expositio super Dionysium De divinis nominibus*
In Ethic.	*Sententia libri Ethicorum*
In Metaph.	*Sententia super Metaphysicam*
In Peri Herm.	*Sententia super Peri Hermeneias*
In Post Anal.	*Sententia super Posteriora Analytica*
In Sent.	*Scriptum super libros Sententiarum magistri Petri Lombardi*
SCG	*Summa contra gentiles*
ST	*Summa Theologiae*
Super Rom.	*Super Epistolam S. Pauli ad Romanos lecturi*

OTHER WORKS

AHDLMA	*Archives d'histoire doctrinale et littéraire du moyen âge*
BGPTM	Beiträge zur Geschichte der Philosophie und Theologie des Mittelalters
BT	*Bulletin Thomiste*
CCSL	*Corpus Christianorum, Series Latina*
CHLMP	*Cambridge History of Later Medieval Philosophy*, eds. N. Kretzmann, A. Kenny, and J. Pinborg (Cambridge, 1982).
DTC	*Dictionnaire de théologie catholique* (Paris, 1899-1953)
EE	Aristotle, *Ethica Eudemia*
EN	Aristotle, *Ethica Nicomachea*
FZPT	*Freiburger Zeitschrift für Philosophie und Theologie*
NCE	*New Catholic Encyclopedia* (New York, 1967-79)

PACPA	*Proceedings of the American Catholic Philosophical Association*
PG	*Patrologiae Cursus Completus, Series Graeca*, ed. J. Migne
PL	*Patrologiae Cursus Completus, Series Latina*, ed. J. Migne
RSPT	*Revue des sciences philosophiques et théologiques*
RT	*Revue Thomiste*
RTAM	*Recherches de théologie ancienne et médiévale*

PART I
The Character of Practical Reason

I

Introduction: Prudence and Moral Theology

TODAY prudence means caution and self-referential care. It seems to be used a lot in reference to handling money. You do not want to see your nest-egg squandered on risky investments, so the advertisement directs you to trust the company's prudent financial managers who will yield you a modest but assured return. Government leaders and officials appeal to 'prudential considerations', usually to decline taking action on a problem which is controversial or expensive, or to indicate that they have half an eye on the next election. This is often a miserable sort of prudence, self-protective, preferring safety to change, far removed from Thomistic prudence.

Thomas Aquinas defined *prudentia* as *recta ratio agibilium*, right reason in dealing with actions, or right practical reason. It is not some quality which is brought to deliberations when there is danger or a great deal at stake, as if the ordinary decisions of life didn't require much prudence. What he had in mind (and took from Aristotle) was a virtue or developed ability which enables an agent to make and carry out good decisions.

Why not use the term 'practical wisdom' instead of prudence? This might help to remove the emphasis on caution and carefulness. It has had some advocates, but there are at least two good reasons to prefer the traditional term, in spite of misunderstandings. First, to bring out the point that self-reference in moral thinking is not necessarily a bad thing. A person who tries to find work she enjoys, who spends time on family matters, hobbies, and friendships, is not only doing this for herself, family, and friends, but is also serving the common good. The dichotomy between self-fulfilment and altruism is a false one. The well-being of society is served by people pursuing individual goals.[1]

[1] There is a point of contact here between economic theory and Thomistic ethics in seeing harmony possible between private actions and public welfare (setting aside the distorting assumptions about the function of the market-place, and a view of individual autonomy and competitiveness foreign to Thomistic common good).

In Thomistic theory this is a fundamental point dealing with the basic conception of agency. Movement towards perfection or completion of a being's nature is described by Thomas as attraction to the good. Moral goodness is established in judgement about actions, but the motivation is attraction, not a sense of duty. Thus the term prudence signals a rejection of a Kantian view of morality based on duty and opposed to inclination.

Second, 'practical wisdom' does not fit well with the wide frame of reference in practical reason, which includes the completion of the action. Wisdom tends to refer to the insight and good judgement in perceiving the correct action, but this is to single out one aspect of prudence, missing out the executive function. Since this omission is a major weakness in most descriptions of practical reason, it is better to avoid a term which reinforces the conception that prudence is basically theoretical.

Practical reason, the focus of much recent interest in the ethics of Aristotle, involves thinking about what you want to do, and how to do it. It is thought applied to action. The primary difference between theoretic reason and practical reason is not between abstract and concrete, but in the purpose: theoretic reasoning is done in order to know something, practical reasoning in order to do something.

There is a process in practical reason, which includes having a goal or a desire to see something happen, deliberating the means to achieve this, deciding on a course of action, and taking the steps to carry it out. This could be fairly trivial, such as wanting to mend a broken fence, examining it, thinking about the tools and procedure, and then doing the job. Or it could be applied to a desire to be a lawyer, getting advice about the options for training, making plans and taking the first of a long series of steps toward the goal, such as saving money, studying for the entrance exams, and so on.

If you did not actually get around to mending the fence, or gave up on the idea of studying law, then your reasoning was not very practical after all, no matter how well thought out your plans were. That is because practical reason is not just a matter of deliberation and decision, but of execution above all.

The common view of prudence is one of good deliberation: thinking things through, looking at options, considering the circumstances, and discerning an appropriate course of action. But this is only an aspect of the flow of action, and not the critical one.

St Thomas's theory of practical reason and prudence was much broader:

The activity of reason goes through three stages. The first is deliberating the possibilities, in order to discover the means to the end; the second is making a judgement about the results of deliberation (so far this is like theoretic reason); but practical reason, which is connected to action, goes further: its third stage consists in executing the results of deliberation and decision. Since the last stage of action is the one closest to the whole point of practical reason, it is the principal act of practical reason and of prudence.[2]

Right practical reason means that the agent carries through from intention to finished action. If that does not happen (and if there is no exterior interference), then there is some fault in the practical reasoning, however excellent the deliberation.

Examples of prudent people are helpful in clarifying the nature of right practical reason. For Aristotle it was Pericles, model statesman. When St Thomas discussed different kinds of prudence he added military leadership and household management, because both are practically oriented. The general (not his theoreticians or advisers) is the example of prudence, because he combines strategy with execution. He must think well, react quickly, and be good at organizing, communicating, and supervising the execution of the plan.

The woman who somehow manages a home, family, and career is not usually in need of more theory or advice. Prudence in this demanding situation is more the ability to manage things, keep the schedule of events, juggle several things at once, respond to emergencies without panic, and maintain a level head in spite of fatigue or irritation.

THE FAILURE TO 'RESTORE' PRUDENCE TO THEOLOGY

Long before the Second Vatican Council forced Catholic theologians to reformulate the foundation and shape of Christian morality, presentations of Thomistic ethics made it clear that the approach of St Thomas was different from the prevailing conception of moral theology in the handbooks. Instead of an emphasis on precepts and obligation, the system of Thomas Aquinas was seen to be based on a metaphysics of the good, a model of human

---

[2] *ST* 2–II 47. 8.

action drawn from Aristotle, and the treatment of moral development as well as particular moral cases within the structure of the
virtues[3]. Specific attention to the importance of prudence was
directed by Garrigou-Lagrange, who noted its centrality in
Aquinas and its neglect in the manual tradition.[4]

The treatments of prudence in this century fall into several
patterns of interpretation: (1) associated with conscience; (2) directive of human action; (3) reformulated conscience; and (4) affective
orientation. The first is more characteristic of the period before
Vatican II, but these general lines continue in contemporary
thought.

1. Some neo-Thomists made attempts to reduce the legalism of
casuistic moral theology and to grant more autonomy to the agent
by associating prudence with conscience[5]. Although opposed by
others on the grounds that this made prudence too subjective, and
that right reason should be an objective, universal, and infallible
rule of morality,[6] this was a useful approach in recognizing the
need for each agent to be aware of his situation, to think and
decide in order to make responsible choices. In this period,
through the 1940s, a number of treatments appeared showing
awareness of the importance of prudence, with an emphasis on the
variability of particular situations and a need for maturity and
wisdom.[7] Instead of simply applying rules in a wooden kind of way, the
prudent person is to be aware of the nuances of a situation and enjoys
some flexibility in his need to make responsible decisions.

---

[3] An important influence was A.-D. Sertillanges, La Philosophie morale de saint
Thomas d'Aquin (Paris, 1916; 2nd edn., 1922, used in this book).
   [4] R. Garrigou-Lagrange, 'Du caractère métaphysique de la théologie morale
de saint Thomas: En particulier dans les rapports de la prudence et de la conscience', RT 8 (1925), 341–55; cf. id., 'La Prudence: Sa place dans l'organisme des
vertus', ibid. 9 (1926), 411–26.
   [5] V. Cathrein, 'Quo sensu secundum S. Thomam ratio sit regula actuum
humanorum?', Gregorianum, 5 (1924), 584–94.
   [6] L. Lehu, 'Si la "recta ratio" de s. Thomas signifie la conscience', RT 8 (1925),
159–66, at 164: 'recta ratio est la règle de la moralité, règle objective, universelle et
infaillible.'
   [7] H. M. Hering, 'Quomodo solvendi sunt casus: recurrendo ad sola principia
an etiam ad prudentiam?', Angelicum, 18 (1941), 311–35; C. J. O'Neil, 'Prudence,
the Incommunicable Wisdom', in R. E. Brennan (ed.), Essays in Thomism (New
York, 1942), 187–204; G. Gundlach, 'Klugheit als Prinzip des Handelns',
Gregorianum, 23 (1942), 238–54; W. A. Gerhard, 'The Intellectual Virtue of
Prudence', Thomist, 8 (1945), 413–56; M. Childress, 'The Prudential Judgment',
PACPA 22 (1947), 141–51.

The equation of prudence with conscience is still faulty: conscience becomes the voice of reason, and the role of prudence is reduced to the perfection of the judgement of conscience. This does not necessarily result in good actions if the agent's will is contrary. Since the will is still primary in decision, prudence is necessary but not determinative of correct action. The position of Josef Pieper is a good case in point. He brought out quite forcefully the need for wisdom, pointing out in his attacks on casuistry that a particular action cannot be calculated in advance, and that there is a gap between a moral rule and a specific situation which is filled by prudence.[8] Yet for all his insight and contribution towards a Thomist view of prudence, he admitted to equating it with conscience.[9] Thus, though in forceful prose Pieper had cleared away certain legalistic attitudes, and had developed something of its right character, prudence still remained basically intellectual, a judgement of the agent which was now to be mature and wise, but which in the process of action could still be ignored if the will didn't follow. In other words, prudence was still seen as a quality which helped the agent only by shaping his preceding moral judgement.

2. The second line of interpretation came closest to a full-blooded Thomistic view as French Dominicans in the 1940s argued for a new appreciation of the directive role of prudence. In the collection *Prudence chrétienne* various writers sought to draw attention to the centrality of the virtue of prudence by relating it to the Bible, the needs of spiritual direction, and also to the family and society in general.[10] Thomas Deman called for a 'restoration' of prudence, arguing that when the casuist approach dominated, obligation replaced the virtue of prudence, so that the Christian life, especially for those in religious orders, came to be seen as a matter of obedience.[11]

[8] J. Pieper, *Traktat über die Klugheit* (Munich, 1949), 53 ff.
[9] Ibid. 25: '. . . wenn man sich bei dem Worte "Klugheit" jedesmal daran erinnert, dass dafür, in einem bestimmten Sinne, auch "Gewissen" gesagt sein könnte'; cf. R. McInerny, 'Prudence and Conscience', *Thomist*, 38 (1974), 291–305, at 299: conscience 'looks to be indistinguishable from the account given of the activity of practical wisdom or prudence'.
[10] See essays by Perrin, Tonneau, *et al.*, in A.-M. Henry (ed.), *Prudence chrétienne* (Paris, 1948).
[11] T. Deman, 'Pour une restauration de la vertu de prudence', in *Prudence chrétienne*, 21–31, at 29–30.

In his influential commentary on the section of the *Summa Theologiae* on prudence Deman noted that in most previous studies the judgement of prudence was really equivalent only to a correct and good conscience.[12] Conscience was understood as the general faculty of specifying the particular action to be done; it may be erroneous or have come to the wrong conclusion, but when conscience functions well and concludes correctly, then the agent is supposedly prudent. This, however, has the problem of stopping short of the action itself—the agent may not actually follow his conscience, and so not carry out his best judgement; and then we are left with the contradiction that a person may be 'prudent' (making good and wise judgements about what to do) but in practice act unwisely. Deman pointed out that this is an intolerable picture of virtue supposedly existing in the mind of an agent who might be quite sinful in actual behaviour, and is in contradiction with what Thomas indicates about prudence. Deman saw that it was not adequate to describe the domain of prudence as the guide of the agent's thinking *up to* the moment of decision, and then to ascribe the decision and its transfer to action as the responsibility of the will. This is to leave the intellect out of the crucial stage.

Deman's solution was to highlight the role of *imperium*, 'command', in Aquinas's account of the process of action.[13] St Thomas treated *imperium* (*ST* 1–II q. 17) as a matter of the intellect (not the will). It follows choice, and is described as the 'principal function of prudence'. This seemed to Deman the rational element needed to balance the role of the will with the participation of the intellect and thus ensure prudent action. In implying, however, that good execution could rectify an erroneous choice, he added confusion to the problem. Because he was not clear about the exact role of reason in choice, he tended to read too much into this final preceptive stage of practical reasoning, and thus he was not able to convince his opponents about the importance of *imperium*.[14]

It is unfortunate that in the discussion of these details the thrust of Deman's position was missed: that prudence was not just good

---

[12] *La Prudence: Somme théologique, 2a–2ae, questions 47–56*, (Paris, 1949), 514.

[13] T. Deman, 'Le "précepte" de la prudence chez saint Thomas d'Aquin', *RTAM* 20 (1953), 40–59.

[14] The controversy with R.-A. Gauthier and O. Lottin is summarized by P. Morisset, 'Prudence et fin selon saint Thomas', *Sciences ecclésiastiques*, 15 (1963), 73–98, 439–58; further discussion in Ch. 12.

conscience but a real principle operating throughout human action. The person with prudence not only applies the right principles to his situation in a wise way, he sees that the right decision is carried out. Deman (and those he influenced[15]) grasped the essential qualities of Thomistic prudence, right reason in action. He saw what was wrong with the legalistic tradition and argued for an understanding of prudence which gives the agent good decisions and correct execution. The lack in his account was his failure to clarify the stages of practical reasoning and the proper relation between reason and will.

One factor preventing wider acceptance and development of Deman's interpretation was the association with situation ethics, the subject of papal warnings in the early 1950s.[16] There was undoubtedly a certain amount of influence from existentialism and other contemporary philosophical positions, but the tendency to identify any new understanding of Thomas Aquinas as a manifestation of secularism made authentic interpretation more difficult. Thus resistance to situation ethics tended to be allied with a continued adherence to the defence of the traditional moral theology, with stress on the objectivity and absoluteness of moral principles, the connection with natural law, and the associated casuistic application.[17] This defensive attitude was probably an important factor in encouraging scholars to stress the differences between the practical reasoning of Aristotle and the Christian doctrine of Aquinas.[18]

On the other hand this has not deterred many from arguing that the legalist tradition was far removed from the ethics of Aquinas,[19]

[15] Such as T. Gilby, in 'Prudence', *NCE* xi. 925–8, and the translation, notes, and appendices in *ST* 2–II qq. 47–56, Blackfriars edn., xxvi (London, 1974).
[16] See *Acta Apostolicae Sedis*, 44 (1952), 413–19, and 48 (1956), 144–5; for background see J. Mahoney, *The Making of Moral Theology: A Study of the Roman Catholic Tradition* (Oxford, 1987), 202 ff.; and for possible lines of interpretation, F. Furger, *Gewissen und Klugheit in der katholischen Moraltheologie der letzten Jahrzehnte* (Lucerne, 1965), 85–102.
[17] See e.g. P. Lumbreras, 'Ethica situationis et doctrina Aquinatis', *Angelicum*, 35 (1958), 139–58.
[18] A. Thiry, 'Saint Thomas et la morale d'Aristote', in *Aristote et saint Thomas d'Aquin* (Louvain, 1957), 229–58, identified in Thomas's teaching these distinctive elements: sin, moral conscience, obligation, and *synderesis*.
[19] See I. T. Eschmann, 'St Thomas's Approach to Moral Philosophy', *PACPA* 31 (1957), 25–33; more recently, V. J. Bourke, 'Is Aquinas a Natural Law Ethicist?', *Monist*, 58 (1974), 52–66; id., 'Aquinas and Recent Theories of Right',

nor from maintaining that an ethics of prudence offers something different from either Kantian morality or a divine command morality[20], nor from attempting to develop a new approach to moral theology, to recast the categories and questions of St Thomas in modern form and examples.[21]

3. The third pattern of looking at prudence is a reversion to conscience, but modified in different ways. Among moral theologians a tension has existed between those who defend the traditional methods of applying objective moral principles and those who claim justification for new approaches.[22]

Though specific treatment of prudence often seems to be lacking in contemporary moral theology, the recognition of it sometimes occurs even if the term itself does not. In commenting on *Gaudium et Spes* (the 'Pastoral Constitution on the Church in the Modern World') Josef Fuchs noted that little attention has been paid to the scholastic concept of the convinced conscience as an inquiry of 'right reason'.[23] The problem of the relation of objective norms to individual conscience is one which requires, in his terms, an 'evaluative comprehension'. Despite these occasional glimpses into the nature of prudence, however, the preoccupation with the definition of natural law, and the problem of the absoluteness of norms and their application in a pluralistic modern world, seem to lead many theologians away from the Thomistic view of prudence as a central moral virtue. In general, the progressive movements since Vatican II have not been very helpful for a better appreciation of St Thomas.

PACPA 48 (1974), 187–95; id., 'Right Reason in Contemporary Ethics', *Thomist*, 38 (1974), 106–24; also H. E. Hartmann, 'St. Thomas and Prudence', Ph.D. thesis (Univ. of Toronto, 1979), and D. M. Nelson, *The Priority of Prudence: Virtue and Natural Law in Thomas Aquinas and the Implications for Modern Ethics* (University Park, Pa., 1992).

[20] See J. Endres, 'Anteil der Klugheit am Erkennen des konkret Wahren und am Wollen des wahrhaft Guten', *Studia Moralia*, 1 (1963), 221–63.

[21] Y. Simon showed a good grasp of the dynamics of prudence and action in St Thomas in 'Introduction to the Study of Practical Wisdom', *New Scholasticism*, 34 (1961), 1–40, reprinted with minor alterations in *Practical Knowledge*, ed. R. J. Mulvaney (New York, 1991), 1–40.

[22] For an example of the latter see F. Furger, 'Prudence and Moral Change', trans. T. L. Westow, in F. Bockle (ed.), *The Social Message of the Gospels* (Concilium, 35; New York, 1968), 119–31.

[23] J. Fuchs, *Personal Responsibility and Christian Morality* (Washington, DC, 1983), 46.

The move away from St Thomas is also true of the approach of some conservatives opposed to the post-Vatican-II liberalizing trends. They agree that there is a need to set aside the manual tradition and develop a different basis for moral theology; but the concern to secure *the underpinnings for a conservative moral agenda (perhaps commendable in some respects) supersedes the desire to understand the teaching of Thomas. Thus for Germain Grisez prudence is much less important than the notion of conscience (reversing St Thomas), and the moral virtues which are the centrepiece of the *Summa Theologiae* are given a Kantian twist to become 'modes of responsibility'.[24]

Another way of modifying conscience and avoiding legalism and Kantianism is by describing its formation in personalist and biblical categories. Bernard Häring in *The Law of Christ* has a section on prudence which, if somewhat vague, has the merit of trying to develop a spiritually enriched view applicable to our current situation. Häring describes prudence in Augustinian fashion as 'love clearly discerning what is helpful and what is hindrance on the path to God', but he takes pains to dissociate Thomas's theory from that of Aristotle.[25] Others have shown that there are rich resources in St Thomas for understanding the connection between prudence, biblical wisdom, and the work of the Holy Spirit in the Christian life.[26]

4. The last view of prudence reacts more strongly against the emphasis on rationality and universality in ethics in the Kantian tradition (which has greatly influenced moral theology in this respect), leading some to stress the importance of affectivity and intuition in the moral life.[27] The appreciation of the importance of the affective virtues, while correcting an earlier imbalance, sometimes threatens to submerge entirely the importance of practical

[24] G. Grisez, *The Way of the Lord Jesus*, i. *Christian Moral Principles* (Chicago, 1983).

[25] B. Häring, *The Law of Christ*, i. *General Moral Theology*, trans. E. G. Kaiser (Westminster, Md., 1961), 498, 505.

[26] See e.g. the emphasis on wisdom and discernment in 'The Holy Spirit and the Moral Life', in J. Mahoney, *Seeking the Spirit* (London, 1981), chs. 6–9; and B. Bujo, *Moralautonomie und Normenfindung bei Thomas von Aquin: Unter Einbeziehung der neutestamentlichen Kommentare* (Paderborn, 1979); see also Ch. 16 n. 29.

[27] D. C. Maguire, 'Ratio Practica and the Intellectualistic Fallacy', *Journal of Religious Ethics*, 10 (1982), 22–39, suggests that the rationalist view of Thomistic ethics should be corrected by 'affective knowledge'.

reason, as in the recent study by Eberhard Schockenhoff.[28] Paul
Wadell's introduction to Thomistic ethics allows only a brief
appearance for prudence. Its quality is wisdom and discernment,
but it has only an ancillary role, 'standing in the service of charity',
with apparently no relation to practical reason, moral principles, or
law.[29]

The emphasis on rules or right reason on the one hand, and the
emphasis on affect and virtue on the other, give the impression that
there is some confusion in Aquinas himself. One interpretation
seeks to assign the legalist approach to the earlier works of Thomas,
with a shift in the later period to an emphasis on virtue.[30] As Jean
Porter reminds us, however, 'the current distinction between
virtue-based ethical systems and rule-based ethical systems cannot
be applied to Thomas';[31] thus an interpretation of Thomistic
prudence, even if restricted to its presentation in the *Summa
Theologiae*, must recognize that Thomas has integrated law and
virtue, and that practical reason must be related to both.

Despite the promising beginning which produced a number of
subsequent studies aimed at a rehabilitation of Thomistic ethics,
the recovery of prudence was partial at best, and often distorted or
ignored crucial aspects of Aquinas's moral theology. The reasons
for this probably include the lingering hold of the legalist tradition;
the suspicion attached to situation ethics; the inability to understand the Aristotelian component; or the influence of Kantian and
other alien philosophies.

It is my conviction that this is only a part of the explanation. In
the last generation there has been an explosion in the studies of
Aristotelian ethics, a firm rejection of or even revulsion against the
legalist mentality, and an appreciation of the dangers of Kantian
categories applied to pre-Enlightenment moral theology. Yet the
understanding of the role of prudence has retreated; it is either
ignored or lamely presented, and certainly not integrated with

[28] E. Schockenhoff, *Bonum Hominis: Die anthropologischen und theologischen
Grundlagen der Tugendethik des Thomas von Aquin* (Mainz, 1987).

[29] P. J. Wadell, *The Primacy of Love: An Introduction to the Ethics of Thomas
Aquinas* (New York, 1992), 129–32.

[30] G. Abba, *Lex et Virtus: Studi sull'evoluzione della dottrina morale di san Tommaso
d'Aquino* (Rome, 1983).

[31] J. Porter, '*De Ordine Caritatis*: Charity, Friendship, and Justice in Thomas
Aquinas' *Summa Theologiae*', *Thomist*, 53 (1989), 197–213, at 213.

metaphysics, psychology, and theology in the way St Thomas achieved.

TOWARDS UNDERSTANDING THOMISTIC PRUDENCE

It is not enough to reject the moral handbooks, or to strip away Kantian moral agency and hope that the Thomistic moral system can emerge by simple exposition of texts. It involves an understanding of what Thomas meant by such terms as conscience, action, passion, free choice, intellect and will, sin, virtue, and the role of law. Much of the confusion in using these terms stems from an inadequate appreciation of the psychology of action in the *Summa Theologiae*. The better understanding aimed at by this study is aided by the extraordinary recent interest in Aristotelian ethics, and Chapter 2 examines the lines of interpretation of Aristotle in order to set the stage for presenting Thomas's theory. The following are major challenges faced by Aquinas in framing his moral theory, and those to be addressed in this book.

  1. To clarify reason and will. It is obvious that both are necessary, but how do they operate, and which is decisive in human action? For Thomas they were like form and matter, so that to ask which is more important would be like trying to decide the relative importance of voltage and current in electricity: it depends on which aspect is considered. They have different functions, but operate together: the intellect relates to truth, the will to good. The metaphysical basis for this relationship is described in Chapter 4, not merely to marvel at the synthesis of Aristotle and Neoplatonism, but because it undergirds Thomas's later teaching about the will which would otherwise be mysterious. The functions of intellect and will and their complementary operation in free choice are covered in Chapters 5 and 6.

  The theory of St Thomas was unique in harmonizing intellect and will not only in the being of God but in human action. Inability to understand his theory, and preference for the voluntarist association of freedom with the will, was a chief factor in the condemnation of certain Thomistic propositions in 1277, and continues to distort present understanding.

  2. To restore order to the process of action. Many descriptions of practical reason are vague in describing the flow from intention to execution, and usually focus on deliberation, where the role of

reason is easier to analyse. Aquinas took seriously the need for an adequate model of human action, but to many readers there has been a sense of confusion and multiplication of stages in the process difficult to harmonize with Aristotle. An interpretation is offered in Part III which restores order and clarity to the process of practical reason. This links the principles of cognition and volition with the stages of action, shows the essential Aristotelian structure, and forms the basis for understanding the different roles of prudence described by St Thomas.

3. To demystify the practical syllogism. When I first began this work on prudence my starting-point was to determine how Aristotle described the practical syllogism, and how Thomas understood this. This proves central to solving the process of decision; when this piece is correctly placed in the puzzle of the process of action, then the process itself and the proper relation of intellect and will are explained. Fundamental questions in the theory of action cannot be solved if the problem of the syllogism is set aside in order to get on with virtues, or spiritual gifts, or natural law. The central role of the practical syllogism as a scheme to explain the process of decision is set out in Chapter 10, but it is also a prominent feature of the explanation by Aquinas of sin and moral weakness analysed in Chapter 14.

4. To make the theory Christian. Aristotelian ethics is often criticized by theologians for neglecting the reality of sin and focusing on natural human life. It is important to see that Aquinas could develop a moral theory faithful to the Aristotelian psychology and description of action, and accommodate the Christian doctrines of sin, grace, the Holy Spirit, and the theological virtues. The final chapter, which relates prudence to love and charity, illustrates this and indicates the spiritual dimension which transforms the relation of intellect and will.

The moral theology of Thomas occupies a major and central place in the *Summa Theologiae* and thus proper understanding of Thomistic ethical theory is crucial for an awareness of his thought as a whole. The new appreciation for the Aristotelian tradition and the search for new moral formulations on the part of both Catholics and Protestants argue the need for new, open-minded, and careful study of the contribution of Thomas Aquinas.

2

The Aristotelian Background

PRACTICAL reasoning is practical because it leads to action. This rests on the belief that there is a causal connection between mind and action; that intentions and reasons are directly linked to behaviour: 'Reasons are the corner-stone of all explanation of human actions, indeed of the very notion of human action itself.'[1] The problem for a theory of practical reason is to describe the connection between the mind of the agent and his action. It would be possible to make a simple link between apprehension by the mind of something good (or desirable) and the activation of appetite leading to action. This is plausible, and is in fact the description of general 'animal' movement: desire, perception, action.[2]

This scheme is inadequate, however, to our experience of human action, and for Aristotle it implied a kind of mechanistic necessity which lacked a proper element for which one could hold a person responsible for his action or award praise or blame. The challenge for him was to explain human action so as to give a coherent account of the links between mind and action (within a causal framework), and yet allow room for the indeterminate element needed for responsibility and for praise and blame; and to allow for an account of growth and the development of virtue.

In Aristotle's general explanation several elements are put between desire and action which involve the human mind and thus differentiate it from the determinacy of ordinary animal action by allowing for choice. Desire posits an end to strive for (and moral virtues are required for right desires); the person then deliberates about the means of attaining it; there is a perception of something being possible to do here and now; then the choice to do it, followed by the action.[3]

The sequence desire–deliberation–perception–choice–act is coherent and introduces the specifically human abilities of reason-

[1] Introduction in J. Raz (ed.), *Practical Reasoning* (Oxford, 1978), 2.

[2] This is Aristotle's explanatory structure in the *De Motu Animalium*; for the contrast between the 'sensitive imagination' of the higher animals and 'deliberative imagination' of human beings see *De Anima* III. 11, 434ᵃ5–7.

[3] W. D. Ross, *Aristotle*[5] (London, 1949), 199.

ing about possibilities and choosing amongst them. As the outcome of this sequence is not 'fixed' (as in animal action) but 'open'
(attested to by human experience), the process can be described as
'voluntary'.[4] Aristotle provided the ground for a rich theory of
human action: the source and determination of desires; the nature
of deliberation and the possible influences on the quality of this
reasoning process; the variability of perception; the nature and
strength of the links between the conclusion of deliberation and
choice, and between choice and action.

Aristotle's treatment in *EN* III, VI, and VII centred on deliberation and choice: thinking about and choosing the right steps to
achieve the desired good. This seems to imply that the crucial
point in Aristotle's ethic is in putting good and evil not in the will
but in the choice of means.[5] This could be interpreted as a
limitation on practical reasoning by assuming that the human
goods that are desired are fixed and not the object of deliberation.
Aristotle's dictum that deliberation is not about ends 'but always
about means' (*EN* III. 3, 1112^{b}11–12) has misled interpreters into
unduly restricting the scope of practical reason. Aristotle did not
mean to deny that an agent can reflect on his values or goals.
Misunderstanding of this point has resulted in distorted estimates
of both Aristotelian *phronēsis* and Thomistic *prudentia*.[6]

---

[4] *Hekousion* in *EN* III is not exactly equivalent to 'voluntary', because the
distinction between *hekousion* and *akousion* also includes our distinction between
'willing' and 'unwilling'; cf. *EE* II. 7; see W. F. R. Hardie, *Aristotle's Ethical
Theory*[2] (Oxford, 1980), 152; for extended treatment, A. Kenny, *Aristotle's Theory
of the Will* (London, 1979), 1–66.

[5] P. Aubenque, *La Prudence chez Aristote*[2] (Paris, 1976), 138: 'La morale
d'Aristote est la seule morale grecque cohérente, parce qu'elle situe le bien et le
mal, non dans l'absolu de la volonté . . . mais dans le choix des moyens.'

[6] In much 19th- and 20th-century interpretation, *phronēsis* was understood to
deal with the means, not the end of an action; for historical survey of the question
see D. J. Allan, 'Aristotle's Account of the Origin of Moral Principles', in J.
Barnes, M. Schofield, and R. Sorabji (eds.), *Articles on Aristotle*, ii. *Ethics and Politics*
(London, 1977), 72–8. Allan influenced R.-A. Gauthier and J. Y. Jolif, *Aristote:
L'Éthique à Nicomaque*[2] (Louvain, 1970), ii. 446–8, who argued for a *phronēsis* that
is aware of the end and the particular at the same time, *contra* P. Aubenque, 'La
Prudence aristotélicienne, porte-t-elle sur la fin ou sur les moyens?', *Revue des
études grecques*, 78 (1965), 40–51. Cf. J. M. Cooper, *Reason and Human Good in
Aristotle* (Cambridge, Mass., 1975), 18: 'And given that all ends other than a
person's ultimate end are considered by him as means to that end, all his ends,
except one, will be subject to deliberative examination'; also Hardie, *Aristotle's
Ethical Theory*, 224–8, and J. O. Urmson, *Aristotle's Ethics* (Oxford, 1988), 53–7.

The function of the practical syllogism holds the key to understanding Aristotle's theory of action, because it is the device Aristotle used to explain the logical and psychological connection between desire and action. Its correct description makes the difference between practical reason as purely deliberative, i.e. determining a specific action, or as the wider description of the process of *prohairesis*, choice of action, which presents the link between thought and action.

THE INTERPRETATION OF THE PRACTICAL SYLLOGISM IN ARISTOTLE

Aristotle devotes little space to a description of the 'practical syllogism' as such.[7] In many cases where a form of the word *syllogismos* is used it means a reasoning process in general rather than the technical sense developed in the *Analytics*;[8] but the fact that the reasoning about what to do involves contingent things rather than necessary does not prevent Aristotle from making the comparison to theoretical reasoning and to the structure of the demonstrative syllogism in particular (*EN* 1142b20–6 and 1143a35–1143b6).

The reasoning process about actions takes place in the steps preceding action itself; but the difficulty arises in describing and identifying them precisely. First the agent has a desire for an end he would like to achieve. Deliberation is the process of reasoning concerned with the 'means' required to achieve the goal. The virtuous man will adopt good goals (because his desires are properly moderated) and thus will deliberate well so that the means he chooses are fitting for the end desired. This is the doctrine of Aristotle up to *EN* III (1112a18 ff).

The process of deliberation can thus be seen to have a three-part structure:

(1) *telos* (an end or purpose);
(2) the means (which may involve more than one step) leading to that end; and
(3) the action to be taken first.

[7] For a summary of Aristotle's examples of practical syllogisms see G. Santas, 'Aristotle on Practical Inference, the Explanation of Action, and Akrasia', *Phronesis*, 14 (1969), 162–89, at 163–6.

[8] See Hardie, *Aristotle's Ethical Theory*, 240 ff.

The tripartite structure of syllogistic reasoning (major–minor–conclusion) fits this process of reasoning about means; and at 1144ᵃ31–2 there is a rare instance of a term approaching 'practical syllogism' applied to the process of reasoning from end to means.

In *EN* VI and VII Aristotle is concerned to add a further dimension to practical reasoning, because a person may deliberate well (i.e. select efficient means) for bad ends (1144ᵃ23–30). Thus practical wisdom (*phronēsis*) needs to be distinguished from cleverness (*deinotēs*). Aristotle wanted to establish a strong connection between choice and character and thus provide a basis for a theory of the development of the virtues and offer a better explanation than the Socratic account of *akrasia*, moral weakness. These are the reasons why Aristotle introduces a stronger comparison to theoretical reasoning and an emphasis on correctness in deliberation (cf. 1140ᵇ3 ff., 1140ᵇ31–1141ᵃ8, and 1142ᵇ16–18). He posits a structure for the reasoning process involving a universal and a particular premiss (1143ᵃ32–ᵇ5), and that the conclusion is the result of the union of the two premisses (1147ᵃ25–8). This dimension of demonstration and correctness in practical reasoning, however, provided by the universal–particular structure (similar to the demonstrative syllogism), is a source of great difficulty in understanding Aristotle.

The conclusion of the practical syllogism determining one's action is the decision 'This here and now is desirable for me and so must be done by me.' How is this parallel to theoretic reasoning? Is not a 'practical syllogism' whose conclusion is the decision to do a particular thing 'a monstrosity from the point of view of Aristotle's theory of knowledge'?[9] The objection has been strongly put:

from the archai of conduct—from the conception of the end and the general rules for its attainment—you cannot reach the conclusion required by any process of reasoning which Aristotle's logic could recognize as scientific. You cannot *prove* what is to be done by you here and now, as you can prove that the angles of the triangle are equal to two right angles.[10]

The crux of the problem is this: in our reasoning we need to reach a specific conclusion; but that very process of reasoning is different from a syllogistic process of establishing the truth of a conclusion.

---

[9] H. H. Joachim, *Aristotle: The Nicomachean Ethics* (Oxford, 1951), 209.
[10] Ibid. 210.

Did Aristotle think the two were basically the same? If he thought them different, did he assimilate one to the other? Some think the problems insoluble.[11] Following the publication of an article by D. J. Allan in 1955 the 'practical syllogism' became the focus of much discussion.[12] Allan considered a passage from *De Anima* III (434ᵃ16–21) where Aristotle gives a brief outline of the process of practical reasoning (the term 'practical syllogism' is not actually used by Aristotle here) which consists of (*a*) a universal judgement of the form 'such a man ought to do such an act'; and (*b*) a two-fold particular application, 'I am such a man and the present act is such an act.'

Allan noted: 'the conclusion is, of course, not another judgement, but the performance of the action.'[13] This was a key insight, because the purpose of the syllogism was understood to give a psychological explanation of the action and was not primarily a means of discovering what to do. This interpretation fits the universal–particular pattern that Aristotle developed in *EN* VI and VII, and can be set out in this way:

First premiss: Universal rule.
Minor premiss: Particular case.
Conclusion: Action.

On the other hand, Allan identified passages from the *De Motu Animalium* where Aristotle shows the agent starting from the 'desirability of some end' and reasoning to an action as a means to that end.[14] Allan concluded:

the practical syllogism may take either of two forms, according as what is expressed in the major premiss is a rule or an end . . . In some contexts, actions are subsumed by intuition under general rules . . . in other contexts, it is said to be a distinctive feature of practical syllogisms that they start from the announcement of an end.[15]

---

[11] Cf. W. K. C. Guthrie, *A History of Greek Philosophy*, vi. *Aristotle: An Encounter* (Cambridge, 1981), 350: 'it is difficult not to feel critical of this attempt to squeeze the springs of action into the framework of scientific reasoning. Aristotle seems to have temporarily forgotten his own principle that a *logos* must be adapted to suit its subject, and that no discussion of human action should aim at the precision of formal logic or mathematics.'

[12] D. J. Allan, 'The Practical Syllogism', in *Autour d'Aristote: Recueil d'Etudes de philosophie ancienne et médiévale offert à Msgr. A. Mansion* (Louvain, 1955), 325–40.

[13] Ibid. 326.   [14] Ibid. 330–1.   [15] Ibid. 336.

If we set this out in a syllogistic structure we have:

Major premiss: End (posited).
Minor premiss: Means (deliberated and chosen).
Conclusion: Action (expressed either as a proposition or in
               the action itself).

There is a noticeable difference between these two forms, and
Allan felt that 'with the texts available it is hardly possible to see
what relation is intended between these two analyses of practical
reasoning'.[16]
Allan was criticized for some errors in his interpretation,[17] but
his study has been crucial in two ways. First, it is now established
that the practical syllogism is a psychological account of action and
shows how the agent can make the transfer from a mental idea to
an action as the result of a reasoning process; this is important for
study of Aquinas and the question of the function of reason and
will in decision. Secondly, because of the tension Allan observed in
two types of reasoning, much of the discussion in the last thirty
years which has resulted in offering diverse positions and explanations can be seen as ways of replying to Allan's dichotomy.
    One position to take is to follow Allan and see the rule–case
format as the more comprehensive, and to assimilate the means–
end reasoning to universal–particular. This involves devising an
implicit (or hypothetical) universal premiss for the desired end,

[16] D. J. Allan, 'The Practical Syllogism', in *Autour d'Aristote: Recueil d'Etudes de
philosophie ancienne et médiévale offert à Msgr. A. Mansion* (Louvain, 1955), 337.
[17] Kenny, *Aristotle's Theory of the Will*, 119, argued that Allan mistook the two
different premisses for two different syllogisms in the *De Motu* examples. Gauthier
and Jolif, *L'Éthique à Nicomaque*, ii. 209–10 (cf. Gauthier, *La Morale d'Aristote*[3]
(Paris, 1973), 42–3), pointed out that Allan's notion of a development from
means–end reasoning in *EN* III to universal–particular in *EN* VI and VII is invalid
in view of the dating of *EN* VI and VII to the *Eudemian Ethics*, therefore
preceding *EN* III (for the uncertainty of dating see A. Kenny, *The Aristotelian
Ethics: a Study of the Relationship between the Eudemian and Nicomachean Ethics of
Aristotle* (Oxford, 1978), and M. Woods, *Aristotle's Eudemian Ethics* (Oxford,
1982), p. xii. Allan replied in a review of Gauthier's commentary, *Classical Review*,
12 (1962), 139, that universal–particular is not meant to be a later development
but a more comprehensive one.
    Allan has also been criticized (e.g. by Hardie, *Aristotle's Ethical Theory*, 249) for
separating deliberation from the practical syllogism, which he did on the grounds
that Aristotle considers deliberation to be theoretical (Allan, 'The Practical Syllogism', 328).

which then becomes a rule of which the action can be an instance.[18] Then human action can be defined as 'practical rule-keeping' in which what the agent needs is the perception that he 'is in the kind of situation to which the rule applies'.[19]

Fr René-Antoine Gauthier, co-author of a substantial commentary on the *Ethics*, sees no problem in subsuming the means–end reasoning under the universal–particular. He sets this assimilation as the proper way to understand Aristotle, and wonders why Allan was troubled by the juxtaposition of the two types in the examples from *De Motu Animalium*.[20] His own explanation for the combination is that the two types of reasoning express complementary aspects of a single process of decision: the universal–particular judgement, inherited from Plato, accounts formally for moral value, but not for motivation. It is Aristotle's contribution of desire for the end which supplies the materially motivating force to practical reasoning, and this was his way of trying to correct the intellectualist account of Plato.[21]

Anthony Kenny has reacted sharply to this way of viewing the practical syllogism, arguing that the attempt to force the process into a rule–case format involving a necessary conclusion is an 'impoverishment of the scope of practical reasoning'.[22] Kenny questions the analogy to theoretical reasoning in respect to logical form. There is a logic in practical reasoning (which he takes to be means–end) which preserves 'satisfactoriness', but this is quite different from the necessity of conclusions in theoretical syllogisms. The forms of reasoning at 1032^{b}19 and 701^{a}18, if looked at from the perspective of demonstrative syllogisms, would seem invalid.

A different approach can be taken. Practical reason begins with a premiss that presents something as a thing to be pursued or avoided, the 'premiss of the good'. It is always the object of desire (*to orekton*) that moves to action, and that is either the good or the apparent good. In this way assimilation is achieved by subordinat-

---

[18] Hardie, *Aristotle's Ethical Theory*, 255, develops from Greenwood the distinction between 'component' and 'external' means to account for the difference.

[19] Ibid. 240.

[20] Gauthier and Jolif, *L'Éthique à Nicomaque*, ii. 209 ff.; cf. Gauthier, *La Morale d'Aristote*, 42 ff.

[21] Gauthier, *La Morale d'Aristote*, 43: 'l'application à l'action morale du schéma moyen-fin répond donc à une intention typiquement aristotélicienne: sa réaction contre l'intellectualisme, excessif à ses yeux, de Platon.'

[22] A. Kenny, *Will, Freedom, and Power* (Oxford, 1975), 71.

ing rules under ends. Thus Aristotle 'may have thought of "rules" as simply summaries of necessary or sufficient means to the final good or some subordinate good . . . then he might also have thought that practical inferences that subsume individual acts under rules are really, in disguise, inferences concerning means to an end.'[23]

The most ambitious attempt to date to harmonize the texts in Aristotle and establish some coherent and suggestive links with current philosophy of action is that of David Charles, which demonstrates the richness implicit in Aristotle's account; in relation to our specific concern for means–end and universal–particular reasonings, Charles helpfully sorts out the two types, noting their respective characteristics.[24] While admitting the differences between them, Charles unites them under the analysis of desire: a desire for the good is the common factor that binds together reasoning to an end and reasoning under a rule. The differences between them, however, are still present:

> In modern terminology, the account of desire brings together two distinct senses of being a *reason for action*; in the first, reason is tied to the *justification* of action, in the second, to the *explanation* of action. Justification shows desire to be conceptually connected with well-being and practical reasoning; explanation suggests a conceptual connexion with action.[25]

Charles notes that the logical form of means–end reasoning is not deductively valid, but that desire 'explains the relevant necessity', because without it means–end reasoning in Aristotle would be obscure. The difference between the logic of means–end and rule–case reasoning also corresponds to the difference in purpose: 'motivational' and 'valuational'; and as desire is common to both, the correct balance of desire in each type is crucial to right choice.[26]

Much of the difficulty in describing the practical syllogism comes from the number of functions being assigned to it: an account of the structure of practical reason; the vehicle for translating desire into action or translating the result of deliberation into action; or the means of establishing the best thing for the agent to do. These functions themselves may be ambiguous, since 'account-

---

[23] Santas, 'Aristotle on Practical Inference', 168.

[24] See D. Charles, *Aristotle's Philosophy of Action* (London, 1984), appendix 3, 262 ff., where the passages are arranged by their form and logic.

[25] Ibid. 232.   [26] Ibid. 161 ff.

ing for the structure of practical reason' may be seen as giving an account of the reasons 'behind' an action, or, somewhat differently, showing the psychological connections between desire, reason, and action. In trying to match the three-part 'practical syllogism' to this agenda one must consider whether the two different schemata for practical reasoning (means–end and rule–case) are interchangeable, or are used in different contexts, or are distinct and complementary in one process, or are alternate modes of explanation depending on the point of view from which one regards practical reasoning.

A strong voice of protest against this project of unwieldy assimilation of conflicting purposes and logics was raised by Martha Nussbaum. Starting from the examples provided by Aristotle in the *De Motu Animalium*, she sees the 'practical syllogism' as a schema for the teleological explanation of activity (means–end), to show the relevant factors and states, in order to give an adequate explanation of act.[27] Holding the means–end model as the dominant one, she sees the conflict with the universal–particular model in some of the *De Motu* examples, e.g. at 701ª17–22, where the agent reasons: 'I need a covering; a cloak is a covering; I need a cloak; what I need I have to make; I need a cloak; I have to make a cloak.' This shows the conflation of two different forms of reasoning.

Referring to the syllogism at 701ª13–15, 'Whenever someone thinks that every man should take walks, and that he is a man, at once he takes a walk', Nussbaum says that this is a 'mistake on Aristotle's part': how can 'I am a man' be a part of a plausible reasoning process? This would 'make sense only in a case in which there is a genuine doubt'.[28]

Aristotle had other items on his agenda, according to Nussbaum, which is why he added the universal–particular model found in *EN* VII. There, in trying to explain *akrasia*, Aristotle needed a type of reasoning process to explain the necessity of action; so his motive is understandable, 'but his interest in deductive validity has led him to make some potentially misleading claims.'[29]

To emphasize further the difference between the two types of reasoning, Nussbaum launched a lengthy (but not very well grounded) polemic against the dangers of following rules for

[27] M. C. Nussbaum, *Aristotle's De Motu Animalium* (Princeton, 1978), 205.
[28] Ibid. 195.   [29] Ibid. 204.

action, particularly against any kind of deductive system of such rules: 'The desire to establish such a deductive science has been a powerful and persuasive one in philosophy, but perhaps the most striking example of an attempt to associate Aristotle with moral deductivism has been the Aristotelianism of Aquinas and the tradition of Christian exegesis descending from it.'[30]

Nussbaum has a very limited knowledge of St Thomas, and her depiction of such a moral science presents a kind of caricature that would be rejected even by those trained in the traditional Catholic handbooks of moral theology.[31] Nevertheless, I believe that Nussbaum has identified (crudely, but arrestingly) the fundamental inadequacy of conceiving human action as determined by a system of rules in which actions are specified by particular rules deduced from other more general rules. Nussbaum takes pains to dissociate Aristotle from such a system, blaming Aquinas for it; but it can be demonstrated that Aquinas did not teach this either.

Other scholars have been sensitive to the problem of practical reasoning by rules. Pierre Aubenque, in his engaging study of prudence in Aristotle, stressed the difference between means–end reasoning and universal–particular, opposing the supposed complementarity of efficient causality and formal causality: there is a profound difference in the purpose and mode of each.[32] The originality of Aristotle lay in the un-Platonic insight of a possible 'dissonance' between ends and means.[33] A great theme throughout Aubenque's study is the contingency of human action—its unpredictability and risks—and the affirmation of human freedom.

It is this element of freedom that Anthony Kenny believes to be jeopardized by a theory of actions determined by rules. He sees in both Aristotle and Aquinas an emphasis on the good rather than 'true or false' in human actions. Practical reason does not necessitate its conclusions; Aquinas saw that the contingen-

---

[30] M. C. Nussbaum, *Aristotle's De Motu Animalium* (Princeton, 1978), 168.

[31] See ibid. 167–73, where Nussbaum constructs the 'content', 'justification', and 'motivation' of a deductive system of rules, the purpose of which is the 'elimination of conflict and regret'.

[32] Aubenque, *La Prudence chez Aristote*, 140: 'car la causalité formelle *se connaît*, alors que la causalité efficiente *s'exerce*.'

[33] Ibid. 141.

cies of the conclusions of practical reason are essential to its freedom.[34]

Gauthier, however, has been a staunch defender of the complementarity and harmony of means–end and universal–particular reasoning as a synthesis of Platonic moral rectitude and an Aristotelian teleological motivation. When criticizing D. J. Allan's observation of the tension between the two types of reasoning Gauthier said that if there were any incoherence here, it would not be the doing of Aristotle alone: Thomas Aquinas himself also juxtaposed the two schemas together.[35] It seems that Gauthier is guilty of what he complained of in other scholars, that is, interpreting Aristotle through the eyes of Thomas, and here he is correct about neither Aristotle nor Aquinas.

In fact, in the present study the case will be advanced for separating the two types of reasoning; what is somewhat unclear in Aristotle, namely the distinction between deliberation and decision, is clarified by Thomas into distinct stages of the process of practical reasoning. There are, however, other issues raised by a comparison of Aristotle and St Thomas on practical reasoning which need to be clarified first.

[34] Kenny, *Will, Freedom, and Power*, 94–5; though the question of locating freedom in the intellect or the will requires clarification, Kenny's basic point about the connection of contingency and freedom remains valid.

[35] Gauthier and Jolif, *L'Éthique à Nicomaque*, ii. 210.

3

Thomistic Practical Reason

THOMAS AQUINAS consciously appropriated much of Aristotle's philosophy not only for his own system of metaphysics, logic, and epistemology, but also for his ethics. The teaching of Aristotle in the *Nicomachean Ethics*, very influential in the early thirteenth century generally, formed the basic ideas and structure of Thomas's thinking right from his period of study with Albert the Great.[1]

Mature assimilation and appreciation of Aristotle is evident in the *Summa Theologiae*, the second part of which is devoted to ethics and begins with a number of questions devoted to an examination of the 'good', desire, deliberation, and choice. The virtue of *prudentia* is modelled directly on *phronēsis* and is described often by Thomas as *recta ratio agibilium*, although the Christian context (its specific treatment directly follows charity in the *ST*) gives it a different aspect. The question arises then of the degree to which the combination with Christian theology changes its Aristotelian character.

CRITICISM OF THE SYNTHESIS

Revisionists of moral theology in the mid twentieth century called into question the assumed synthesis of Aristotle and St Thomas and asserted the problems for Aquinas's theology caused by relying too much on Aristotle: an intellectualism concerning the end of man (the idea of contemplation); rationalism in his doctrine of God; intellectualism in evaluating man's highest power; and an a priori method tied too closely to Aristotle. It was said that where we find a weakness in St Thomas, it is almost always reducible to his esteem

---

[1] On the *EN* in the Middle Ages see G. Wieland, *Ethica-scientia practica: Die Anfänge der philosophischen Ethik im 13. Jahrhundert* (BGPTM 21; Münster, 1981), and more generally, 'The Reception and Interpretation of Aristotle's Ethics', *CHLMP* 657–72. For Thomas's use of the *EN* see D. Papadis, *Die Rezeption der Nikomachischen Ethik des Aristoteles bei Thomas von Aquin* (Frankfurt, 1980).

for Aristotle.[2] This was a reaction against a line of neo-Thomist interpretation which seemed able to present Aristotelian-Thomism as a natural synthesis but which did not explore too carefully the sources of tension between the two.[3] On the Aristotelian framework were added the theological concerns of creation, the doctrine of man and sin, redemption, grace, and eschatology, and the resulting synthesis is prima facie a difficult one; at the very least it should not be taken for granted. Because of Thomas's skill at blending, the places where Aristotelianism ends and Thomism begins are not always easy to detect, either in the commentary on the *EN* where Aristotle's thinking is explicated, or in the *SCG* and *ST* where theological concerns seem to dominate.

If excessive attachment to Aristotle concerned some theologians, it was the opposite fault—innovation and change—for which Harry Jaffa blamed Thomas. While paying tribute to his understanding of Aristotle and his ability to comment insightfully, Jaffa charged that his theological agenda ended up in a distortion of Aristotle. There is a clear trend of 'falsely harmonizing' Christianity with Aristotelian doctrines on such points as providence, immortality, creation, and, in the area of ethics, 'a divinely implanted "natural" habit of the moral principles'.[4] The net result, according to Jaffa, is an apparent harmony; but looking at the facts, there is 'a manifest and striking difference between pagan and Christian ethics'.[5] The most specific focus for his attack on Thomas's treatment is the notion of 'principles naturally known'; this idea of indemonstrable principles, and the generation of a 'natural law' and regulated morality, which he associated with Thomism, were a major stumbling-block for Jaffa.

R.-A. Gauthier did not hesitate to expose the limitations of Jaffa's scholarship[6], but he admitted the central point of essential

[2] J. Leclercq, *La Philosophie morale de s. Thomas devant la pensée contemporaine* (Louvain, 1955), 171: 'Si saint Thomas n'avait pas eu pour Aristote une vénération aussi profonde, il eût sans doute été un peu plus en garde et aurait trié ses arguments.'
[3] e.g. J. Gredt, *Elementa Philosophiae Aristotelico-Thomisticae*[6] (Freiburg im Breisgau, 1932).
[4] H. V. Jaffa, *Thomism and Aristotelianism: A Study of the Commentary by Thomas Aquinas on the Nicomachean Ethics* (Chicago, 1952), 187.
[5] Ibid. 22.
[6] R.-A. Gauthier's review of Jaffa in *BT* 9 (1954–6), 157–9, questions his knowledge of Greek and his awareness of the methodology of Thomas.

differences between Thomas and Aristotle. In reaction to an assumed synthesis between the two philosophies, Gauthier tells us that what makes it possible for us to see Thomas as an Aristotelian, when in reality their systems are quite different, is that we are looking at Aristotle himself through Thomist eyes.[7]

In a more specific list of differences between the ethics of Aristotle and Aquinas[8], the primary changes are these:

(1) man's happiness is not only in this life;
(2) the interpretation of man's quest for happiness is a function of a general theory of the good;
(3) the notion of 'human nature' which explains man's desire for happiness is inserted in the universal teleology of nature; and
(4) the introduction of a 'special faculty responsible for moral value, the will'.

Secondary changes by Thomas include: the roles of will and reason as principles of choice; the distinction between inner choice and outward action; the interiorization of will and morality; the distinction between happiness as a subjective end and God as objective end; merit and reward; the inversion of Aristotle's virtues; and the additional doctrines of natural law and *synderesis*.[9]

There is no doubt that Aquinas had to make changes to do justice to Christian theology; the question is to what extent these changes affected or distorted Aristotle's system. The two factors noted above which chiefly bear on practical reason are the relation between reason and will and the conception of natural law and *synderesis*.

Gauthier in effect agrees with Jaffa that Thomas's theological themes, though they appear 'subrepticement et comme par acci-

---

[7] Gauthier and Jolif, *L'Éthique à Nicomaque*, i. 275: 'pour pouvoir utiliser la philosophie morale d'Aristote dans une théologie animée par un esprit étranger à l'esprit d'Aristote et construite selon des exigences étrangères aux exigences de la philosophie, il lui a fallu en bouleverser le sens et l'équilibre; or, ce qu'on lit bien souvent aujourd'hui chez Aristote, ce ne sont pas les pensées d'Aristote, mais les réinterprétations thomistes, fussent-elles la négation de l'enseignement exprès de l'Aristote historique.'

[8] P. Mercken, 'Transformations of the Ethics of Aristotle in the Moral Philosophy of Thomas Aquinas', *Tommaso d'Aquino nel suo settimo centenario: Atti del Congresso Internazionale* (Naples, 1974), v. *L'agire morale*, 152.

[9] Ibid. 160–1.

dent', essentially change what Aristotle was trying to construct.
Thomas, according to Gauthier, in his moral philosophy was not
really dealing with human action, but the action by which man is
united to God; thus in the *prima secundae* of the *Summa*, when the
beginning, structure, and subject-matter seem to follow Aristotle,
Gauthier says that it is only the terminology and not the spirit of
Aristotle which Aquinas manages to preserve.[10]

In focusing his criticism Gauthier charges Thomas with narrow-
ing the scope of practical wisdom. While *phronēsis* for Aristotle
included knowledge of the end as well as the means, the end for
Thomas, being beyond this life, cannot be known and thus is not
part of *prudentia*. Beyond this, practical wisdom is further limited to
knowledge of the ends of human action by the teaching of *synderesis* and the first principles of natural law, which appear to take
away responsibilities included in Aristotelian *phronēsis*.[11]

If Thomistic *prudentia* for Gauthier is restricted at the point of
knowing the ends of human action and thus deals only with the
means, it is also restricted at the point of the transition from
reasoning to action. Where Aristotle had posited a structure of
deliberation–perception–choice, for Thomas the factor of the will
seems to come into prominence. According to Gauthier it is the
will which makes accountable the movement from the conclusion
of deliberation to its transformation into action. Since in his view
Aristotle's account of action was not able to surpass the Socratic
explanation of error without the notion of the will, Gauthier
understood Thomas's account, modified by the element of
voluntas, to have supplied a deficiency in Aristotle's theory.[12]

Gauthier thus has identified *synderesis* and the will as the major
innovations in Aquinas's account of practical reason as compared
to Aristotle's. The first reduces the need for prudence to understand the ends of action, while the second reduces the executive
role of practical reason. Gauthier wants us to think that Thomas
radically altered Aristotle's account of *phronēsis* by his theological
concerns. Because Thomas added the concept of sin, which for
Gauthier means that human choice must be explained in terms of

---

[10] Gauthier and Jolif, *L'Éthique à Nicomaque*, i. 276: 'Saint Thomas dès lors
pourra bien en garder des mots, des formules, jamais l'esprit.'
[11] Ibid. i. 277.
[12] Ibid. ii. 218: 'dans la psychologie d'Aristote *la volonté n'existe pas*'; the lack is
often noted, e.g. at ii. 170 and 193–4.

will, the result is that Aristotelian 'practical wisdom' in Aquinas has only a limited, formal role; it is no longer the manager of human life; and right action depends more on the will and on God's grace than on prudence.[13]

This understanding of Thomas's relation to Aristotle is fundamentally flawed, and the following chapters can be seen to be an answer to these charges and an argument for the restoration of *prudentia* in Thomas. There is nevertheless a prima-facie plausibility to Gauthier's assessment. Because of the ambiguities in determining the 'first principles' of practical reason, Thomas incorporated the non-Aristotelian factor of *synderesis* which can seem to remove from the domain of prudence certain aspects of understanding the basic ends of human action.[14] Even if one observes a de-emphasis on *synderesis* in the *Summa Theologiae* as compared to earlier works, the link still remains between practical reason and natural law in 1-II q. 94, which can give the impression of a system of basic ends, 'fixed' by natural law, the role of practical reasoning then being to deliberate and decide on the best means to obtain these predetermined ends. This might indeed be a limitation on the scope of practical reason, and requires further clarification.

The central concern of a theory of practical reason is to show the connection between reasoning and action, giving an account of the integration of desire, calculation, perception, and decision. If deliberation is taken to be the essence or central aspect of practical reason, then we can see that the difficulties inherent in a cohesive account involve the stages before and after deliberation: i.e. the process of presenting objects to the practical reason for deliberation, and the transmission of the result of deliberation into action. The disagreement between Aristotle and Aquinas is thus not so much on the nature of deliberation (the correct adaptation of means to ends) but in their accounts of what ends are chosen, and

---

[13] Gauthier and Jolif, *L'Éthique à Nicomaque*, i. 279: 'Mais parce que le "choix" que dirige la prudence est à ses yeux un acte de la volonté, la prudence ne peut plus avoir pour saint Thomas qu'un rôle limité de régulation formelle: l'efficacité lui est refusée. Elle reste pour l'action un guide, elle n'est plus comme l'était la *phronèsis* d'Aristote maîtresse de vie. C'est de la volonté et de la Grace que dépendent désormais notre bonne action ou notre péché, et il fallait que s'efface la sagesse d'Aristote pour faire place à la puissance de Dieu et à la faiblesse de l'homme.'

[14] *ST* 2-II 47. 6 ad 3: unde relinquitur quod prudentia sit nobilior virtutibus moralibus, et moveat eas. Sed synderesis movet prudentiam, sicut intellectus principiorum scientiam.

how the particular action specified at the conclusion of deliberation is translated into action. Aquinas is supposed to have changed
Aristotle in regard to the first aspect by his concept of natural law,
and in regard to the second with the conception of the will.
Accordingly, Gauthier sees *prudentia* in Thomas to be without the
full intellective function of Aristotle's *phronēsis*, and also without its
executive function, which is transferred to the will.

Our primary task in this study is to describe practical reason in
the thought of Thomas; but in considering its nature, extent, and
function we confront the difficult issues of the role of law and the
function of the will. The significance of their effect on our project
should first be assessed before we take up our primary task.

LEGALISM AND PRACTICAL REASON

The view that Aquinas fundamentally changed the role of
prudence by the concept of *synderesis* and natural law depends on
seeing the function of law as an entire system of principles to guide
action. This is what Jaffa thought Thomas was doing: 'Thomas
appears in the context to regard the natural law as a kind of
geometrical system.'[15] He admits that there really is no such
'Euclidean system' worked out by Thomas (in contrast to later
developments), but 'one could properly infer the possibility of such
a system.'[16]

Even when we exclude the notion of a carefully consistent
geometric quality from a system of moral principles (which no one
could envision without denying that he was dealing with contingent actions), the fact remains that there is a traditional interpretation of Thomist moral theology which sees the process of moral
reasoning as moving from a body of moral principles (*scientia
moralis*), deduced from the naturally known and therefore certain
first principles of practical reason, to the application in a particular
situation.[17]

Even after the second Vatican Council this may still be con-

[16] Ibid. 223 n. 23.
[17] On the science of moral theology see B.-H. Merkelbach, *Summa theologiae
moralis ad mentem sanctae Thomae*[3] (Paris, 1938), i. 10: 'cognitio evidens et certa
veritatum quae ex principiis certis deducuntur et in synthesim logico nexu et
ordine inter se coordinantur.'

sidered the dominant interpretation, as reflected in the definition of practical reason from the *New Catholic Encyclopedia*:

Human action is concerned with the particular and the contingent. But there are first principles in the practical order, as in the speculative, and a corresponding habit that enables man to come to knowledge of such principles, viz., synderesis. Right reason (*recta ratio*), starting with the principles furnished by synderesis and using the rules of reasoning (exactly as in the speculative order), establishes conclusions that constitute the rules of morality. Conscience applies these rules to particular situations, to what must be done by the individual here and now.[18]

This must be also what Gauthier has in mind when he speaks of the creation of moral science as deductions from *synderesis*. If this had been the understanding of Aquinas, then Gauthier would surely have been right to stress the difference between open-ended *phronēsis* which begins with desire for an end, and a limited *prudentia* which works within a framework of principles already developed (and furnished by a different form of knowledge) and whose function is merely to select and apply.

The concept of a system of 'natural law' for determining morality has come in for heavy criticism from philosophers and theologians, and dissatisfaction has grown in Roman Catholic circles to the point where 'crisis' would not be too strong a word to describe the state of moral theology let loose from its Tridentine moorings. Among those who reject it, however, it is not always clear just what is being discarded or retained: the legalist mentality, the inflexible structure, the belief in absolute principles, the idea that nature provides norms, or the particular applications of 'natural law' in recent teachings of the Roman Catholic Church.

The ethic of Aquinas seems to breathe a different atmosphere from the later tradition of legalistic moral theology, and there is ample reason to reconsider the association of legalism with the process of practical reason in the theology of Thomas. There is, first, the total absence, as even Jaffa noted, of any precise system. There is nothing approaching a comprehensive set of deductions from general rules to particular situations. This in itself may not be decisive, as Thomas was usually more interested in establishing the broad theoretical foundations for theology than in detailing the specific applications. But not only is there is no system of rules,

Thomas did not even describe the process of derivation or show how this is to be done, which has been seen as a lack on his part.[19]

The organization of the *secunda pars* of the *Summa Theologiae* should also cause us to question this association of legalism and practical reason, because the section on law, *ST* 1-II 90–108, is well removed from the account of human action and morality at the beginning of 1-II and also from the section on prudence in 2-II. Vernon Bourke and others have argued that we should move away from seeing Thomas as primarily a theorist of natural law.[20]

It is clear that a certain tension exists in accounts of practical reason between the themes of contingency and freedom on the one hand, and on the other, necessity and truth. Since all of these elements are stressed at various times by Aristotle, we should be careful not to minimize them; one theme may be stressed more than the other, depending on the interests of the commentator, not without risk of distortion at times.[21]

To combine the two themes in one process of reasoning seems virtually impossible in the case of Thomas's teaching, where the requirements of freedom seem to contradict the requirements of truth. What can be regarded as an ambiguous attitude to truth in Aristotle—which produces a more flexible system—becomes in Thomas, because of his theological concerns, an assertion of truth in the connection of natural law and eternal law. If, in our understanding of the ethics of Aristotle, it is possible to hold in uneasy tension the countervailing demands of freedom to deliberate the means for attaining good ends and of the requirements of good judgement, this seems impossible with Aquinas. One must choose either to emphasize the Aristotelian teleological

[19] 'Aquinas is silent about the procedure by which *derived* deontic propositions are obtained', T. Potts, *Conscience in Medieval Philosophy* (Cambridge, 1980), 53. J. Finnis is more sensitive to the nature of practical reasoning in Aristotle and Thomas, and recognizes the need for wisdom on the part of the agent in applying norms; yet he speaks of the need for a process of inference from first principles to moral norms, and refers to 'the gap which Aquinas failed to fill'; see *Fundamentals of Ethics* (Oxford, 1983), 69.

[20] Bourke, 'Is Aquinas a Natural Law Ethicist?; and V. Punzo, 'Natural Law and the Normative Function of Reason', *PACPA* 54 (1980), 197–206.

[21] In Aristotelian scholarship contrast the extreme emphasis on necessity by S. Etheridge, 'Aristotle's Practical Syllogism and Necessity', *Philologus*, 112 (1968), 20–42, with the heroic virtue of prudence connected with freedom by Aubenque, *La Prudence chez Aristote*; an emphasis on truth is stressed by J. Owens, 'The Ethical Universal in Aristotle', *Studia Moralia*, 3 (1965), 27–47.

element (and soften his teaching on law and truth in the practical syllogism), or to emphasize the absolute starting-points and the importance of truth but lose some of the Aristotelian freedom.

How is it that Aquinas can seem so Aristotelian in his description of human action and yet be so Augustinian in his insistence on the need for conformity to the eternal law (*ST* 1-II 93. 6)? How does one reconcile the frank admission of uncertainty in deliberating about the contingencies of life (1-II 14. 3) with the need Thomas feels for right judgement, and especially with his statement that the judgement of reason (even when errant) is put forward as the truth (1-II 19. 5 ad 1)? How could Thomas be satisfied with such tensions? Perhaps the synthesis between Aristotle and Christian doctrine is illusory after all.

Though the suspicion of an incompatibility between Aristotle's anthropology and the human being viewed under the law of God was current in the thirteenth century, and remains strong in our own day, Aquinas was not of this mind himself, and we are belatedly coming to realize the dimensions of his achievement in combining Aristotle with the Christian theology of Augustine. It is instructive to note the progress in the estimation of Alasdair MacIntyre on this score. Moving from a view which saw an inherent tension between biblical theology and Aristotelian teleology,[22] he more recently expresses admiration for their integration by Aquinas:

So an Aristotelian account of nature, both theoretical and practical, was not merely harmonized with an Augustinian supernatural theology but shown to require it for its completion . . . so that Aristotle's account of the rational world became recognizably the prologue required for an Augustinian theology.[23]

It has been recognized that part of our problem with legalism and the combining of law with teleological morality has to do with an erroneous understanding of the basis of law in its relation to the human mind. There is a great difference between seeing law as a function of the intellect, as Aquinas did, and seeing law primarily in terms of will, as Scotus and much of the tradition following him

---

[22] A. MacIntyre, *After Virtue: A Study in Moral Theory*[2] (Notre Dame, 1985); note that Jaffa is said (p. 278) to present 'the most cogent statement of the case' against Thomas.

[23] A. MacIntyre, *Three Rival Versions of Moral Enquiry* (Notre Dame, 1990), 123.

did.[24] Much of the perceived need to emphasize the primacy of will had to do with providing the force or obligation which seemed to be lacking in a view of law which was based on reason. The further explanation of this quite probably lies in the implications of nominalist philosophy, which changed the connection between thought, motivation, and freedom, and between man, God, and the world.[25]

One merit of the work of Germain Grisez and John Finnis is to call attention to the discrepancy that has developed in Western thought between natural inclination to human goods and the obligation of law.[26] Suarez represents the shift in Western thinking which depreciated the motivation and goodness of inclinations, requiring the imposition of divine sanction on 'natural law' to give motivational force.[27]

The later scholastic creation of a system of rules or laws does not represent the teaching of Thomas, and is a misunderstanding of the nature of practical reason on more than one count. Not only does it find its basis in the will rather than the reason of God (and so takes on the character of obligation rather than guidance), but it

[24] T. E. Davitt, *The Nature of Law* (St Louis, 1951), contrasted the Scotist-Ockhamist tradition of the primacy of will with the Albertian-Thomist tradition of the primacy of the intellect in relation to law; cf. V. Bourke, *Will in Western Thought* (New York, 1964), 171–89.

[25] S. Pinckaers, *Les Sources de la morale chrétienne* (Paris, 1985), has pointed to the 'demolition' of Aquinas's moral theology by Ockham, and of the rupture between liberty and reason, and the development of a false, voluntaristic view of freedom encapsulated in the concept of the 'liberty of indifference'.

There are still those who assert that St Thomas himself shared in the development of the voluntarist view, and attach to him the concept of 'indifference'; cf. K. Riesenhuber, 'Der Wandel des Freiheitsverständnisses von Thomas von Aquin zur frühen Neuzeit', *Rivista di filosofia neo-scolastica*, 66 (1974), 946–74, at 957–9.

[26] G. Grisez, 'The First Principle of Practical Reason: A Commentary on the *Summa Theologiae*, 1-2, Question 94, Article 2', *Natural Law Forum*, 10 (1965), 168–201, somewhat abridged in A. Kenny (ed.), *Aquinas: A Collection of Critical Essays* (London, 1969), 340–82. J. Finnis, *Natural Law and Natural Rights* (Oxford, 1980), acknowledges the influence of Grisez.

[27] The problem with Suarez and the voluntarist theory of law is often thought to be at the stage of *imperium*: instead of being an act of reason, it becomes one of will (see T. Gilby's note 'd' on *ST* 1-II 17. 1, Blackfriars edn., xvii. 183; and Finnis, *Natural Law*, 339). More crucial, however, is whether the decision of the agent is made by his intellect or his will. Moral theology went wrong with a voluntarist theory of law, but even more fundamentally with a voluntarist psychology.

distorts the nature of human agency. To consider that practical reason requires or consists of a detailed set of rules is to conceive the mind of the agent as in need of detailed laws. There is a link here with an emphasis on the will, because if the primary responsibility for decision is given to the will of the agent, then the will needs instructions to obey, and these must come in particularized form (hence rules) if the role of the agent's intellect in the actual choice has been reduced. The reason is still involved, of course, but its sphere becomes one of formulating specific applications of norms and rules, and when this takes place prior to the agent's choice, then this reasoning takes on an abstract and legalistic flavour. This approach to morality is again characteristic of the later scholastics rather than of Aquinas.[28] If this connection between legalism and voluntarism holds, then Thomas's teaching on prudence will be clarified by giving attention to the problem of the relation of intellect and will in the psychology of action.

THE PROBLEM OF THE WILL

Many scholars have identified the will, along with natural law, as one of the major changes which Aquinas made to Aristotelian ethics. Typical is the claim that in Aristotle the will is more 'conspicuously absent' than the concept of human nature, while in Aquinas the will is 'the very root of morality, since its quality determines the moral character of the human act and of the agent'.[29] Now if the problem of law itself relates to the question of the will and needs to be illumined by considering its relation to a psychological account of practical reasoning, then the question of the will becomes central indeed for a consideration of the ethical theory of Thomas Aquinas.

The will in much modern theology, philosophy, and cultural ethos in general is the centre of decision and the locus of freedom. The fact that scholars can assume that *voluntas* must substantially alter *phronēsis* indicates the extent to which modern conceptions of the will have shaped (and distorted) the received understanding of Thomas's account of human action and practical reasoning. If one agrees with the common view that the will is the pivot in human

[28] For some of the contrast between Aquinas and Suarez see D. Westberg, 'Reason, Will, and Legalism', *New Blackfriars*, 68 (1987), 431–6.

[29] Mercken, 'Transformations', 158.

action, then one will have a distorted impression of Thomas's view of the interaction of reason and will in the process of deliberation and choice and in the possibilities for error and sin. If the will is seen as the primary factor in the process of deciding, then it follows that if a wrong decision is made, the will is the responsible factor.

A more exact assessment of the place of the will in a theory of action is provided by asking, 'what happens when a person knows he should do *x*, but then fails to do *x*?' For Socrates, the fault is in the intellect: the agent has simply failed to understand his best course of action. Aristotle's account is difficult to assess. Some regard his explanation of *akrasia* to be basically an intellectualist account—that the akratic did not really see the right conclusion—so that Aristotle's account is not really an improvement on the Socratic explanation.[30] This is also the view of Gauthier, who explains that the struggle is really a contrast between reason and irrational desire; and because this (by definition) cannot be decided by the reason, it shows that Aristotle needed a concept of the will, and that without it he could not improve on Socrates.[31]

Did Aristotle need (and fail to supply) an account of the will? Gauthier does not hesitate to answer this affirmatively, and many others simply assume that this is a lack in Aristotle's account.[32] Yet the attention given to analysing the practical syllogism in Aristotle's works has shown that even if agreement is lacking on the exact form of reasoning and the content of the premisses, yet in general the practical syllogism can furnish the basis of a psychologically convincing account of human action and an explanation of *akrasia* without an emphasis on will.

The key is to understand human choice and action not as a process of reasoning followed by an 'act of will' to carry it out, but as an operation combining both belief and desire. This is the way in which Anthony Kenny and David Charles have directed us, allowing us to question the notion that Aristotle lacks a concept of

---

[30] This is the view of J. J. Walsh, *Aristotle's Conception of Moral Weakness* (New York, 1963), 1–2.

[31] Gauthier and Jolif, *L'Éthique à Nicomaque*, ii. 603: 'Si l'on ignore la volonté, il faut nécessairement admettre la théorie socratique de l'incontinence.'

[32] See e.g. Ross, *Aristotle*, 199–200; and Etheridge, 'Aristotle's Practical Syllogism', 21, says that any analysis of moral actions seems to require a distinct concept of the will for which there is no equivalent in Aristotle.

the will.[33] This view of practical reasoning may actually be more precisely described in the *Eudemian Ethics* than in the *EN*: 'choice is not either opinion [*doxa*] or wish [*boulēsis*], neither one of them nor both . . . it must result from both of these; for both of them occur in one who chooses.'[34]

Did Thomas Aquinas add this notion of will to Aristotle's practical reason to explain human action? Even if the will is given a prominence and definition by Aquinas lacking in Aristotle, it does not have the role given it by most interpreters. *Voluntas* is important, but is not the exclusive factor in choice, and perhaps not even the 'decisive' one.

A common view of *akrasia*, often presented as the view of St Thomas, is that the agent's will is at fault—he 'decides' not to abide by what his reason tells him.[35] Aquinas, however, closely follows Aristotle's model.[36] He sets it up in terms of two parallel syllogisms,[37] and presents the problem as a case of deciding which major premiss to syllogize under. The two syllogisms show that the alternative decisions are arrived at by a reasoning process for both the self-controlled and the akratic; and in Aquinas's explanation a good case can be made for arguing that *akrasia* is a failure of the agent to perceive the correct principle in the circumstances, which is a failure of his powers as a whole: his mind, appetite, and emotions, rather than just a failure of his will-power. It is instructive to note, in view of the difference that Thomas is supposed to have made to Aristotle by invoking the will, that some see in Aquinas the same inability as in Aristotle to surpass the Socratic account of *akrasia*.[38]

There is good reason to doubt that Aristotle's account of action

[33] Kenny, *Aristotle's Theory of the Will*, 69–80; Charles, *Aristotle's Philosophy of Action*, develops the view that the agent in his practical reasoning expresses both belief and desire, so that his decision is expressive of his whole personality and not just his intellect.

[34] *EE* II. 10, 1226^{b}1–6, trans. M. Woods, (Oxford, 1982), 33.

[35] R. P. Reilly, 'Will and the Concept of a Person', *PACPA* 53 (1979), 71–7, at 74, says of the incontinent person that 'He "wills" not to exercise rational control of his behavior'.

[36] *EN* VII, 1147^{a}25–36; Aquinas, *In VII Ethic.*, lect. 1345–9.

[37] This may be the interpretation Thomas inherited rather than Aristotle's own teaching; see A. Kenny, 'The Practical Syllogism and Incontinence', *Phronesis*, 11 (1966), 163–84, at 180–4; but see the reply of Santas, 'Aristotle on Practical Inference', 179 n. 12.

[38] D. Davidson, *Essays on Actions and Events* (Oxford, 1980), 33.

needs to be supplemented by the notion of will; if so, and if Aquinas was developing a properly Aristotelian doctrine himself, then there is no inherent reason why 'will' had to be supplied by him. The fact that generations of readers have assumed it to be the critical factor in the Thomistic theory of action (and have even tried to read Aristotle in that light) reflects the dominance of voluntarism in post-nominalist Western philosophy. Some may reply that Christian anthropology is different from Aristotle in this respect, and that Aquinas, in so far as he was a Christian theologian, was bound to emphasize the dominance of the will in spite of his faithfulness to Aristotle.

The proper relationship between intellect and will has thus become the crux of the problem in understanding the nature of *prudentia* in St Thomas, and this reaffirms the point made a generation ago that moral philosophers badly need to develop an 'adequate philosophy of psychology'.[39] Therefore this study begins not with the problems of natural law, *synderesis*, and conscience, which have been the traditional themes in connection with prudence, but rather with the attempt to establish a sound understanding of Aquinas's metaphysics and psychology of action.

[39] G. E. M. Anscombe, 'Modern Moral Philosophy', *Philosophy*, 33 (1958), 1.

PART II
Intellect, Will, and Action

4

The Metaphysics of Agency

ST THOMAS developed his philosophy of action not from a doctrine of law but from a profound metaphysics of being. (This is not
a disjunction, however, since the harmony of law and human
action is achieved in the doctrine of participation in the mind of
God, who governs the universe with wisdom and love.) Thomas's
theory of being, truth, and good is conspicuously absent from
Protestant ethics as well as from much post-Tridentine Catholic
moral theology, but not because it is obscurely buried in a great
field: it is prominent at the beginning of the *Summa Theologiae*, is
found throughout his works, and underlies his description of
intellect and will. When this metaphysical doctrine is played down
or ignored then the explanation of the motivation for action will
inevitably take false turns.

Thomas in *ST* I 5 not only agrees with the Aristotelian definition that 'the good is what all things seek' but greatly expands its
scope. Aristotle's conception of good is basically in reference to
human relations and character,[1] and reflects something of the
Greek bias towards defining ethics in human terms only; for
Thomas, the notion of good encompasses all of reality.[2]

THE DYNAMICS OF BEING

All created beings (excluding spiritual beings) are understood as
composites of matter and form.[3] Matter, in order to exist in a

---

[1] In Aristotle the good is discussed in terms of the end of human action, what
produces well-being; see Hardie, *Aristotle's Ethical Theory*, ch. 2; cf. J. L. Ackrill,
'Aristotle on "Good" and the Categories', in Barnes *et al.*, *Articles on Aristotle*, ii.
17–24.

[2] Aquinas also incorporates the Ciceronian-Augustinian distinction of good as
honestum, *utile*, and *delectabile* in his metaphysics of good in general. Although he
recognizes that these qualities primarily relate to human good, he generalizes
them into attraction, rest, and final end, allowing the framework to be applied to
the movement of all being; cf. Papadis, *Die Rezeption der Nikomachischen Ethik*, 11
n. 3; and W. Kluxen, *Philosophische Ethik bei Thomas von Aquin* (Mainz, 1964), 167.

[3] For a recent and comprehensive treatment of many of the metaphysical
topics touched on here, see J. Aertsen, *Nature and Creature: Thomas Aquinas's Way
of Thought* (Leiden, 1988).

being, receives form, its organizing principle. Form is what gives definition to matter, what defines its identity and characterizes it from other beings.[4] One can also describe the form as the principle which makes a being intelligible, the aspect of being which enables a mind to know what it is.[5]

Matter and form are not static but provide the principles which account for change and movement in being. Change is expressed in terms of acquiring new form, while the continuity with the previous state is provided by the principle of matter. The notions of 'potency' and 'act', which Thomas appropriated from Aristotle,[6] can be used to express and elucidate this relationship of being towards change and to new being. If act is used to signify matter and form in existence, then a being which is capable of receiving such form is said to be 'in potency' to that act.[7]

Thomas employed these principles very early in the *ST* in his discussions of the existence, perfection, and simplicity of God; he defined movement or change as 'bringing something from potency to act'.[8] This implies a certain capacity in a thing to be changed, because nothing is moved unless it is in potency to the thing towards which it is moved. Acorns can become oak trees; wood has the capacity to be burned, asbestos much less so. Thus the description of change in terms of potency and act implies that change is not arbitrary but is in accordance with the nature of a being.

There is also in the above definition of movement the element of bringing forth (*educere*), which implies exterior action. Seeds do not of themselves (without soil, air, water, and sun) become plants; they have the capacity in their natures to do so, but change in seeds and in all other natural beings requires movement from something

---

[4] *In II Metaph.*, lect. 4, 320: considerandum est quod unumquodque con-stitutitur in specie per propriam formam.

[5] *In VII Metaph.*, lect. 10, 1496: materia, quae principium est individuationis, est secundum se ignota, et non cognoscitur nisi per formam, a qua sumitur ratio universalis.

[6] G. Verbeke, 'The Meaning of Potency in Aristotle', in L. P. Gerson (ed.), *Graceful Reason: Essays in Ancient and Medieval Philosophy Presented to Joseph Owens, CSSR* (Toronto, 1983), 59: potency is 'the possibility of a particular being to be transformed in a certain way under the influence of an external cause'.

[7] *ST* I 77. 3: Potentia, secundum illud quod est potentia, ordinatur ad actum.

[8] I 2. 3: Movere enim nihil aliud est quam educere aliquid de potentia in actum.

else. This is expressed in the Aristotelian principle used by Aquinas, 'everything which is moved is moved by another',[9] because a being in potency is not reduced to act except through some other being in act.[10]

This movement from potency to act can also be described as the movement towards perfection or completion. A thing is said to be perfect according as it is in act; for perfection is ascribed to it when it lacks nothing in the mode of its perfection.[11] A blade of grass or an entire lawn is complete when it has all it needs to thrive, a piece of paper is perfect when it is completely suitable for its purpose (which may imply very different qualities depending on whether it is meant to absorb ink well or to decorate a wall).

A number of principles can be summarized at this point: a thing must exist before it can be moved or changed; movement is in accord with what a thing's nature is meant to be, described as potency to act; movement requires another being already in act; and the completion of movement from potency to act can be described as perfection.

Yet these principles describe reality from the point of view of an observer; this is not the language of agency. From the perspective of a seed becoming a tree, or ice melting, or a man walking to the store, there is a different level of terminology which treats beings as agents. Note that when Thomas says that every agent acts for an end, he is speaking not just of persons or animals, but in the broadest way possible, of all substances in potency to act.[12] The Thomistic metaphysics of agency is expressed in the terms good, end, and desire, which Aquinas uses in question 5 of *ST* I.

Good, unity, and truth are transcendentals, aspects of being common to all things, which express different relations. Being and good are identical in reference to the thing and so are 'convertible' with each other; but they differ in character.[13] The good is a

---

[9] I 2. 3: Omne autem quod movetur, ab alio movetur.

[10] I 4. 1 ad 2: cum ens in potentia non reducatur in actum, nisi per aliquod ens in actu.

[11] I 4. 1: dicitur aliquid esse perfectum, secundum quod est actu: nam perfectum dicitur, cui nihil deest secundum modum suae perfectionis.

[12] M. J. Kelly, 'Agency in Aquinas', *Laval théologique et philosophique*, 33 (1977), 33–7, at 36: 'For Aquinas, the universe of substances is a universe of agents'; cf. n. 15 below.

[13] *ST* I 5. 1: bonum et ens sunt idem secundum rem: sed differunt secundum rationem tantum.

function of something being desirable:[14] it refers to a thing in its capacity to be desired. All movement and change in the universe, hence the dynamic quality of being, is contained in this.

Thomas goes beyond Aristotle by linking appetite for the good to the movement of every being to its completion. 'Something is desirable to the extent that it is perfect, for all things desire their own perfection.'[15] The notion of perfection or completion is not a vague ideal, but is rooted in the reality of being. Each thing is perfect to the extent that it is in act, or actualized; therefore each thing is good to the extent that it is a being.[16]

The basis for agency in the universe is that beings do not simply exist, nor are they merely the subjects of events and forces which cause change; they desire their perfection. A thing is perfect when it is in act; therefore the extent that something is good (and therefore something which attracts) is a function of its being. The aspect of being which conveys the notion of ability to attract, which also contains the notion of perfection or fulfilment, is what the term 'good' adds to the mere notion of being.[17]

The notion of good allows a further elucidation of agency in terms of final causality. Since the good is what all things seek, says Thomas, this means that good carries the notion of an end.[18] Final causality presupposes the operation of formal and efficient causality, which Aquinas explains in this way: that which is first in the process of causing is the last thing in the thing that is caused, because in the process of causation the first element is the good, or the end (or purpose) which is what moves the efficient cause (i.e. gets the process going); second, the action of the efficient cause, moving towards form; third, the form, the completion, arrives. But the process is in reverse when considered from the point of view of what is brought about: first comes the form itself, which a thing must have to be or become; then we consider its power of

---

[14] *ST* I 5. 1: Ratio enim boni in hoc consistit, quod aliquid sit appetibile.

[15] Ibid.: Manifestum est autem quod unumquodque est appetibile secundum quod est perfectum: nam omnia appetunt suam perfectionem.

[16] Ibid.: Intantum est autem perfectum unumquodque, inquantum est actu: unde manifestum est quod intantum est aliquid bonum, inquantum est ens.

[17] Ibid.: sed bonum dicit rationem appetibilis, quam non dicit ens; see L. Dewan, 'St. Thomas and the Causality of God's Goodness', *Laval théologique et philosophique*, 34 (1978), 291–304, at 297.

[18] I 5. 4: cum bonum sit quod omnia appetunt, hoc autem habet rationem finis; manifestum est quod bonum rationem finis importat.

movement; then follows the character of good, through which perfection in a being is established.[19]

FORM AND INCLINATION

In *ST* I 5. 5 Aquinas brings together the notions of good, perfection, form, and movement, to explain how good is the principle of action. A thing is good because it is complete and therefore attractive. A perfect or complete thing is something which lacks nothing according to its mode of perfection. Since each thing is what it is through its form, the determinants of a thing's form are a combination of the material and productive factors. This movement towards form can be expressed in terms of an inclination to an end, either to an action or to something of this kind; because each thing, as far as it is in act, acts and tends toward that which is fitting for itself according to its form.[20]

This is summarized by Thomas in a later discussion: a natural thing has its existence in act through its form. Each thing has a 'habitude' toward its natural form, so that when it does not have the form, it tends towards it; and when it has it, it rests in it. This is true of any natural perfection, which is a good of nature.[21] In things which lack cognition this habitude to good is restricted to natural appetite.

Thus action is closely linked with the nature of a thing: as substance will tend to act in a certain way, in keeping with its nature which in part is defined by this tendency to act for certain ends. For example, the term 'acid' describes certain substances which have a characteristic tendency (nature) under certain circumstances to donate protons.[22]

[19] Ibid. In causando autem, primum invenitur bonum et finis, qui movet efficientem; secundo, acto efficientis, movens ad formam; tertio advenit forma. Unde e converso esse oportet in causato: quod primum sit ipsa forma, per quam est ens; secundo consideratur in ea virtus effectiva, secundum quod est perfectum in esse . . . tertio consequitur ratio boni, per quam in ente perfectio fundatur.

[20] I 5. 5: Ad formam autem consequitur inclinatio ad finem, aut ad actionem, aut ad aliquid huiusmodi: quia unumquodque, inquantum est actu, agit, et tendit in id quod sibi convenit secundum suam formam.

[21] I 19. 1: Quaelibet autem res ad suam formam naturalem hanc habet habitudinem, ut quando non habet ipsam, tendat in eam; et quando habet ipsam, quiescat in ea. Et idem est de qualibet perfectione naturali, quod est bonum naturae.

[22] See S. Makin, 'Aquinas, Natural Tendencies, and Natural Kinds', *New Scholasticism*, 63 (1989), 253–74, at 264–5.

   This expansion of the description of movement toward good as
the dynamic of all being was taken further by Aquinas as he made
the bold equivalence between the appetite of being for perfection
and the force of love.[23] Though Thomas described the inclination
of all things to the good on the lines of Aristotelian metaphysics
(modified to emphasize the centrality of being), the description can
be seen to be compatible with a certain line of Neoplatonic
thinking and of the Pseudo-Dionysian account of the unity of
being and love. This connection is made most explicit in *ST* I-II
27. 1: since love pertains to the appetitive power, its object is
related to it as the cause of movement or of action itself. The
proper object of love is the good, because love connotes a certain
connaturality of the being which loves towards what is loved.
Since what is good for each thing is what is connatural or
proportionate to itself, it follows that good is the proper cause of
love.[24]

   The dynamics of movement are more obviously characterized
by love in the case of living beings, although their movement is
also more complicated to describe. Things are said to be living
when they act from themselves, and not moved by other things.[25]
This definition of life as self-movement is not in contradiction
with the principle that everything that moves is moved by something else. Movement always depends on inclination toward form;
but the way in which the agent relates to form becomes more
complex in certain beings and allows for degrees of self-movement. The principle which allows this is the soul, by which the
living being is composed of a part which is moved (the physical
body) and the other part which is the mover, the active principle
(the soul).

   At one level there are plants. These are beings which move

---

[23] *ST* I-II 26. 1: Dicendum quod amor est aliquid ad appetitum pertinens: cum
utriusque obiectum sit bonum. See J. Laporta, 'Pour trouver le sens exact des
termes *appetitus naturalis, desiderium naturale, amor naturalis*, etc., chez saint Thomas
d'Aquin', *AHDLMA* 40 (1973), 37–95.

[24] I-II 27. 1: Oportet igitur ut illud sit proprie causa amoris quod est amoris
obiectum. Amoris autem proprium obiectum est bonum: quia . . . amor importat
quandam connaturalitatem vel complacentiam amantis ad amatum; unicuique
autem est bonum id quod est sibi connaturale et proportionatum. Unde relinquitur quod bonum sit propria causa amoris.

[25] I 18. 3: cum vivere dicantur aliqua secundum quod operantur ex seipsis, et
non quasi ab aliis mota.

themselves in a very limited way, only with respect to the execution of movement and not by the relation they have to form or purpose; the form through which they act and the purpose for which they act are determined for them by nature. They move themselves in increase and decrease according to a form inherent in them by nature.[26] (Modern science perhaps allows us to expand the description of organic motion to include such phenomena as the movement towards or away from light or moisture, and other responses to environmental stimuli, as characteristic of even the lowest forms of life.)

There is a higher order of beings which move themselves not just with respect to execution but also in relation to the form which is the principle of movement, which they can acquire by themselves. These are animals, whose principle of movement is not built in by nature but is received through sensation.[27] Among animals there are degrees of having sensation: the more complete the sensation, the more self-movement. Those which have only the sense of touch, such as the oyster, are moved by dilation and constriction. The higher animals which have a complete sensitive power are able to recognize not only things which are touching them but things at a distance, and so they move themselves accordingly.

Yet as self-movers such animals are limited in the ends they have. Although they receive the principle of movement, the form, through sensation, they do not set for themselves the purpose of their action or movement; this is given to them by nature, and they are moved by instinct to do something through the form apprehended by sensation.

This is given some expansion by Thomas at *ST* I 80. 1 in the discussion of appetitive powers. Animals are beings which share to some extent in cognition. Things like fire, which lack cognition, have a natural inclination which follows a natural form. In animals which have cognition each being is determined to its proper natural being through a natural form, but nevertheless is capable of receiving images of other things. Thus the forms exist in a higher way in beings with cognition, above the mode of natural forms, so

[26] I 18. 3: Et huiusmodi sunt plantae, quae secundum formam inditam eis a natura, movent seipsas secundum augmentum et decrementum.

[27] Ibid.: Et huiusmodi sunt animalia, quorum motus principium est forma non a natura indita, sed per sensum accepta.

that they have an inclination which is above the natural inclination (of things such as acid and fire), which is called the natural appetite. 'This superior inclination belongs to the appetitive power of the soul, by which an animal is able to desire the thing that it apprehends, not only those things to which it is inclined by a natural form.'[28]

Thomas was willing to call the apprehension and appetite of animals an imperfect kind of cognition and volition. In explaining voluntary action in the *secunda pars* Aquinas says that perfect cognition is when a thing which is the end is not only perceived, but the character of the end (*ratio finis*) and its relationship to it are recognized, which belongs only to a rational nature. Imperfect cognition of the end is that which consists only in the apprehension of the end without the nature of the end, or the relationship of action to purpose being recognized.[29]

With the complete kind of cognition, the agent is able, by deliberation, to move or not move towards an end. An animal with imperfect cognition, apprehending the end, does not deliberate, but is immediately moved towards it. Thus Thomas concludes that animals do not have the voluntary action that corresponds to perfect cognition, but they have a lesser kind in accordance with their imperfect cognition.

INTELLECT AND WILL

The split of human personality into various 'faculties' such as will, intellect, and emotion has led to problems and is now widely called in question. Thomas Aquinas, however, emphasized the unity of thought and will in action;[30] they are meant to work closely together, and he even says explicitly that they include each other.[31]

---

[28] *ST* I 80. 1: Et haec superior inclinatio pertinet ad vim animae appetitivam, per quam animal appetere potest ea quae apprehendit, non solum ea ad quae inclinatur ex forma naturali.

[29] 1-II 6. 2: Imperfecta autem cognitio finis est quae in sola finis apprehensione consistit, sine hoc quod cognoscatur ratio finis, et proportio actus ad finem.

[30] See T. Gilby, 'Thought, Volition and the Organism', *Thomist*, 2 (1940), 1–13.

[31] *ST* I 16. 4 ad 1: voluntas et intellectus mutuo se includunt. Cf. 2-II 109. 2 ad 1.

Why separate these functions? Why not simply identify intellect and will and simply assert the essential unity of the human agent, refusing to divide the human personality at all into subcapacities such as reason and will? To speak about thinking and desiring is sometimes needed for analysis, but perhaps it is better to say that the whole person 'understands' or 'feels' or 'wants to do something' without trying to relate these activities to specific elements of the psyche.

One line of reasoning which Thomas uses in the *ST* to establish the real differences between the potencies of the soul is based on the difference between essence and action. Considering the intellect (*ST* I 79. 1), one could say that it was the essence of the soul if it were the immediate principle of operation. In this case the potency would be related to its operation and to its act in the same way that essence relates to being. Only in the case of God, however, is being identical with understanding; therefore in God intellect is identical with essence; but in all created intellectual beings, the intellect is a kind of capacity, since it exists in a 'lower mode' of actuality.[32] This means that being able to understand is a capacity of the soul, distinct from the essence of the soul itself.

Thomas expanded on this in his *Quaestiones de anima*. On the part of the agent that which is the immediate principle of operation must be an accidental form.[33] The essence of the soul is not the immediate principle of its operations, but it functions by mediating accidental principles. This means that the potencies of the soul are not its essence but are properties of it.[34] This conclusion can also be reached by considering the very diversity of actions. These are not only different, but are diverse in kind and cannot be reduced to one immediate principle. Actions and emotions differ from each other, and so it seems right to attribute them to diverse principles.[35]

The difference between intellect and will is based on the difference between their objects. In *ST* I 77. 3 Thomas states that a power is related to its act, so that the nature of a power is taken

[32] L. Dewan, 'St. Thomas and the Integration of Knowledge into Being', *International Philos. Quart.* 24 (1984), 383–93, at 392.

[33] *Quaestiones de anima*, 12: necesse est quod ex parte agentis illud quod immediate agit sit forma accidentalis.

[34] Ibid.: Manifestum est igitur quod ipsa essentia animae non est principium immediatum suarum operationum, sed operatur mediantibus principiis accidentalibus. Unde potentiae animae non sunt ipsa essentia animae sed proprietates eius.

[35] Ibid.

from the act to which it is directed. The nature of an act is differentiated according to the diverse nature of the object.[36]

The relationship between a power, its object, and the resulting activation are explained by Aquinas in his commentary on the *De Anima*: the specific natures of acts and operations are taken from their relationship to objects. Every operation of the soul is of either an active or passive power. The objects of passive powers are active in relation to passive powers, because they bring the powers to the point of action, as what is visible activates sight, and what is sensible activates sensation. The objects of active powers relate to activations of the powers as ends (*fines*), for the objects are also the effects of the powers themselves.[37]

This is not needlessly subtle; it allows intellect and will (and sensation) to be moved by reality ('omne movens movetur ab alio'), but also to be active. This double aspect of the powers of the soul is reflected in the consideration of the object. The object is active in terms of activating a power, but is an end in relation to the power now activated.

Say there is a bicycle; it can be noticed by beings which have powers of sight or touch. As an existing object it is what activates the perceptive powers of a soul (no one can see a bicycle which is not there). As an object of the intellect the bicycle can now be examined and understood, and as such is the *finis* of the activated intellectual power. It can also be seen as something desirable (for riding, or for possessing) and thus an object of the will.

The metaphysical principles of understanding and willing are most clearly set forth by Thomas in the *ST* in the section on angels.[38] Since they are creatures, they share with human beings the

---

[36] *ST* I 77. 3: potentia, secundum illud quod est potentia, ordinatur ad actum. Unde oportet rationem potentiae accipi ex actu ad quem ordinatur: . . . Ratio autem actus diversificatur secundum diversam rationem obiecti.

[37] *In II De Anima*, 415ª16, 305: Species enim actuum et operationum sumuntur secundum ordinem ad obiecta. Omnis enim animae operatio vel est actus potentiae activae vel passivae. Obiecta quidem potentiarum passivarum comparantur ad operationes earum ut activa, quia reducunt potentias in actum, sicut visibile visum et omne sensibile sensum. Obiecta vero potentiarum activarum comparantur ad operationes ipsarum ut fines; obiecta enim potentiarum activarum sunt operata ipsarum.

[38] For a comparison of the *ST* with the earlier treatment in the *De veritate* and the subtle improvements made by St Thomas see L. Dewan, 'The Real Distinction between Intellect and Will', *Angelicum*, 57 (1980), 557–93.

mixture of potency and act which separates them from the unity of essence and action found in God alone. But because they have thought and will without the need for sensation the operations of intellect are purer and illustrate the principles of rational nature more precisely.

The object of understanding is the truth (*verum*) and the object of willing is the good (*bonum*). Each of these objects is interchangeable with being, which means that in themselves the corresponding powers are able to relate to all of reality. Each of the intellectual powers receives its specification from the object.[39] Such powers can be called operative powers or virtues because operation is the act to which an operative power relates.[40]

The will of angels is discussed in question 59, which offers an excellent summary of the appetite of all being to good and the different kinds of inclination to good based on the differing modes of cognition. Some things are inclined to good through a 'natural habitude' alone, without cognition, such as plants and inanimate bodies. This is natural appetite. Others are inclined with some cognition, because they recognize some particular good, as sensation can recognize something pleasant, or white, and so on. This kind of inclination is called sensitive appetite. Other beings are inclined to the good with cognition, by which they recognize the very character of good (*ipsam boni rationem*), and which is the property of the intellect. These are not inclined to the good by being directed by something else, nor towards a particular good only, but are inclined only towards universal good itself; and this inclination is called the will.[41]

When St Thomas discusses the will in the context of human action in *ST* I-II, he makes it clear that the underlying metaphysics is still one of natural inclination to good, and that every inclination follows some form. The natural appetite follows a form existing in nature, while the sensitive appetite, and also the rational appetite

---

[39] *ST* I 54. 2: Simpliciter quidem, sicut intelligere, cuius obiectum est verum, et velle, cuius obiectum est bonum, quorum utrumque convertitur cum ente; et ita intelligere et velle, quantum est de se, habent se ad omnia; et utrumque recipit speciem ab obiecto.

[40] I 54. 3: proprius actus respondet propriae potentiae . . . Actus autem ad quem comparatur potentia operativa, est operatio.

[41] I 59. 1: sed quasi inclinata in ipsum universale bonum. Et haec inclinatio dicitur voluntas.

(the will), follow a form which is apprehended.[42] The good which
the natural appetite seeks is good actually existing (*bonum existens in
re*);[43] while the good to which the will is inclined need not be truly
good, provided that it is perceived under the character of good.
This is of the greatest importance, because in Thomistic theory it is
not necessary to secure the freedom of the will by removing the
will from the created order and from natural inclination.[44]

THE MUTUAL INFLUENCE OF INTELLECT AND WILL

The relationship between intellect and will is determined by the
nature of their respective objects, truth and good. Both are natural
powers, and combine a wide-ranging freedom with natural necessity. Although the will does not necessarily will its particular
objects, it does naturally adhere to the ultimate end, the universal
good, just as the intellect of necessity must adhere to the first
principles.[45]

The natural necessitation of the will to the universal good is its
participation in the metaphysics of all being, inclination to perfection. This perfection is beatitude, which for creatures with reason
consists only in the vision of God. This implies that the will would

[42] I-II 8. 1: appetitus naturalis consequitur formam in natura existentem:
appetitus autem sensitivus, vel etiam intellectivus seu rationalis, qui dicitur
voluntas, sequitur formam apprehensam.

[43] Laporta, 'Pour trouver le sens exact', 49.

[44] Kant's placement of the will in a noumenal sphere separate from the material
world is fundamentally different and (from a Thomistic point of view) fatal. But
the split between knowledge of reality and the freedom of the will had already
been decisively made by Duns Scotus, who considered the intellect a natural
power (and therefore moved by objects) but denied this of the will, which was for
him entirely self-moved. See R. Effler, *John Duns Scotus and the Principle 'Omne
quod movetur ad alio movetur'* (St Bonaventure, NY, 1962), 165–6. More than a few
interpreters have brought this alien view to their reading of St Thomas, with
inevitable distortion. The description of the will in terms of 'infinite Spirit' in
comparison to the intrinsic limitations of the intellect has more to do with
modern romanticism than with the philosophy of Aquinas. See e.g. K. Riesenhuber, *Die Transzendenz der Freiheit zum Guten: Der Wille in der Anthropologie und
Metaphysik des Thomas von Aquin* (Munich, 1971), 302: 'Doch gehört die Erkenntnis aus ihrem Wesen und Ursprung zum Sein des Menschen und damit zur
ruhenden Substanz, durch die etwas schlechthin ist. . . . Der Wille ist aber das
Vermögen des endlichen Geistes, das sich wesentlich auf das Andere bezieht.'

[45] *ST* I 82. 2: sicut intellectus naturaliter et ex necessitate inhaeret primis principiis, ita voluntas ultimo fini.

be naturally inclined to those things which have a necessary connection to the beatific vision, just as the will to eat necessarily implies taking the steps to procure nourishment. But although the will for beatitude is a necessary one, the inclination to any specific good in this life is not. Until the certitude attaching to the vision of God demonstrates the connection between our particular choices and our final good, the will cannot be said to incline necessarily even to God, or to divine things.[46]

If something were presented to the will as perfectly good, the will would necessarily be drawn to it; but the nature of good is not presented to us in this life as anything absolutely good with no qualification, but as something pluriform and complex which does not necessarily determine the will.[47] This is precisely why the intellect must be involved in the determination of the will: no single good (apart from God himself) will act as an object to draw the will, and hence every good requires the intellect to provide it with its character or formality of goodness.

Intellect and will can be compared to each other in reference to the objects which actualize them. Simply considered, in their operations as powers, the intellect is higher than the will because the object of the intellect is simpler and 'more absolute' than that of the will: the object of the intellect is the very character of the attractive good, while the object of the will is the attractive good thing, the rationale of which is in the intellect.[48] This is another way of saying that for an object to move the will it must be given its character as good by the intellect.

It is also possible to compare intellect and will in reference to the nature of the objects, and in this fashion the relationship is more complex, and varies because of the different way in which each power relates to its object. Following the teaching of Aristotle,

---

[46] *ST* I 82. 2: Sed tamen antequam per certitudinem divinae visionis necessitas huiusmodi connexionis demonstretur, voluntas non ex necessitate Deo inhaeret, nec his quae Dei sunt. Against the widely held interpretation of Cajetan, positing a natural human desire for God, cf. Laporta, 'Pour trouver le sens exact', 38: 'L'erreur de Cajetan est de considérer le désir naturel de la vision comme une activité psychique.'

[47] I 82. 2 ad 1: Sed quia bonum est multiplex, propter hoc non ex necessitate determinatur ad unum.

[48] I 82. 3: Obiectum enim intellectus est simplicius et magis absolutum quam obiectum voluntatis: nam obiectum intellectus est ipsa ratio boni appetibilis; bonum autem appetibile, cuius ratio est in intellectu, est obiectum voluntatis.

good and evil, the objects of the will, are in exterior things; but true and false, the objects of intellect, are in the mind. Thus when something lower than the mind is being considered (e.g. some material reality such as a stone) then the reality of the object in the mind is higher than the object as an attractive good for the will. But when something higher than the soul is considered, the relationship changes, because the object existing in its own reality, and acting as attractive good, is higher than that being considered as an object of the intellect which exists in the mind.

This of course applies to a person's relationship to God, and implies that love of God is better than knowledge ('Unde melior est amor Dei quam cognitio'). Since willing requires cognition, there can be no question of love without knowledge, no separation of powers, no independence of will and intellect, and no retraction of the basic superiority of intellect over will.[49] The relative difference of intellect and will presented here is strictly in terms of metaphysical relation to object: the object of the intellect, as truth, is in the mind, the object of the will, the attractive good, is outside. (The important implications of the need for both powers to be perfected in the virtues of faith and charity will be presented in the final chapter on prudence and love.)

The relation of intellect and will can also be described in terms of potency and act, and adds further clarification to their respective operations. The will is moved not simply by the good, but by good which is understood. This means that the operation of intellect is prior to that of the will, as act is prior to potency. Thus the relation of intellect to will is one of mover to movable, or active to passive.[50]

In the next article (82. 4) Thomas explains that though the intellect moves the will *per modum finis*, because the understood good which functions as end is what moves the will, it is also true that the will also moves the intellect *per modum agentis*, from the point of view of the agent. The will moves the intellect and all other powers of the soul, because being the power which relates to the universal end, it moves the powers which relate to particular ends. Thus the operation of each power can be seen in relation to

[49] Thomas summarizes the entire article with the statement, 'simpliciter tamen intellectus est nobilior quam voluntas'.

[50] I 82. 3 ad 2: Et hoc modo intellectus est prior voluntate, sicut motivum mobili, et activum passivo: bonum enim intellectum movet voluntatem.

some kind of good proper and fitting for it, as vision relates to the perception of colour, and cognition to truth.[51] The operation of intellect can be seen as the movement towards the good of truth, which is the *finis* of its operation; and while there is a natural inclination to knowledge in general, the operation of the intellect towards any particular truth (understood as an end and something good) is an operation governed by the will.

It is one thing to establish the metaphysical relationships between intellect and will and explain the different aspects in which one is 'higher' than or prior to the other. But in an actual decision or process of action, can one say which causes the other? If I find a book to read, did I see it first and then decide I wanted to pick it up? Or did I have a desire to read (or a general desire for diversion) and then notice the book? Which comes first, the desire or the noticing? Even if our cognition is metaphysically prior to our volition, is it not true that we regard the things that we want to regard and notice those things which we are willing to notice?

In *ST* I 82. 4 arg. 3 Thomas points out the possibility of an infinite regress here: if the will causes understanding by willing the act of understanding, another act of understanding must precede that willing; and that understanding will have another prior willing, and so on. In his answer Thomas says: there is an end to this series because it begins in the understanding. Every act of the will requires that cognition (*apprehensio*) precede it, but a motion of the will does not precede every act of cognition.[52]

There is a text in Aristotle's *Eudemian Ethics* which also raises the same question of the ultimate cause of our deliberations. Aristotle concludes that the starting point of our thinking is not thought, but is a higher principle than our intellect, namely a god, or a divine element, who moves everything in the universe, including operations of the soul.[53] The way in which Thomas uses this text provides a point of comparison between the possible development of his thought between the *prima pars* and the *secunda pars* of the

---

[51] I 82. 4: Obiectum autem voluntatis est bonum et finis in communi. Quaelibet autem potentia comparatur ad aliquod bonum proprium sibi conveniens; sicut visus ad perceptionem coloris, intellectus ad cognitionem veri.

[52] I 82. 4 ad 3: non oportet procedere in infinitum, sed statur in intellectu sicut in primo. Omnem enim voluntatis motum necesse est quod praecedat apprehensio: sed non omnem apprehensionem praecedit motus voluntatis.

[53] *EE* VIII. 2, 1248ᵃ17–29; see also Ch. 6 n. 37.

ST. In *ST* I 82. 4 ad 3 Thomas says that 'the *principium* of advising and understanding is another intellectual principle higher than our intellect, which is God, as even Aristotle says'.[54]

In *ST* 1-II 9. 4 (in the main reply) Thomas seems to treat the matter in the context of the will: it is necessary to posit that for the first movement of the will, the will proceeds from the impulse of another exterior mover.[55] Thomas seems to shift the ground of the original principle of movement from the intellect to the will, or rather that God as first cause relates to the human agent as an object of the will, which is more fundamental than the relation to the agent as an object of the intellect. Much has been made of this supposed shift in Thomas's teaching away from God as formal causality to the pre-eminence of final causality. This question can be resolved, however, by attending to the fundamental metaphysical principles of Aquinas.

To make final causality dominant over formal causality would be to make good transcendent over being. Though this may indeed be the case with Platonism, in Thomas's doctrine the good is not transcendent over truth and reality. Being is the fundamental reality which is convertible into the three transcendentals.[56] One could argue that considered in themselves neither *bonum* nor *verum* is primary over the other, and that therefore the intellect does not have priority over the will; but it would be wrong to draw from this the conclusion that Thomas thereby emphasizes the freedom of the will.[57]

The voluntarist approach is possible for those who believe in a Platonic 'sovereignty of the good', but its divergence from Aquinas

[54] *ST* I 82. 4 ad 3: principium consiliandi et intelligendi est aliquod intellectivum principium altius intellectu nostro, quod est Deus, ut etiam Aristoteles dicit.

[55] 1-II 9. 4: necesse est ponere quod in primum motum voluntatis voluntas prodeat ex instinctu alicuius exterioris moventis.

[56] J. Crosby in 'Are Being and Good Really Convertible? A Phenomenological Inquiry', *New Scholasticism*, 57 (1983), 465–500, at 499, argues for the transformation of the theory of good into one of 'value', just as absolute as Thomistic *ens*. His reasons are Kantian: the Thomistic theory of *bonum* means that moral obligation is reduced to something hypothetical and not unconditional. More accurate are M. Hönes, *Ens et bonum convertuntur: Eine Deutung des scholastischen Axioms unter besonderer Berücksichtigung der Metaphysik und Ethik des hl. Thomas von Aquin* (Freiburg im Breisgau, 1968), 91 ff., and J. A. Aertsen, 'The Convertibility of Being and Good in St. Thomas Aquinas', *New Scholasticism*, 59 (1985), 449–70.

[57] As e.g. K. Riesenhuber does; see n. 44 above.

is seen by paying heed to the connection in Thomistic theory between being itself and the intellect. Though the will relates to *bonum*, and the intellect to *verum*, being itself (*ens*) is an object of the intellect. This is established as a fundamental principle at the beginning of the *Summa*: the first stage in intellectual conception is being, for everything is knowable to the extent that it actually is, following Aristotle's *Metaphysics*.[58] Thus if we consider a rational agent's relation to an object purely on the level of being it is through the intellect that the relation exists.

Transferring these relations to the order of causality and rational agency, the will corresponds to the efficient cause, the intellect to the formal cause, and the object itself, the *bonum intellectum*, to the final cause. It has been supposed that Thomas in the *De veritate* associated the final cause with the intellect, and that the treatment we find in the *ST* represents the new understanding that final cause is a matter of the will,[59] but this misrepresents Thomas's teaching. What moves the will as end (according to the *De veritate* text) is not the intellect but the object seen as something good, the *bonum apprehensum*.[60] In other words, though intellect is said to move the will *per modum finis*, it is by providing (so to speak) the will with an appropriate *bonum* for it to be moved. The will is already inclined to universal good. To be activated at all, however, this general orientation of the will to good must be particularized, directed towards an object, which requires cognitive apprehension. There can be no end for action, and thus no final causality, without the apprehension of the intellect. There is no being (not even God) which can be a good for the agent, as something which engages the will, without being understood or perceived as good.

Thus it is correct to conclude that the good, in order to operate as final cause, presupposes the operation of efficient and of formal causality. Though an agent may be inclined to an object as something good and experience the primacy of this 'final causality', yet with respect to knowledge, being is prior to good.[61] In the process

[58] *ST* I 5. 2: Primo autem in conceptione intellectus cadit ens: quia secundum hoc unumquodque cognoscibile est, inquantum est actu.

[59] O. Lottin, 'Liberté humaine et motion divine', *RTAM* 7 (1935), 52–69, 156–73; this has influenced many other scholars.

[60] *De veritate*, 22. 12 ad 3.

[61] *ST* I 5. 2: secundum rationem prius est ens quam bonum; see Dewan, 'St. Thomas and the Causality of God's Goodness', 299.

of causation (cf. *ST* I 5. 4) the order of causality is: final cause first, then efficient, then formal. But in considering the actual thing which is caused, the order is reversed: first is the form, by which the being exists; then the power which perfects it in being; finally the aspect of good which perfects the being.

This inverse relationship in orders of causality is not just an obscure point in understanding the relation between good, being, and agency; it also underlies the account of motivation in human action. The purpose or end of an action is the starting point in terms of cognition and deliberation, but it is the last in terms of being.[62] Expressed in terms of affective motivation, there are two sequences of the ordering of love, desire, and delight. In terms of intention, the delight can act as a *finis* and inspire desire and love, moving the person to action; but in the order of execution love is first, prompting desire, and when the object is attained then delight is experienced as the fruit of love.[63]

[62] I-II 14. 5: Principium autem in inquisitione consilii est finis, qui quidem est prior in intentione, posterior tamen in esse.
[63] I-II 25. 2.

5

Cognition and Volition

IT might be argued on metaphysical principles that since truth is
the object of the theoretic intellect, while action is the object of
the practical, this implies separate powers. Thomas did not agree:
whether something is huge or small, it is of course still perceived
by the same power; likewise the same intellect is the means by
which something is perceived, whether the object is related to
action or not.[1]

Thomas makes it clear that truth is not excluded as an object of
practical thinking: 'the object of the practical intellect is something
good in relation to action, under the aspect of truth. For the
practical intellect, like the speculative, knows truth, but it relates
the known truth to action.'[2] Studying the general account Thomas
gives of the mind's operation lays the foundation for a study of the
process of practical reasoning as well.

COGNITION AND REALITY

Since cognition covers such a wide territory—from the stone a
person trips over to speculation about angelic being, as well as the
field of practical reasoning—the general description of cognition
must be very broad indeed. A further obstacle to understanding
Aquinas on this is the development and influence of theories since
his time. The further distinctions introduced by Scotus into
scholastic discussion, the influence of Descartes, Locke, and Kant,
have produced rival versions, which are often imported into discussions of Thomistic theory.

---

[1] *ST* I 79. 11. This is Thomas's mature position, since in earlier works there
may have been a tendency towards separation of theoretic and practical: see J.
Naus, *The Nature of the Practical Intellect according to St Thomas Aquinas* (Rome,
1959), 17–34.

[2] I 79. 11 ad 2: ita obiectum intellectus practici est bonum ordinabile ad opus,
sub ratione veri. Intellectus enim practicus veritatem cognoscit, sicut et speculativus, sed veritatem cognitam ordinat ad opus.

St Thomas provided his best summary in the *Summa Theologiae*.[3] Although he recognised that Plato's theory of intellection was developed to give certainty to human knowledge in the face of the agnostic implications of a Heraclitean view of reality (*ST* I 84. 1), Thomas did not hesitate to express clear opposition to the Platonic theory. At the basis of all human knowledge for Thomas there is sense perception, because there are no innate ideas, and the human mind must make use of sense experience for thinking.

Thomas was able to be consistent with this principle and at the same time explain the possibility of acquiring knowledge of abstract sciences and even of immaterial reality by describing three different elements of cognition: sense perception, judgement, and reasoning.

There is an order in the elements or aspects in the process of knowing an object (*ST* I 85. 5). The human intellect does not reach perfect cognition in the mere apprehension of an object. First it apprehends the essence or the 'quiddity' of the object (i.e. it recognizes what it is); and then it adds further understanding of the thing's properties, accidents, and other aspects. Depending on the nature of the object, an analysis or reasoning process may be required to apprehend it fully. In the second stage there is the 'judgement of existence', the judgement that something *is* indeed the case.[4] In this operation the mind asserts the being or reality of that which is discovered by apprehension. The process of gaining knowledge can thus be seen at its most basic level as an accumulation of true judgements. The first operation of the intellect gathers the data, so to speak, while the second operation judges the veracity of the information.

The intellect understands material things by a process of abstraction from 'phantasms', that is, the sensible images.[5] This process of abstracting general knowledge from the images of things is different from the positing of an 'idea' in the Platonic sense, but as Thomas explained, it is 'to consider the nature of a species without

[3] For discussion of other works see B. Lonergan, *Verbum: Word and Idea in Aquinas*, ed. D. Burrell (Notre Dame, 1967); cf. G. Klubertanz, *The Philosophy of Human Nature* (New York, 1953), and A. Kenny, 'Intellect and Imagination in Aquinas', in Kenny (ed.), *Aquinas* (London, 1969), 273–96.

[4] P. Hoenen, *Reality and Judgment according to St. Thomas*, trans. H. F. Tiblier (Chicago, 1952), 36 ff.

[5] *ST* I 85. 1: intellectus noster intelligit materialia a abstrahendo a phantasmatibus.

considering the individuating factors which are represented in the phantasm'.[6] This is not the same thing as saying that this quality or form 'exists' apart from the matter in which it is.

The relation between the intellect and phantasms is described as the ability of the agent intellect to abstract 'intelligible species' from the phantasms provided by sensation. This power is imparted by the intellect, which is also able to separate and consider specific natures without the individuating factors.[7] The process of abstracting intelligible species from phantasms occurs at the same time as one understands these in the phantasms (85. 1 ad 5); in other words, the sense image is necessary for cognition, whether provided directly by sensation or by imagination (84. 7 ad 2).

The intelligible species relates to the intellect as that by which the intellect understands; i.e., just as one sees by means of an image of a visible thing, so one understands by means of the intelligible species which is the likeness of the thing understood.'[8] In this way, a person can know things which are outside the soul.

Thomas's clarification of the relation of phantasm to the intellect was profound and a great advance on previous theories, including that of his mentor St Albert.[9] He was able to explain the need for and the role of sense experience and yet preserve the dominant function of the intellect. He did this by attributing an efficient causality of the phantasm in the production of the intelligible species, but subordinating it to the concurrent causality of the agent intellect which performs the abstraction and separation—a kind of illumination—to produce the intelligible species. The potential intellect is passive with regard to the phantasms, but these are not able to make an impression by themselves: the agent intellect is also required, whose action on the phantasms results in a kind of likeness, the intelligible species, by which we understand.[10]

[6] I 85. 1 ad 1: considerare scilicet naturam speciei absque consideratione individualium principiorum, quae per phantasmata repraesentantur.

[7] I 85. 1 ad 4: Abstrahit autem intellectus agens species intelligibiles a phantasmatibus, inquantum per virtutem intellectus agentis accipere possumus in nostra consideratione naturas specierum sine individualibus conditionibus, secundum quarum similitudines intellectus possibilis informatur.

[8] I 85. 2: Unde similitudo rei visibilis est secundum quam visus videt; et similitudo rei intellectae, quae est species intelligibilis, est forma secundum quam intellectus intelligit.

[9] See G. C. Reilly, *The Psychology of Saint Albert the Great Compared with that of Saint Thomas* (Washington, DC, 1934), 56–8.

[10] *ST* I 85. 1 ad 3; see Klubertanz, *The Philosophy of Human Nature*, 158–202.

For Thomas, the connection between cognition and reality was most important, because this constituted the ground of certainty. The object of understanding is thus a real thing, of which the intelligible species is a likeness.[11] The description of the relation of sensation and intellection provides the direct connection between being and cognition. Although it is on a different level, the object of cognition has being in the mind. There is an 'intentional' existence in the mind of the knower. An object passes from real being into cognitional being by means of the senses; but the link is established by the real being as formal cause of the intentional being.[12]

JUDGEMENT

A two-stage theory of cognition made up of perception or the apprehension of the object with a judgement following had been in the philosophical tradition since Plato and Aristotle,[13] but Thomas Aquinas made a major contribution by clarifying the functions and by assimilating it to his metaphysics of being.

Judgement as an aspect of cognition has both a wide and a narrow sense in Aquinas. Sometimes judgement follows perception; elsewhere it is the conclusion of a reasoning process; and it is also a critical part of practical reasoning.[14] Judgement even has a role to play in apprehension itself, since a sort of process of affirmation and denial is involved, and it is not wrong to speak of a 'sense judgement'.[15]

In regard to the function of cognition in knowing truth, however, judgement is more properly restricted to the operation of the mind which reflects on the results of apprehension. This sequence of apprehension and judgement is found in the earliest teaching of Thomas:

[11] I 85. 2: id quod intelligitur primo, est res cuius species intelligibilis est similitudo.

[12] See R. W. Clark, 'Aquinas on Intentions', *Thomist*, 40 (1976), 303–10.

[13] Background and texts, including judgement in St Augustine, are treated by B. Garceau, *Judicium: Vocabulaire, sources, doctrine de saint Thomas d'Aquin* (Montreal, 1968).

[14] Garceau, *Judicium*, 265–78, lists the important text references under the different categories of usage.

[15] J. Owens, 'Judgment and Truth in Aquinas', *Mediaeval Studies*, 32 (1970), 138–58; cf. Garceau, *Judicium*, 272–3.

As the intellect forms things, however, it has only a similitude of the thing existing outside of the soul, just as the sense has when it receives the sense-impression of a thing; but when it begins to judge concerning the perceived object, then that judgement itself is something proper to it, which is not found outside the mind.[16]

True knowledge is found not in the stages of apprehension but in the judgement following perception, which is the act of affirming or denying in the mind the reality of the apprehensions made. This move from apprehension to judgement is natural for the mind to make because it wants to know.[17]

The most basic judgement is that of existence; for example, 'Here is a chair'. Further examination allows another judgement such as 'This chair is wooden'. Such a proposition takes the form 'A is B', but this is not a statement of identity between two things joined by the copula 'is'. There are only two logical elements in the proposition: a subject and predicate, which relate as matter and form. When we say 'Socrates is white' the predicate element 'is white' functions as a verb; we are not making a statement of identity but saying something about the subject, Socrates.[18]

In order for the judgement to be considered true, and not simply an assertion, it is compared with what has been grasped by the act of judgement. Thus the separate cognition of two objects is required, and this is what makes the act of judgement something new in the process of cognition. One object is 'the existence actually synthesizing the components in the thing that is being apprehended' and the other object is the judgement itself.[19] Though the proposition expresses the judgement of the mind, the act of judgement involves not just the enunciation of the proposition but the knowledge that it is correct. For the judgement to be true, the object apprehended must be seen to correspond to the judgement made about it.

[16] *De veritate*, 1. 3: Intellectus autem formans quiditatem rerum non habet nisi similitudinem rei existentis extra animam, sicut et sensus inquantum accipit speciem rei sensibilis. Sed quando incipit iudicare de re apprehensa, tunc ipsum iudicium est quoddam proprium ei, quod non invenitur extra in re.

[17] This is based on the metaphysical tendency or 'desire' of the human being to know; *ST* I 12. 8 ad 4: naturale desiderium rationalis creaturae est ad sciendum omnia illa quae pertinent ad perfectionem intellectus.

[18] H. McCabe, 'The Structure of the Judgment: A Reply to Fr. Wall, O.P.', *Thomist*, 19 (1956), 232–8.

[19] Owens, 'Judgment and Truth', 156.

It would be a mistake to think that a judgement can be made only after a process of investigation or reasoning, because judgement can be a kind of immediate discernment. We recognize immediately the meaning of 'I ain't gonna go nowhere', or 'me not go', and that both are incorrect grammatically, but in different ways (an adult native speaker of English might say the first but not the second). The use of a language can be seen as a manifold series of judgements about the selection and ordering of words; fluent command of a language is not (indeed cannot be) simply a matter of following grammarians' rules, nor is it an intuitive process; it is the ability developed by experience and training to make proper judgements about the use of words.

REASONING

Though *ratio* is often used for cognition or the operation of the mind in general, there is also a narrower sense which contrasts with understanding or *intellectus*. Where Thomas makes this distinction in his treatment of the human mind he defines their separate functions: 'Intellection is to apprehend intelligible truth directly; reasoning, however, is a matter of proceeding from one understood thing to another in order to know intelligible truth.'[20] The contrast between understanding and reasoning of course does not follow a clear dividing line; yet there is in general a difference between the direct apprehension of understanding and the process of thinking something through from principle to conclusion which is characteristic of discursive reasoning.[21]

The distinction between reasoning and understanding becomes clearer when one considers that reasoning is something one has to resort to because a clear judgement cannot be made. In other words the mind wants to be able to ascertain reality; from past

[20] *ST* I 79. 8: Intelligere enim est simpliciter veritatem intelligibilem apprehendere. Ratiocinari autem est procedere de uno intellecto ad aliud, ad veritatem intelligibilem cognoscendam.

[21] J. Peghaire, Intellectus *et* ratio *selon s. Thomas d'Aquin* (Paris, 1936), 13 ff., pointed out that though 'intellect' and 'reason' have diverse senses, they overlap sometimes, and in some passages in Thomas they seem to be identified, while elsewhere they are opposed. When they are distinguished, however, the synonyms associated with *ratio*, e.g. *cogitare, conferre, inquirere*, and *discurrere*, serve to distinguish between human reason which requires a process to think something through, and angelic or divine intellect which is able to know simply (pp. 85 ff.).

experience a person may be able to make immediate judgements about the objects he sees; if he cannot do so with certainty then he resorts to a process of reasoning in order to be able to make a judgement.

A doctor, for example, may examine a young patient. After some years of experience when a patient presents a certain set of symptoms the doctor can tell immediately 'This is chicken-pox.' Another case may offer a similar set of symptoms which might lead a hasty or inexperienced examiner to the same judgement, but which would then be wrong. A wiser physician might say to himself 'This *looks* like chicken-pox, but I'm not sure.' Then a process of reasoning occurs, of checking other symptoms, consulting medical texts and colleagues, a process of investigation to determine the correct judgement of the connection between the constellation of symptoms and the underlying causes.

The relation of reasoning to understanding is that of the incomplete to the complete, analogous to the relation of 'moving' to 'resting', or 'acquiring' to 'holding'. Reasoning is a way of discovery, while understanding is the process of judgement.[22] These two processes of reasoning, the *via inventionis* and the *via iudicii* (see Fig. 1), can be seen as good descriptions of the stages of reasoning and knowledge in cognition in general.[23] The process of discovery by reasoning needs a discerning judgement based on first principles to establish certainty about the conclusions.[24] This distinction also forms the basis for later analysis of the stages of deliberation and decision in practical reasoning.

[22] *ST* I 79. 8.
[23] J. Isaac, 'La Notion de dialectique chez saint Thomas', *RSPT* 34 (1950), 481–506, drew attention to the nature of *iudicium* in the general process of reasoning and especially in its most particular context, the administration of justice and the pronouncement of a sentence or judgement. The parallel between scientific and judicial reasoning holds in respect of the fact that in both cases reasoning follows a two-step pattern: *inquisitio* and *iudicium*, a process of discovery and a process of judgement; and these are two successive psychological steps (p. 485).
The division allows the clarification of the distinctive character of each process. *Inquisitio* is free to be an inquiry for the facts of the matter, while *iudicium* becomes more clearly a decisive judgement, 'yes' or 'no', on the truth of what one has discovered.
[24] Cf. *In I Post. Anal.* 1. 1-6, where Thomas distinguishes different acts of reason and compares them with the different parts of logic. The intellectual operation which deals with necessity and certitude is *iudicativa*, based on resolution to first

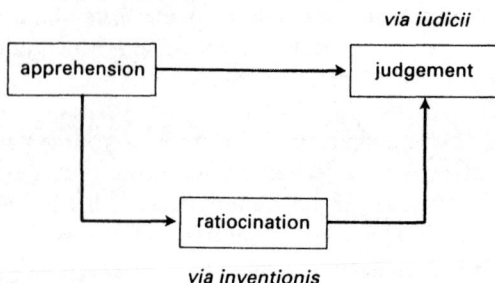

FIGURE I

Rationality in general should not be confused with the reasoning process. God's intellect is able to see all parts in relation to the whole, and does not need to consider them in succession in order to understand them. Likewise God does not reason from principles to conclusions or from effects to causes as humans do.[25] Human minds acquire the knowledge of truth by a discursive process, reasoning from one known thing to another, because of 'a weakness of intellectual light'.[26]

ILLUMINATION AND CERTITUDE

The implications of the teaching on cognition by Aquinas become clear when one considers the knowledge of spiritual realities— immaterial substances. The doctrine of illumination (as used by other theologians) is a means to explain the possibility of knowing angels, for example, or God, or even one's soul. If Thomas is to be consistent about the dependence on phantasms for knowledge, then how does he explain how one can come to a knowledge of immaterial beings? This is squarely faced by Thomas in *ST* I 88. 1:

principles. The second type of logic is *inventiva*, without certitude until established by judgement.

---

[25] *ST* I 14. 7. Angels, although more limited and not able to see the relation of cause and effects with the directness of the mind of God, are intellectual beings not requiring discursive reasoning, since they are able to know all the conclusions which follow from knowing the principles of things. Thus they do not need to acquire knowledge by composition and division; cf. I 58. 3, 4.

[26] I 58. 3: Quod quidem contingit ex debilitate intellectualis luminis in eis. Cf. G. M.-M. Cottier, 'Intellectus et ratio', *RT* 88 (1988), 215–28, at 224: 'C'est pourquoi *ratio* est un nom d'imperfection et de limitation.'

he does not try to steer a middle course between Plato and Aristotle; he rejects Plato's position on the primacy of Ideas. Aristotle taught that our intellect understands nothing except by turning itself to the phantasms, and Thomas adheres to this: we cannot understand immaterial things according to our mode of knowing, because they do not come under sense or imagination.[27] Following a lengthy refutation of the Averroist explanation of the agent intellect, Thomas ended up in an isolated position here, with a theory of cognition which was shared by very few, if any, contemporaries.

Thomas does accept the Augustinian point that the human mind understands and judges all things 'in the light of the first truth', but he changes the meaning of the 'light'. Instead of its being part of the process of cognition and meeting the continual need for knowledge of higher things, Thomas makes the intellect itself the light, and it is connected to God because it is a kind of impression of the first truth.[28] The light in the intellect is not the content (*quod intelligitur*), but the means by which we understand (*quo intelligitur*).

Illumination of the intellect had also been considered by Thomas in *ST* I 84. 5, where the question dealt with the Augustinian *rationes aeternae*. There the distinction is also made between knowing the ideas of God directly (which applies only to the beatific vision) and knowing by a principle of cognition; this knowing is like saying we see things in the sunlight (*in sole*) when we mean 'by the sun' (*per solem*). In this latter sense the soul knows all things *in rationibus aeternis*, understood as knowing all things *per quarum participationem*, by participating in the eternal exemplars: 'For the intellectual light in us is nothing other than a certain participated likeness of the uncreated light in which the eternal exemplars are held.'[29] It is clear that illumination is not exterior to the intellect but that it itself has, by its operation, the light to see and judge things in the world.

[27] I 88. 1: . . . unde nihil intelligit nisi convertendo se ad phantasmata, ut ex dictis patet. Et sic manifestum est quod substantias immateriales, quae sub sensu et imaginatione non cadunt, primo et per se, secundum modum cognitionis nobis expertum, intelligere non possumus.

[28] I 88. 3 ad 1: ipsum lumen intellectus nostri, sive naturale sive gratuitum, nihil aliud est quam quaedam impressio veritatis primae.

[29] I 84. 5: Ipsum enim lumen intellectuale quod est in nobis, nihil est aliud quam quaedam participata similitudo luminis increati, in quo continentur rationes aeternae.

What about the certainty of the mind's knowledge? The most decisive aspect of St Thomas's theory of cognition lies at this point, where he differs from Albert and others who followed Augustine. If no outside illumination is required for acts of cognition, even for the 'higher' areas of knowledge, then no illumination is required, either, for the certainty which attaches to its knowledge. The nature of the intellect itself and its connection to reality are the basis for a person's knowledge of truth, not intuition or a process of deduction.[30]

This was the teaching of Aquinas from the start of his career. At the beginning of one of his earliest works, the *De veritate*, he defined truth as the proper relationship between reality and the intellect.[31] This is based on the fact that all cognition is accomplished by the assimilation of cognition to the thing recognized; thus this assimilation is the cause of cognition.[32] The object by itself does not produce truth, neither does the intellect by itself; but both together, when properly related, furnish the mind with truth.

This is the epistemological corollary of his theory of the role of the phantasm and of the agent intellect, and is further explained in *De veritate* 1. 9 in considering whether truth can be in sensation. Thomas says that truth is in both the intellect and the sense, though not in the same way—truth in sensation is there as a consequence of its act but not as known by the sense.[33] The intellect, however, can reflect on its act (*reflectitur supra actum suum*), knowing both its act and its relation to reality.[34] It is of the nature of the intellect that it be conformed to real things; therefore it recognises the truth of the intellect because it reflects on itself.[35]

The question of illumination is dealt with in *De veritate* 11. 1. A

---

[30] T. S. Hibbs, 'Against a Cartesian Reading of *Intellectus* in Aquinas', *Modern Schoolman*, 66 (1988), 55–69, at 68 n. 41: 'The contrast with Descartes, who sought to construct a deductive system grounded in indubitable principles grasped by intuition, could not be sharper.'

[31] *De veritate*, 1. 1: prima ergo comparatio entis ad intellectum est ut ens intellectui concordet, quae quidem concordia adaequatio intellectus et rei dicitur.

[32] Ibid.: Omnis autem cognitio perficitur per assimilationem cognoscentis ad rem cognitam, ita quod assimilatio dicta est causa cognitionis.

[33] Ibid.: 1. 9: Sed veritas est in sensu sicut consequens actum eius; . . . sed tamen non est in sensu sicut cognita a sensu.

[34] Ibid.: non solum secundum quod cognoscit actum suum sed secundum quod cognoscit proportionem eius ad rem.

[35] Ibid.: . . . in cuius natura est ut rebus conformetur: unde secundum hoc cognoscit veritatem intellectus quod supra se ipsum reflectitur.

rather lengthy case is made against Avicenna's agent intellect and other misunderstandings. Knowledge is acquired by discovery (*inventio*) or by teaching (*disciplina*); in either case 'the process of the reason arriving at the knowledge of something unknown is by means of discovery, as it applies universal principles to specific matters and thence proceeds to particular conclusions, and from these to others.'[36] Now the light of reason (or its illumination) can be seen as that power by which principles of this kind are known, which has been placed in it by God.[37] Thus every human teaching, because it depends on the truth of the first principles, cannot have efficacy without the virtue of this light.[38] Thomas explains that God's light is behind all knowledge in that it underlies the truth of the first principles, and not that it is directly required as a supplement for specific acts of cognition.

In the *Summa* the question of certitude is discussed more indirectly in relation to cognition. In *ST* 112. 5, in the question on whether one can know whether one has grace, Thomas writes that 'one cannot have certitude about anything unless one is able to judge by means of the correct principle; thus certitude about demonstrative conclusions is had through indemonstrable universal principles.'[39] It is the truth of the principles, resting on the fundamental truth of the basic principles, which certifies the truth of one's knowledge. The element of certainty is not some quality which can be added to knowledge—it is part of the definition of knowledge: the character of knowledge (*scientia*) is connected to certainty: a person has certainty about those things of which he has *scientiam* (*ST* 1-II 112. 5 ad 2).[40]

This is different from a Platonic view of knowledge in which comparison to the ideal form of something furnishes certitude.

---

[36] *De veritate*, 11. 1: Processus autem rationis pervenientis ad cognitionem ignoti inveniendo est ut principia communia per se nota applicet ad determinatas materias et inde procedat in aliquas particulares conclusiones et ex his in alias.

[37] Ibid.: rationis lumen quo principia huiusmodi nobis sunt nota, est nobis a Deo inditum.

[38] Ibid.: Unde cum omnis doctrina humana efficaciam habere non possit nisi ex virtute illius luminis.

[39] *ST* 1-II 112. 5: Certitudo enim non potest haberi de aliquo, nisi possit diiudicari per proprium principium: sic enim certitudo habetur de conclusionibus demonstrativis per indemonstrabilia universalia principia.

[40] For certitude in relation to faith and the supernatural gifts of knowledge see *ST* 2-II 4. 8 and 9. 1.

When we make the judgement 'this is a tree' or 'this material is
wood', the certainty of judgement is based on experience of these
things and ultimately on the principle of non-contradiction underlying all the judgements made to build up knowledge. Sometimes
things will be difficult to judge: is the material of bamboo, since
technically the plant is a grass, to be considered 'wood'? But this
does not mean that the general categories to describe reality are
purely nominal, or that the lack of certainty in some judgements
undermines the quality of certainty in the whole range. The fact of
twilight, as Samuel Johnson said, does not mean that we cannot tell
the difference between night and day.

THE OPERATION OF THE WILL

The moral section of the *Summa*, the entire *secunda pars*, is a careful
description of human action based on the metaphysical principles
already established. In the first article of *ST* i-II Thomas states that
all actions which are produced by any potency are caused by it
according to the character of the object.[41] This emphasizes that the
will does not exercise an independent function—it is shaped by its
object, and must function in relation to the potency which can
delineate the character of an object, namely the intellect.

The will cannot, of its nature, simply be attracted to an object or
course of action by itself. Whatever action a person undertakes, it is
pursued on the basis of a final end (*ST* i-II 1. 6). There are two
reasons to back up this point: first, whatever a person desires, it is
desired under the aspect of 'good'. Even if it is not the final good, it
is desired as tending towards complete good, because the incomplete state of something is directed towards its perfection.[42]
Secondly, the final end relates to the appetite as the prime mover
relates to other movements. Thus secondary objects of desire do
not move the appetite except in relation to the primary desirable
thing.[43]

Thomas's teaching about natural and rational appetite (will) can

[41] i-II 1. 1: omnes actiones quae procedunt ab aliqua potentia, causantur ab ea
secundum rationem sui obiecti.

[42] i-II 1. 6: necesse ut appetitur ut tendens in bonum perfectum: quia semper
inchoatio alicuius ordinatur ad consummationem ipsius.

[43] Ibid.: secunda appetibilia non movent appetitum nisi in ordine ad primum
appetibile, quod est ultimus finis.

be put this way: human beings (like all other beings) by nature are already 'programmed' to seek the good, their perfection. But because they have a rational nature, only the final good, which could be described as perfect excellence or fulfilment, moves the will by necessity. Any particular object must be seen in relation to this goal in order to move the agent into action.[44] In other words, since the good as final end is not presented to us directly, all objects in life must be chosen under the aspect of good. This is not contradicted by the fact that people do actually differ in their values and understanding of the purpose of life.[45]

It is not necessary, of course, for the agent to be conscious of this connection to the ultimate end whenever he does something: 'the force of the primary intention, which is in respect of the final end, remains in any desire for any kind of thing, even if there is no actual thought about the final purpose.'[46] In Thomas's example, a person who goes on a journey does not need to be thinking about the purpose or destination at every step of the way.

The comparison to non-rational animals is useful here. In *ST* 1-II 6. 2 Thomas argues that the character of an action being 'voluntary' requires that the principle of action be interior, with some awareness of purpose (*cum aliqua cognitione finis*). Complete awareness of purpose occurs when a thing is not only apprehended as an end, but also its character as end is recognized, including the relation of the means to the end. Such awareness of purpose belongs only to rational nature. An animal may have desire for food, see some food (as an object of desire), and decide to move toward it. In this process there is cognition and appetite, and the animal is the source of the action. This is a kind of voluntary

[44] D. Schlüter, 'Der Wille und das Gute bei Thomas von Aquin', *FZPT* 18 (1971), 88–136, at 125 n. 129: 'das konkrete Einzelgut ist deshalb und insofern gut, als es in Beziehung zum Endziel steht.'

[45] See W. VanderMarck, 'Ethics as a Key to Aquinas's Theology', *Thomist*, 40 (1976), 535–54. Even if there were agreement on a set of 'basic human goods' as suggested by Finnis, *Natural Law and Natural Rights*, 85–90 (life, knowledge, play, aesthetic experience, sociability, practical reasonableness, and religion), no necessity attaches to them. St Thomas would agree that playfulness and humour do not need to be related to some other purpose in life, that they have their own intrinsic worth. But people may reject play, or sociability, or religion, or even physical life itself, for the sake of some higher good.

[46] *ST* 1-II 1. 6 ad 3: sed virtus primae intentionis, quae est respectu ultimi finis, manet in quolibet appetitu cuiuscumque rei, etiam si de ultimo fine actu non cogitetur.

action, but it is 'imperfect'. What the animal lacks is not cleverness or computational skills, but awareness of purpose, and how the action fits into a scheme of purposes. The word 'will' (*voluntas*), says Thomas, means the rational appetite,[47] the kind of inclination to good in general which requires the ability to understand ends and means, and by definition does not occur in beings which lack rational nature.

A dog has a certain range of objects which it can be attracted to as food, and other objects which might be appealing to gnaw on even if inedible. At various times the dog might find resting attractive, or running, or chasing squirrels. There is even some choice involved, we can presume, between jumping up to chase a cat or preferring to stay still and enjoy its rest. While there are differences amongst individual animals (some dogs enjoy hunting more than others), human beings can consider an enormously wide range of objects and actions under the aspect of 'good'. Climbing a cliff, watering the garden, reading a novel in bed, and so on, can be seen as attractive (or unattractive) depending on the circumstances and the mood, taste, ability, and level of cultivation of individual persons.

But the difference between human will and animal appetite lies not primarily in the wider range of objects open for consideration, but in the ability of the human agent to see actions in relationship to a goal. A rational agent is able to see the connection between the goal and actions which may not be attractive at all in themselves (such as undergoing surgery), and willingly choose them for the purpose they achieve. The woman who wants to become an expert on Russian affairs chooses to spend her time on the tedium of learning Russian verbs, while the man who desires to excel on the playing-field may willingly spend hours jogging and lifting weights.

Thomas considered various arguments that can be directed against his scheme of *bonum* as that which moves the will, which gave him an opportunity to clarify the nature of this general inclination. First, since an appetite can be directed toward an object or its opposite, can we not say that the will is drawn to *malum* as well as *bonum*? (This is the essence of *ST* 1–II 8. 1 arg. 1 and 2.) Aquinas insists that the object of volition is *bonum*. If an

---

[47] 1-II 6. 2 ad 1: voluntas nominat rationalem appetitum.

object is perceived as bad it is avoided. Now it is true that there can be opposite actions such as being active or resting, speaking or being silent, but the will is drawn toward one or the other under its aspect of good (*sub ratione boni*).

Another argument concerns the relation of good to being. If Thomas argues that the fundamental quality of the good is sought inasmuch as it has being, then there is a problem in explaining our desires for non-existent things such as 'not walking' or 'not speaking'; or less trivially, for future states of affairs which do not exist (arg. 3).

Here Thomas's theory of cognition and intentional being is important. Things can have being in the mind, although not in the natural realm (*in rerum natura*). Such things as logical constructs and so on have a kind of being; and because the mind can give being to things in this way, future things, as objects apprehended by the mind, are also real beings.

An architect's vision of a new building may exist only in his head or on paper, but the idea now exists where it did not before. It can be described in some detail, and it is possible for it to be an object of desire and action; therefore one may say that the mind has given this building a cognitional existence. Although never built, Frank Lloyd Wright's 'mile-high building' was conceived and put down in a drawing—and so we may indicate the point when it came into existence—though its being is of a different sort from what it would have had if actually erected.

THE POTENTIALITY OF THE WILL

In *ST* 1-II 9. 1 Aquinas considers the complex relationship between the activation of the will and intellect. That which is in potency is reduced to act by something already in act. This is the meaning of moving something or imparting change (*movere*). A psychological power is in potency in two respects: (1) to be active or inactive; and (2) to do this or the other. A mover (something in act) is required to activate the power in both respects: exercise (doing or not doing) and the determination or specification of the act.[48] Note that in the first respect it is a binary operation: doing/

---

[48] 1-II 9. 1: Indiget igitur movente quantum ad duo: scilicet quantum ad exercitium vel usum actus; et quantum ad determinationem actus.

not doing, on/off. In the second respect there can be many possible determinations. In Thomas's example of vision (as a potency) the first respect is simply seeing or not seeing; the second, in regard to colour, could be not only black or white but a host of different colours and shades.

Now the will (as rational appetite) needs a mover in both respects. The first, the exercise, comes from the subject, i.e. the agent, who can be acting or not. The second comes from the object (towards which the agent is inclined), according to which the action receives its specification.

The first respect relates to the end, because since every agent acts for a purpose, the principle of motion derives from the purpose. The good in general has that character of purpose and is the object of the will. All the actions of the agent are comprehended in the will's fundamental desire for the good in general. The will then moves the other powers of the soul to their respective actions. This is true, according to Thomas, because the potency or skill set on a general end will move a skill or power to a more particular end which is included in the general end.

If a person plans to do the weekly shopping, the will directed to that purpose will set in motion the process of action leading to driving a car, going to the bank, thinking about menus for the coming week, and so on, without forming a special intention for each separate action.

The second respect of moving from potency to act deals with the object in the manner of formal cause. All actions in nature are specified by form. The prime formal principle is being and universal truth, the object of the intellect. Thus in this aspect of movement the intellect moves the will by presenting to it its object. For this object to be able to move the will into act it must be apprehended not as simply 'there' but as something good and attractive (ad 2). Any apprehension of being without this character of attractiveness will leave the will unmoved.

It is also true to say that the will moves itself (1–II 9. 3). As the intellect moves from potency to act through the knowledge of the premiss to a knowledge of the conclusion, so the will can move itself to willing a particular means which is related to the end it already wills. In other words the desire for a general end will prompt the agent to consider various possible means and carry on

to the identification of a particular means to that end. The two
aspects of will as being moved and moving can be clarified by
distinguishing act and potency. The will is in act with reference to
the end, in potency in relation to the means (I-II 9. 3 ad I).
Willing the end can be seen as the will moving itself to act.

Thomas is consistent with his principles by asserting (I-II 9. 4)
that the will is not self-actualized. One might, however, argue
from experience that the will does begin to will something when
it didn't before. The conclusion that many might draw from this is
that the will then decides to turn to something new. But not
Thomas: when we will something new, 'it is necessary that it be
moved to the willed object by something else.'[49] The reason
behind this is metaphysical: everything which is sometimes an
agent in act and sometimes in potency, needs to be moved by some
other mover. The will never moves into act totally on its own; it
does not actuate itself. It always requires an object, and this is a
requirement of the Aristotelian-Thomist account of all being and
change.

The objection can be made, of course, that this would contradict the principle of voluntary action, namely that it originates
from an *interior* principle and not an external object (9. 4 arg. I).
Thomas replies that though it is true that we can speak of the will
as an 'intrinsic principle of action' it does not mean that it is the
first principle, not moved by something else.

It is important to see here what Thomas is *not* saying. When he
asserts that the will is never its own first cause and that it is moved
in act by something else he is not describing a range of objects. He
does not mean that various ideas, objects, goals, and good things to
pursue all take their turn in being exterior objects moving the will
in action. There is only one exterior being who moves the will,
namely God (I-II 9. 6). And there are two reasons for this: first,
because God is the creator of the human soul, and therefore the
cause of its potencies; the second reason follows from the nature of
the universal good: since nothing motivates the will except good in
general, only God, who is universal good, can move the will in this
way. Everything else (in creation) is considered good by participation and is a kind of particular good. A particular cause does not
yield a general inclination.

[49] I-II 9. 4: Necesse est ergo quod ab aliquo moveatur ad volendum.

INTELLECT, WILL, AND EMOTION

Though the principle of human action is the mutual influence of intellect and will, some account must be given of the place of emotion in the psychology of human action, especially with the revival of interest in this amongst philosophers and psychologists.[50] In general, there is an 'affective' quality to all thinking and action, since it is part of the dynamic of movement toward or away from the object perceived as *bonum* or *malum*.[51] Thus the will in its fundamental role of inclining the agent to various goods (or avoiding evils) has an affective orientation, and it is appropriate to use, as Thomas does, such emotional terms as love, desire, joy, sorrow, hate, and so on to describe its function.

It is the more restricted sense of emotion, related to physiological change, which Thomas explores in the section of the *Summa* dealing with the passions (1-II qq. 22–48). As with all the powers of the soul, the Thomistic understanding of the activation of the passions relates them fundamentally to their object. In relation to something good, there may be love, desire, joy (depending on the degree of attainment), hope or despair (depending on the perception of the likelihood of attainment). In relation to a bad object, there may be sadness, aversion, or hatred. In relation to the possibility of something bad occurring, there may be fear, or its opposite, courage (in the face of the perceived danger), or anger.

These emotions can also be categorized in reference to the two sensitive appetites, 'irascible' and 'concupiscible', the former relating to the difficult good, the latter to what is pleasurable. Thus in these two appetites there may be opposing movements (attraction or aversion), so that in the irascible appetite there may be hope or despair, or courage or fear. Anger is here as well, but it does not have an opposite emotion, since it is related both to evil (such as an injury suffered) and towards good (in terms of a victory to be achieved).

The emotions do not lead to action directly. Although Thomas

---

[50] See J. Jacob, *Passiones: Ihr Wesen und ihre Anteilnahme an der Vernunft nach dem hl. Thomas von Aquin* (Mödling, 1958), and M. Jordan, 'Aquinas's Construction of a Moral Account of the Passions', *FZPT* 33 (1986), 71–97.

[51] See D. von Hildebrand, 'The Role of Affectivity in Morality', *PACPA* 32 (1958), 85–95; and R.-T. Caldera, *Le Jugement par inclination chez saint Thomas d'Aquin* (Paris, 1980).

treats of the emotions at some length, his philosophy of human action is not at all an 'emotive' one in that passions are not the primary agencies for decision or execution of action. They may help to shape or motivate action, but in Thomas's scheme the sensitive appetite is subject to the rational part of the soul.

For Thomas the sensitive appetite is controlled by both reason and will. Attention should be paid to his teaching here, as common discourse about human emotion often attributes control to 'will-power' *or* to intellect. The teaching in *ST* I 81. 3 is quite clear. The passions are subject to reason with regard to their activation—they are, like the will, prompted by the character given to the object by the reason.[52]

If one considers sensitive appetite in an animal, the emotion follows directly from the 'estimative' power which moves the sensitive appetite. For example, a sheep, when it recognizes an enemy such as a wolf, will feel fear. In human beings, however, there is a 'cogitative' power in place of the estimative, which by nature is able to be moved by reasoning, i.e. by the consideration of general principles, logical deduction, and the generation of particular conclusions. So, Thomas says, 'it is clear that general reasoning commands the sensitive appetite (including both irascible and concupiscible) and thus the appetite is obedient to it.'[53] Anyone can see that this is true from experience, says Thomas: we can by reasoning mitigate our anger or fear. For example, when we are angry at someone for bumping into us, by considering whether it was done accidentally or not, whether or not it could have been helped, we can affect the state of our anger. The same with fear: we can calm our fears, of the dark, for example, by reminding ourselves that the door is locked and that we checked through the house when it was light.

Emotions are subject to the will with regard to execution. In the case of non-human animals, motion will follow the appetite immediately. Using the example of the sheep, when the wolf is seen, and fear is felt, then the sheep will flee—there is no 'superior appetite' to resist this. A human being, however, is not immediately moved into action in response to the activation of the

---

[52] W. Lyons, *Emotion* (Cambridge, 1980), 35, has misread Aquinas as less a cognitive account than 'an impulse or conative account of emotion'.

[53] *ST* I 81. 3: Et ideo patet quod ratio universalis imperat appetitui sensitivo . . . et hic appetitus ei obedit.

sensitive appetite (whether to pursue or avoid), but awaits the command of the superior appetite. Though it is often convenient for people to excuse their eating habits or sexual behaviour on the basis of the strength and irresistibility of sensation and the natural sequence of desire and action, Thomas will have none of this: 'the lower appetite is not sufficient to move us into action, unless the superior appetite consents.'[54]

Passion or emotion is not a sufficient explanation for human action, even for sinful or 'irrational' actions, or what are called 'acts of passion'. Thomas does not resort to the easy explanation that in sinning the agent is ruled by passion, because all voluntary action involves choice, and choice is determined by intellect and will. The intricate way in which intellect and will combine in *liberum arbitrium* as the principle of all human action is the subject of the next chapter.

[54] *ST* I 81. 3: unde appetitus inferior non sufficit movere, nisi appetitus superior consentiat.

6

Liberum Arbitrium, Principle of Action

WHEN the focus of the *Summa Theologiae* shifts from God and creation to human morality, the link Aquinas offers is that God is the exemplar of the human, that human beings are constituted in the image of God. The essence of this image is stated clearly in the prologue: 'a human being is the principle of his own actions, having as it were *liberum arbitrium* and power over his own acts.'[1] Mastery over actions comes through both reason and will, and thus *liberum arbitrium* (which distinguishes human action from that of irrational animals) is said to be a power both of the will and of reason.[2]

The term *liberum arbitrium* was used in classical literature and legal formulations to indicate the 'power to decide' or 'freedom of action'.[3] As it was used by Boethius and much of the medieval tradition, it was understood to be a matter for both reason and will, (as indicated in the *Sentences* of Peter Lombard which St Thomas quoted), but with St Bernard and the development of the Franciscan tradition there was a growing tendency to put the emphasis on the will as the decisive factor, until *liberum arbitrium* largely became synonymous with free will.[4]

That *liberum arbitrium* is still translated as 'free will' and not 'free choice'[5] indicates the truth of the observation that the later em-

---

[1] *ST* 1-II *prol.*: restat ut consideremus de eius imagine, idest de homine, secundum quod et ipse est suorum operum principium, quasi liberum arbitrium habens et suorum operum potestatem.

[2] 1-II 1. 1: Est autem homo dominus suorum actuum per rationem et voluntatem: unde et liberum arbitrium esse dicitur facultas voluntatis et rationis. See also the next article, 1-II 1. 2: Illa ergo quae rationem habent, seipsa movent ad finem: quia habent dominium suorum actuum per liberum arbitrium, quod est facultas voluntatis et rationis.

[3] *The Oxford Latin Dictionary* cites Livy, Seneca, Tacitus, Ulpian, and Gaius.

[4] O. Lottin wrote a series of articles on the history of *liberum arbitrium*, first published in 1926–7 and gathered into his *Psychologie et morale aux XIIᵉ et XIIIᵉ siècles* (Gembloux, 1942), i. 11–389.

[5] The English Dominican translation of 1915 and T. Suttor in the Blackfriars edn. (vol. xi) use 'free will' for *liberum arbitrium*, while 'free choice' is used by J. F. Anderson in his *ST* selections in *The Treatise on Man* (Englewood Cliffs, NJ, 1962).

phasis on will in the scholastic tradition has affected the proper understanding of St Thomas.[6] The basic underlying error is to conceive the will and intellect to function independently, if not in opposition to each other. When they are pictured as operating sequentially, then it is inevitable that the locus of decision is resolved either by positing a judgement of the intellect followed by an acquiescent will (so that the 'real decision' is made by the intellect), or by an intellectual description of options presented with 'indifference', leaving the will free to make the decision ('free will').[7]

The only way for choice to be the genuine product of both reason and will is for both to be active at the same time, and this is the right way to interpret Thomas. This is explained by a metaphysical distinction between the potencies: intellect and will (as described in Chapters 4 and 5) are different *kinds* of potencies, based on the different ways in which a person relates to an object, and they activate and guide each other.

CHOICE, FREEDOM, AND ERROR IN THE EARLY WORKS

The problem of *liberum arbitrium* is treated competently by Thomas in two early works, the commentary on the *Sentences* (1254–6), and *De veritate* (1256–9). The main lines of Thomas's insight into the problem and towards its solution can be seen in these writings and remain basically unaltered.[8]

Thomas wanted to emphasize that free choice is a combination of both reason and will. Choice involves the forces of discretion and

---

[6] Bourke, *Will in Western Thought*, 88, observed that most Catholics have read St Thomas on the topic of the will through the eyes of Duns Scotus; Pinckaers, *Les Sources de la morale chrétienne*, attacked the voluntarist tradition inherited from Ockham, especially the concept of 'indifference' in practical judgement, which should not be associated with Aquinas. The reader will find that Lottin also identified free choice with the will, and considered Thomas to be a voluntarist.

[7] Lottin no doubt understood the problem in this fashion, because he tried to assign the terms 'intellectualist' or 'voluntarist' to the subjects of his study; cf. *Psych. et morale*, i. 222.

[8] Lottin saw a change in the teaching on free choice from an emphasis on the intellect in *De veritate* to an emphasis on the will in *De malo*, but this approach can be convincing only to those who are determined to make Thomas a voluntarist; see n. 32 below. There are later developments, new insights and changes in terminology, but these should be regarded as clarifications in response to questions and challenges, and not fundamental changes in position.

desire, and so requires the power of both reason and will.[9] Thomas saw the combination of reason and will as an integral harmony in a single process of action, and he applied the terms 'cognitive' and 'affective' to designate the different but complementary roles of reason and will in the choice of action.[10]

On the question of whether the nature of *liberum arbitrium* is a potency, a *habitus*, or a combination of two potencies, Thomas agrees with Bonaventure that it cannot be one rational power without the other, nor can it be a third potency separate from intellect and will as Albert the Great had thought.[11] Thomas would probably have solved this question rather differently if he had felt less constrained by the traditional boundaries of the debate. He states that free choice properly signifies an act (and not a potency, faculty, or habit); but since long usage has established the different meaning, he agrees to regard it as the 'principle' behind the act.[12]

All human actions are a product of a choice which is the result of a judgement of reason—this is the essence of *liberum arbitrium*.[13] This ability to choose is the mark of all intelligent beings, including God and angels, and is what distinguishes man from beasts.[14] This judgement is very closely related to will. Reason apprehends the good which the will desires; the judgement of what to do is perceived under the aspect of good, and can therefore not be essentially contrary to appetite or will.[15] The basic harmony of reason and will is presupposed: reason apprehends what is good, and will desires it.

[9] *In II Sent.* 24. 1. 2: Eligere enim, quod actus eius ponitur, importat discretionem et desiderium; unde eligere est alterum alteri praeoptare. Haec autem duo sine virtute voluntatis et rationis perfici non possunt.

[10] Cf. *In II Sent.* 24. 2. 4 ad 2.

[11] *In II Sent.* 24. 1. 3; cf. *De veritate*, 24. 6.

[12] *De veritate*, 24. 4: Liberum arbitrium, si vis vocabuli attendatur, nominat actum, sed ex usu loquendi tractum est ut significet id quod est principium actus. Thomas's use of terms often involves concessions to the tradition of discussion. This applies to the treatment of conscience and *synderesis* as well.

[13] *De veritate*, 24. 1: Homo vero per virtutem rationis iudicans de agendis potest etiam de suo arbitrio iudicare in quantum cognoscit rationem finis et eius quod est ad finem.

[14] Ibid. 24. 2; the discussion of free choice in angels and God is in art. 3; cf. *In II Sent.* 25. 1. 1.

[15] *De veritate*, 24. 2: Appetitus enim cognitionem sequitur, cum appetitus non sit nisi boni . . . sed iudicium de hoc particulari operabili ut nunc, numquam potest esse appetitui contrarium.

Even an act such as fornication is not 'chosen' by the will in opposition to a dictate of reason which pronounces it to be wrong (as a common model of moral reasoning has it); it is selected by the reason (and will) as an object of good. In fact, all people choose each of their actions on the basis of doing something good (or desirable), because no one can act on the basis of an intention for evil.[16]

What about the anti-Pelagian contention, so important in the _Sentences_, that humans need grace in order to accomplish good? Thomas was able to resolve the relationship of grace to _liberum arbitrium_ by distinguishing two different meanings of good: not according to any difference in the thing or action itself (_secundum substantiam_) but according to the attitude of the agent (_secundum modum agendi_). Giving alms, for example, would be a kind of good action as it stemmed from a natural generosity; but it would be different from a giving which sprang from true charity. Free choice without grace is not able to choose this latter kind of good (i.e. properly motivated), which is beyond human nature. That good, however, which is proportionate to human nature is possible for _liberum arbitrium_ to fulfil. Thomas says, for example, that we are able to cultivate fields, to build homes, and to do many other good things without the aid of grace.[17]

Thomas does not set up right and wrong as a matter of the will obeying or disobeying the voice of reason. Choice is the result of a combination of reason and will—both of which may err, both of which need to be right in order for good choices to be made. According to Thomas there can be error in judging, both in theoretical and in practical matters.[18] In actions this may happen by poor reasoning itself (for instance, inappropriate use of a practical syllogism for the circumstances) and thus wrong conclusions may be arrived at; or passion can bind reason so that its judgement of the

---

[16] _De veritate_, 24. 2: Nullus enim intendens ad malum operatur. Thomas cites Pseudo Dionysius, _De divinis nominibus_; the text (4. 31) in the Migne edition (_PG_ iii. 731) reads 'nemo enim proposito sibi malo facit quae facit'; the text in Thomas's commentary says 'nullus enim ad malum respiciens facit quae facit', on which Thomas has a long section; he puts it more positively and clearly establishes his basic principle that even when we do bad things we act on the basis of desiring what is good: 'non enim faciamus mala, nisi ex desiderio alicuius boni' (_In De div. nom._ 4. 22, no. 581).

[17] _De veritate_, 24. 14.   [18] _In II Sent._ 24. 3. 3.

particular action is affected. Thus Thomas affirms that it is not the will that should be looked to as the only source of error and wrong choice. There are many ways in which reason also can go wrong. Thomas says that reason is the cognitive potency and directive of the will: therefore error cannot occur in the will unless it in some way occurs in the reason.[19] Thomas here does not exonerate will and 'put the blame' on reason—that would be to make the same mistake in the opposite direction. The delicate and intimate complementarity of cognition and affection means that for good action both need to be well-ordered; when evil action is done, both have been disordered. Both reason and will acting together (and this joint operation is what is called *liberum arbitrium*) are the principles of choice, of freedom, and of error.

A difference noted by his contemporaries in his doctrine of free choice (and which was later included among articles for censure) was Thomas's teaching of the will as a passive potency: 'The appetite is passive because it is moved by something desirable; a desirable thing has motive force only when it has been apprehended in a certain way.'[20] The rational appetite or will desires good, but cannot be moved by good in general: it must be apprehended as something useful or desirable in particular. This is the function of reason: to particularize and specify the good for the will to seek. In this respect, the will depends on the intellect to present a good object to desire. But because no good is absolute except God, any other good perceived by reason and presented as desirable to the will has an ambiguous quality about it, in that it lacks the fullness of good, so that the will need not accept a good object merely because it has been presented with it. On this metaphysical point of the contingency of all being and the ambiguity of all good apart from God Thomas grounds his profound doctrine of the radical freedom of free choice—of both reason and will.

Thomas emphasized the freedom of *voluntas* and that it is not 'forced' to follow the judgement of reason. That is not because the

[19] *In II Sent.* 24. 3. 3 ad 1: non potest esse peccatum in voluntate nisi sit aliquo modo in ratione . . . unde malam voluntatem aliquo modo praecedit falsa aestimatio.

[20] *De veritate,* 25. 1: Motus enim appetitivae partis ex apprehensione quodam modo oritur, quia omnis operatio passivi ab activo originem sumit: appetitus autem potentia passiva est, quia movetur ab appetibili quod est movens non motum, ut dicitur in III *De Anima*; appetibile vero non movet appetitum nisi apprehensum.

actual decision, the choice, is left finally to the will (as most other theologians held) but because the judgement of reason may be fallible. Any particular action might be good, but it might also not be good if considered from a different point of view.

Thomas shifted the discussion of free choice to a different level, and so enriched it that in investing traditional terms and references with new meaning he was and continues to be misunderstood. If one has not appreciated the mutual involvement of reason and will, then one can be confused by statements such as that the will is what moves the reason by ordering its act, and the reason moves the will by proposing to it its object.[21] The teaching that choice (*electio*) is principally an act of the will (*ST* 1-II q. 13) seems difficult to reconcile with the notion of the priority of the intellect and of the will as a *potentia passiva*. But things become clearer when one sees *liberum arbitrium* in the context of the stages of the process of action. Each act of volition is preceded by an act of cognition to apprehend the good; but each stage in the process is initiated by a preceding act of will which moves the intellect to the next stage.

The *Summa contra gentiles* uses the same principles to defend man's freedom against deterministic theories and to explain the nature of error and sin. Human action as the product of both cognition and volition working together is made even clearer: every choice and activation of the will by us is caused directly by an intellectual apprehension, because understood good is the object of the will.[22] The object of desire is not only in the intellect but also in the will of the person who desires—in the intellect as an image of its representation, and in the will as the end of motion.[23]

What is the explanation for defective action? Thomas starts with the possibility of the will, the usual explanation. If there were in it a natural defect, then we would always be committing this bad action. If it is 'voluntary', i.e. if we can control it, then we have to look further for its cause, which will lead us into an infinite regress. Thus

---

[21] *De veritate*, 24. 6 ad 5: Voluntas quodam modo movet rationem imperando actum eius, et ratio movet voluntatem proponendo ei obiectum suum, quod est finis.

[22] *SCG* III 85: Omnis electio et actualis voluntas in nobis immediate ex apprehensione intelligibili causatur: bonum enim intellectum est obiectum voluntatis.

[23] *SCG* IV 19: Sic igitur quod amatur non solum est in intellectu amantis, sed etiam in voluntate ipsius . . . in intellectu enim est secundum similitudinem suae speciei: in voluntate autem amantis est sicut terminus motus.

we must posit two principles which precede volition: the *vis apprehensiva* (cognition) and the *obiectum apprehensum*, which is the goal or end. Thus reason is the proper mover of the will. Moral error or sin in an act of the will can arise when the will follows an apprehension of sense, or when there is something in the reason representing another good, which diverges from the proper good.[24] Thomas did not make use of the practical syllogism in the *SCG*, so he was not able to give more than a general explanation of the combination of reason and will in error.

LIBERUM ARBITRIUM IN THE SUMMA THEOLOGIAE

Thomas placed his discussion of *liberum arbitrium* (*ST* I 83) after a general treatment of intellect, will, and other psychological powers. This removed it from the context of sin and grace where it had been normally discussed (in commentaries on the *Sentences*), placing it under the doctrine of creation and anthropology. Thomas also kept it removed from the actual discussion of the details of human action in *ST* I-II; thus the general and theoretical relationship between reason and will in choice are discussed in terms of *liberum arbitrium*, while the details of the process of human action could be treated separately using different terminology.

In *ST* I 82. 4, Thomas explains how the will and intellect mutually move each other. The intellect moves the will through the end it presents, or in the manner of final causality, because 'understood good is the object of the will'. The will, however, moves all the potencies of the soul, and thus as efficient cause moves the intellect to cognition.[25]

Thomas begins his section on *liberum arbitrium* (83. 1) by saying that man has free choice because he acts by a judgement (*iudicium*) that something should be done or avoided; this judgement is not made by instinct (as in brute animals) but through a cognitive

---

[24] *SCG* III 10: Cum autem voluntas in actionem prorumpit ad apprehensionem apprehensivae sensualis; vel ipsius rationis aliquod aliud bonum repraesentantis a proprio bono diversum; sequitur in actione voluntatis peccatum morale.

[25] *ST* I 82. 4: aliquid dicitur movere dupliciter. Uno modo, per modum finis; sicut dicitur quod finis movet efficientem. Et hoc modo intellectus movet voluntatem: quia bonum intellectum est obiectum voluntatis, et movet ipsam ut finis.

Alio modo dicitur aliquid movere per modum agentis; sicut alterans movet alteratum, et impellens movet impulsum. Et hoc modo voluntas movet intellectum et omnes animae vires.

power (*per vim cognoscitivam*). Because particular actions are contingent, there is no necessity, and human reason is free in selection. This is the same doctrine as we found in the *De veritate*.

Thomas identifies the principal act of choice (*electio*) with the appetitive potency (83. 3) and ends his main response with the bald statement 'And so free choice is the appetitive potency.'[26] It is in a formal way that choice is connected properly to appetite: since choosing has to do with selecting means to an end, and means are considered under the aspect of good, and good is the object of the rational appetite (the will), the choice is properly an act of the appetitive power.

As in the *De veritate*, this statement of the connection between choice and will is not at all the same as an assertion that it is the appetite alone that chooses. In fact what Thomas understands to be the proper relationship of intellect and will is maintained throughout this question: 'for choice, however, there come together something of the cognitive power and something of the power of appetite.'[27] Further, in all three replies to the arguments the point is made that appetite requires something from cognition for its activation: 'apprehensive powers' accompany appetite (ad 1); counsel or the judgement of reason precedes choice (ad 2); and 'the appetite has the power to make comparisons because of the cognitive power by which it is moved.'[28]

Throughout much of this article Aquinas has shifted to the use of *electio* for choice, and he gave his rationale at the beginning of the response: 'What we mean by free choice is that we are able to receive one thing while refusing another, which is choosing.'[29] This shows that Thomas regarded *liberum arbitrium* and *electio* to be equivalent to Aristotle's *prohairesis*, understood in both a general and a particular sense. *Prohairesis* in *EN* III is treated as the principle of action, while in books VI and VII it is more specifically the act of choice leading to action. The terminology available in the Latin discussions allowed Aquinas to use *liberum arbitrium* for the general

---

[26] *ST* I 83. 3: Et sic liberum arbitrium est appetitiva potentia.

[27] Ibid.: Ad electionem autem concurrit aliquid ex parte cognitivae virtutis, et aliquid ex parte appetitivae.

[28] Ibid. ad 3: Appetitus enim, quamvis non sit collativus, tamen inquantum a vi cognotiva conferente movetur, habet quandam collationis similitudinem.

[29] I 83. 3: Proprium liberi arbitrii est electio: ex hoc enim liberi arbitrii esse dicimur, quod possumus unum recipere, alio recusato, quod est eligere.

sense and *electio* for the particular (which may be distinguished as 'free choice' and 'choice'). The citation of Aristotle's description of *prohairesis* as *intellectus appetitivus vel appetitus intellectivus* is meant to underscore the primary contention, found in all of Thomas' treatments, that human choice involves an intimate combination of both reason and will.

The final article in the question (83. 4) deals with the relationship between willing in general (*velle*) and *liberum arbitrium* or *vis electiva*. Following a distinction made by John Damascene between *boulēsis* and *thelēsis* (83. 4 ad 1), Thomas distinguishes between simple willing and choosing after deliberation, i.e. selecting a means to an end. This is analogous, Thomas says, to the distinction between *intelligere*, simple apprehension of something, and *ratiocinari*, the process of arriving from one thing to knowledge of another. This is not just a subtle scholastic distinction for Thomas but is at the heart of his understanding of the psychological process of action. We have a willing for the good in general; but we do not choose the good in general, but only in particularized form, and it is the reason that performs the function of specification. *Liberum arbitrium* does not occur without the particularization, and because of the nature of being and mind there is an indeterminacy about every particular good specified by reasoning, which is the source of possible error, or evil, and also of freedom. The difference in the nature of the apprehended good as intellect translates it from general to particular is the essence of the psychological process of action.

De Malo 6: 'ON HUMAN CHOICE'

The sixth of the series of questions *De malo* was probably disputed publicly and written in 1270 when Thomas's views on *liberum arbitrium* were being criticized, and the question of freedom and the will was certainly part of the general controversy in Paris concerning the soul.[30] The topic of discussion is *electio* and not *liberum arbitrium*, which allowed Thomas to discuss more freely the aspect of the will in choice without entering into the discussions of

---

[30] Though quest. 6 has been thought to have been inserted into a series written previously (see Lottin, *Psych. et morale*, i. 253), the unity of the work is now being affirmed (see Leonine edn., pref., 3–5.)

intellect and will which were associated with the question in Lombard's *Sentences* at II. 25.

Thomas's arguments form a clear attack on both cosmological and intellectual determinism, the former presented by Arabic philosophers such as al-Kindi, and the latter by the 'radical Aristotelians' such as Siger of Brabant. Thomas wanted to make a robust defence of the free function of the will. He even distances himself from the concept of *potentia passiva*, and by putting the condemned proposition in the seventh argument is able to present arguments against this misunderstanding of his teaching.[31]

Thomas here is understandably careful in the use of terms and guarded in the choice of arguments. The emphasis on the will is to make it clear that on the point of freedom and responsibility he is on the side of the Augustinian theologians against the determinists; but this does not mean that there has been a change to a voluntarist position.[32] Thomas's whole argument here should be seen as a clarification and defence of the position of the mutual interdependence and freedom of intellect and will which he held all along.

The question is put as to whether man has free *electio* or whether he chooses from necessity. Thomas begins his answer by saying that some (undoubtedly Siger's group) try to combine Aristotle's principle of voluntary action with a theory of determination. They say that an action may be necessitated, but that if it is not imposed by force it is still voluntary, as long as its *principium* is internal and not external. As long as necessity is internal and not external (which would make it imposed) it is consistent with voluntary action.[33]

---

[31] *De malo*, 6, arg. 7; voluntas est potentia passiva, et velle est pati. Sed omnis potentia passiva ex necessitate movetur a suo activo si sit sufficiens. Ergo videtur quod voluntas de necessitate moveatur ab appetibili . . .; Aquinas presents this as Aristotle's teaching from *De Anima* and the *Metaphysics*, and it is not a repudiation of the teaching of *De veritate* where he said that appetite is a passive power (see n. 20 above). In his reply (ad 7) Thomas makes use of the distinction between universal and particular good: no particular, limited good has the character of necessity.

[32] Cf. O. Lottin, 'La Preuve de la liberté humaine chez saint Thomas d'Aquin', *RTAM* 23 (1956), 323–30, at 327–30. Though B. Lonergan and others have pressed even further this voluntarist reading, Lottin's view was correctly criticized by (among others) J. Lebacqz, *Libre Arbitre et jugement* (Paris, 1960), 35, as based on 'une méconnnaissance foncière'; for further analysis see D. Westberg, 'Did Aquinas Change his Mind about the Will?', *Thomist*, forthcoming.

[33] *De malo*, 6, ll. 240–7.

This opinion is heretical, declares Thomas, for it removes praise and blame and subverts all the principles of moral philosophy. If we are moved by necessity to will something, then there is no longer need for deliberation, exhortation, command, or punishment. Thomas explains that the motive or active principle in human action is in both the intellect and the will, citing an authority they would accept, Aristotle's *De Anima*.[34] Thomas expounds his metaphysical principles: there is in human beings a *forma intellectiva*, and an inclination of the will which follows the apprehended form; and from the conjunction of these follows the exterior act. In irrational animals, the form apprehended is determinate, and has one result. In humans, however, because of the many possibilities included under a universal form, there is no such determination.

The main body of Thomas's answer is based on the important distinction between the specification and the exercise of an action.[35] The specification of the act is related to truth, which belongs to intellect and to the order of formal causality; the exercise of the act is related to good, which is the object of the will and belongs to the order of final causality. The teaching is very similar to that found in *ST* I 82 and 83, and the more exact definition of this point should not prevent perception of the basic continuity of teaching, right from *De veritate*, in seeing specification and exercise as descriptions of the complementary roles of intellect and will.

The notion of final causality has to do with the ends (*fines*) of action, and all ends are comprehended under the good; therefore it is the will that is moved in the order of final causality. The deep metaphysical and theological relationship between *verum* and *bonum* which is the relationship between intellect and will admits of no separation or emphasis of one over the other. The order of truth is combined with the order of good in all action, because 'good, to the extent that it is apprehensible, is contained under truth, as something true; and truth itself, to the extent that it is the end of an intellectual operation, is contained under good as a

---

[34] *De malo*, 6, ll. 248–75.

[35] Ibid. ll. 339–45: Si ergo consideremus motum potentiarum animae ex parte obiecti specificantis actum, primum principium motionis est ex intellectu; . . . si autem consideremus motus potentiarum animae ex parte exercitii actus, sic principium motionis est ex voluntate.

particular good.'[36] Could there be a more brilliant or profound analysis than this?

There is still the need to sort out the psychological process of action; and here the question of intellect and will cannot be left merely by saying they are interdependent. The will is not moved without reasoning preceding it; but then a movement of the will (desire) is required before we take counsel. This would lead to infinite regress, however, unless there is some first mover. Now some, says Thomas, have posited that this initial movement is instilled by a celestial body; and this gives him the opportunity to reject decisively cosmological determinism, again quoting from the *De Anima*.

The answer Thomas supplies to the question of the prime mover is God; but the authority here is still Aristotle.[37] What first moves both will and intellect is something beyond them both: God is the ultimate principle behind all knowing and all desiring. Though Thomas does not cite them here (because they would not convince his opponents in the context of this dispute), his authorities in his doctrine of 'bonum intellectum movet voluntatem' are just as much St Augustine and Pseudo-Dionysius as Aristotle.[38]

The foundation is now laid for an explanation both ingenious and profound of why when the will is presented with a particular *bonum intellectum* it is not moved by necessity, even though the

---

[36] *De malo*, 6, ll. 333–8: Unde et ipsum bonum inquantum est quaedam forma apprehensibilis, continetur sub vero quasi quoddam verum, et ipsum verum in quantum est finis intellectualis operationis, continetur sub bono ut quoddam particulare bonum.

[37] In the *EE*, 1249^b14–24, Aristotle says that God is not a ruler in the sense of issuing commands, but is the End for which *phronēsis* dictates, the goal of all other choices. For the use of that section of *EE* known to medieval theologians, see T. H. Deman, 'Le "Liber de bona fortuna" dans la théologie de s. Thomas d'Aquin', *RSPT* 17 (1928), 38–58, and C. Fabro, 'Le "Liber de Bona Fortuna" chez saint Thomas', *RT* 88 (1988), 556–72. For a recent study of *EE* with reference to Aquinas, see A. Kenny, *Aristotle on the Perfect Life* (Oxford, 1992), 76–85.

[38] E.-H. Wéber, *Dialogue et dissensions entre saint Bonaventure et saint Thomas d'Aquin à Paris (1252–1273)* (Paris, 1974), 329: 'Face aux affirmations antiintellectualistes qui se développent en 1270 chez les théologiens conservateurs, Thomas rappelle le grand principe d'Augustin: rien n'est objet d'amour s'il n'est d'abord connu'; in the *De malo*, however, his opponents were the extreme Aristotelians, and quotations of Augustine would not be useful. Wéber, ibid. 321, sees the Neoplatonism of Pseudo-Dionysius as the source of two doctrines for Thomas: (1) the 'passivity' of the will relative to the motive role of the desired object; and (2) the hierarchical view of 'natural love'.

object is good, and even though, let us say, the apprehension by the intellect has not been faulty in any way. Only something which is good in every possible way (*secundum omnia particularia*) will move the will by necessity, and this can be true only of beatitude itself, which is the perfect good everyone seeks. Any other object or goal, however, lacks this perfection, and one may consider whether it is really good or fitting in respect to a particular characteristic. For example, something unquestionably good for one's health is not necessarily desired by the will because it is not good from the point of view of being pleasurable.[39] Medicine may be rejected for its unpalatibility or its cost; healthy food declined in preference to 'junk' food for its taste or convenience; exercise refused for the effort it requires, and so on.

If the metaphysical argument was not convincing enough, Aquinas offers further evidence from experience to show why the will is not moved by necessity. The will may simply incline to one thing more than another, and this may happen in three ways: (1) one consideration may have more weight than another; (2) a person may ponder over one particular circumstance or aspect and not another, applying different perspectives; and (3) dispositions vary in people, and moods may also change in the same person. The will of an angry man will be moved differently from that of a calm man, just as the reaction to food will be one way in the case of a healthy person and another in that of a sick person.

The concept of a disposition is also important for freedom, responsibility, and growth. If dispositions were part of nature and not subject to will, then the will would be choosing from natural necessity, just as all people have the very basic desires to be, to live, and to understand. But if the disposition is not natural but subject to the will, then 'when something seems either good or bad to the agent in this particular case, being affected by a disposition or passion, then the will is not moved by necessity; for it is possible to change this disposition so that something will not appear to him in

---

[39] *De malo*, 6 ll. 441–9: Si autem sit tale bonum quod non inveniatur esse bonum secundum omnia particularia quae considerari possunt, non ex necessitate movebit, etiam quantum ad determinationem actus: poterit enim aliquis velle eius oppositum, etiam de eo cogitans, quia forte est bonum vel conveniens secundum aliquod aliud particulare consideratum; sicut quod est bonum sanitati non est bonum delectationi, et sic de aliis.

the same way: as when a person calms down his anger so as not to make his decision on something in anger.'[40]

In sum, Aquinas saw the inseparable combination of cognitive and affective components in choice and insisted on their joint operation; in seeing a process from general to particular involving stages of thinking and willing, Thomas saw that reason and will alternate, and thus each influences the other. Decisions to act are free by virtue of both intellect and will.

The more precise description in *De malo* of the influence of disposition and character on the question of freedom of choice shows the thinking that Thomas was doing to clarify his understanding for his definitive treatment of these important questions and for his presentation of the problems of intellect, will, and human action in the context of character and virtue in the *secunda pars* of the *Summa Theologiae*. To appreciate Thomas's brilliant solutions to the problems of moral psychology, the differences in fundamental principles from other theologians need explaining.

---

[40] *De malo*, 6 ll. 472–81: Si autem sit talis dispositio quae non sit naturalis, sed subiacens voluntati, puta cum aliquis disponitur per habitum vel passionem ad hoc quod sibi videatur aliquid vel bonum vel malum in hoc particulari, non ex necessitate movebitur voluntas: quia poterit hanc dispositionem removere, ut sibi non videatur aliquid sic, ut scilicet cum aliquis quietat in se iram ut non iudicet de aliquo tamquam iratus. Facilius tamen removetur passio quam habitus.

7
The Distinctiveness of Thomist Psychology

I T is not surprising that medieval thinkers found it difficult to assimilate Aristotle's psychology with the traditional biblical and theological views of the Augustinian tradition mediated through Peter Lombard. The terms of reference set down by the *Sentences* for the powers of the soul were *liberum arbitrium*, sensuality, and reason (which was divided into 'higher' and 'lower').[1] Besides compartmentalizing the mind, this classification encouraged a solution of the problem of sin in terms of identifying choice with will.

The position of Thomas Aquinas can be better appreciated by comparison with Albert the Great and Bonaventure. Both were open to the teaching of Aristotle and were great thinkers in their own right. The former was Thomas's mentor and fellow Dominican, while the latter represents the Franciscan tradition in its least hostile stance, and all three saw themselves as theologians interpreting the great Augustinian heritage.

COGNITION AND ILLUMINATION

Theories of cognition are important for moral theory because the account of the process of the origin of ideas, knowledge of truth, and certitude affects the ability of the doctrine to account for the possibility of error in human action. In general, the more one relies on illumination for cognition, the less one can adequately explain error in the intellect. This naturally leads to regarding the will as the principle agent in human action, with the explanation of error centring primarily on the disposition of the will. Having already considered the Thomistic account of cognition we turn to Augustine, Albert, and Bonaventure.

St Augustine modified Plato's doctrine of Ideas, rejecting the 'innatist' knowledge of the soul and the pre-existence of the soul

---

[1] *Sentences*, II. 25; see P. Michaud-Quantin, 'La Classification des puissances de l'âme au XIIᵉ siècle', *Revue du moyen âge latin*, 5 (1949), 15–34, at 33–4.

associated with it. Instead, Augustine developed the biblical metaphor of God as light to explain the source of truth for the human
mind. This teaching of 'illumination' became a major point of
discussion in the thirteenth century in reaction to the Aristotelian
model of cognition, and it has been seen as the most characteristic
doctrine of the Franciscan-Augustinian school, and one of the
points of greatest contrast between Bonaventure and Aquinas.[2]

   In *De Trinitate* ix Augustine speaks about the way the human
mind is able to see the truth not by the different perceptions people
have, but by gazing upon 'indestructible truth'. 'Even in the case of
images of things corporeal which are drawn in through bodily
sense . . . even here, too, we are convinced either to accept or
reject, within ourselves, by other rules above our mind which
remain altogether unchangeable, when we approve or reject anything rightly.'[3] When comparing objects of memory to imaginary
objects (Augustine's example is the walls of Carthage and
Alexandria), there is a judgement of the truth from above made
firm by most permanent rules (*incorruptissimis regulis*) even though it
is hidden in a kind of cloud of corporeal images.[4] Towards the end
of the chapter Augustine summarizes by saying that 'we see by
forming images of objects in the mind or through bodily sensation;
but we grasp in a different way, by simple understanding, what is
above the sight of the mind, namely the exemplars and the un-
speakably beautiful art of such forms.'[5] The precise way to
interpret this teaching still remains difficult to establish,[6] because it

---

[2] L. Veuthey, 'Les Divers Courants de la philosphie augustino-franciscaine au
moyen âge', in *Scholastica ratione historico-critica instauranda* (Rome, 1951), 627–52,
at 632: 'L'élément caractéristique essentiel de l'augustinisme est l'*illumination*'; see
also E. Gilson, 'Pourquoi s. Thomas a critiqué s. Augustin', *AHDLMA* 1 (1926),
1–127, at 111.

[3] *De Trinitate*, ix. 6. 10: Unde etiam phantasias rerum corporalium per corporis
sensum haustas. . . aliis omnino regulis supra mentem nostram incommutabiliter
manentibus vel approbare apud nosmetipsos vel improbare convincimur cum
recte aliquid approbamus aut improbamus.

[4] Ibid.

[5] *De Trinitate*, ix. 6. 11: aliter figurantes animo imagines corporum aut per
corpus corpora videntes, aliter autem rationes artemque ineffabiliter pulchram
talium figurarum super aciem mentis simplici intelligentia capientes.

[6] J. Hessen, *Augustins metaphysik der Erkenntnis* (Leiden, 1960), 256, understood
Augustine as wanting to establish the divine and eternal ground of our certainty:
'Nicht in uns, sondern in Gott liegt nach augustinischer Lehre der Quell der
Wahrheit.'

is difficult to know to what extent illumination contains 'information' rather than principles for judgement.[7]

Later medieval interpreters tried to read precision into the texts which was not there, because Augustine's purpose was theological and spiritual rather than philosophical and psychological.[8] Thus it is a mistake to try to read from (or into) Augustine's writings a coherent and consistent theory of cognition on the natural level. Many scholastics in the thirteenth century attempted to do this, however, in the face of the new theories entering in with the texts of Aristotle and Arabic commentators such as Avicenna and Averroes for whom the soul's relation to the body and the operation of the intellect were major issues.

Albert the Great, indefatigable commentator on Aristotle, follows his psychology of sensation but mediated by Avicenna.[9] Sensation relates to the potential intellect, which is developed as a passive potency, and the doctrine here is Aristotelian in that the intellect is passive with respect to the sensible impressions it receives.[10] This emphasis on the passivity of the potential intellect,

---

[7] E. Gilson, *The Christian Philosophy of Saint Augustine*, trans. L. E. M. Lynch, (New York, 1960), 91, preferred to see in the concept of illumination a 'regulative and formal role'; cf. F. Copleston, *A History of Philosophy* (Westminster, Md., 1950), ii. 64–5: 'Augustine's problem is one concerning *certitude*, not one concerning the content of our concepts or ideas.' But F. van Steenberghen, *Introduction à l'étude de la philosophie médiévale* (Louvain, 1974), 386–7, held that illumination for Augustine was not a purely formal matter; he sees *De Trin.* viii. 3. 4 as teaching that the intellect, illumined by God, is capable of immediate and a priori intuition of 'meta-empirical' ideas and of the principles involved in them, while lower ideas or concepts of things result from a spontaneous application of this knowledge to the things presented by the sense (or represented by images).

[8] R. A. Markus in A. H. Armstrong (ed.), *Camb. Hist. of Later Greek and Early Medieval Philosophy*, 368, writes of Augustine's illumination theory that 'fundamentally it is a statement in completely general terms of what Augustine considers the ultimate ground of the possibility of rational knowledge, that is to say, God's intimate presence to the human mind'. Markus says (p. 367) that texts can be found to support a theory of illumination as providing concepts and as providing the 'yardstick' for regulating judgements; it did not occur to Augustine to try to make a radical distinction between them.

[9] See E. P. Mahoney, 'Sense, Intellect, and Imagination in Albert, Thomas, and Siger', *CHLMP* 602–22, at 604; cf. Gilson, *History of Christian Philosophy in the Middle Ages* (New York, 1955), 285.

[10] *Summa de creaturis*, II 34. 1 (Borgnet edn., xxxv. 295): Sensus autem dicitur potentia passiva, non quod recipiat formam quae transmutat substantiam suam in substantiam secundum esse, sed potius transmutatur in speciem sensibilem secundum intentionem.

which deals with sensation, is combined with a stress on the action of the agent intellect, which deals with the intelligibles, and here his teaching is a heightened Augustinianism. The phantasm or sensible form is dealt with by the agent intellect whose action is compared to light which makes the object intelligible.[11] Albert's teaching here turns out to be a full-blown illuminationism. The light of the agent intellect is necessary to produce the intelligibles themselves, so that the agent intellect is really the form of the intelligible and of the potential intellect.[12] In other words, the potential intellect is informed not only by the intelligible but also at the same time by the light of the agent intellect itself, so that the process of abstraction requires the continual direct illumination by the agent intellect.[13]

This doctrine would imply that the human intellect really does not need sensation for knowledge; but Albert taught that intelligibles, though present in the agent intellect, are undivided; and thus the phantasms have a role in limiting and dividing the light of the agent intellect into distinct intelligibles. The potential intellect, because of being tied to bodily sensation, is darkened, and has to receive light from the agent intellect in a gradual way. The ultimate goal is to possess a perfected intellect, rising to a knowledge of spiritual nature, angels, and God.[14] This makes his doctrine more Neoplatonic than Aristotelian, and his successors here can be seen to be Meister Eckhart and the mystics.[15]

By comparison Bonaventure is more of an Aristotelian, with a coherent, integrated scheme of cognition, but remaining true to Augustine's insights and theology. In his account of sensation he followed the explanation of Aristotle, but his doctrine of intellectual knowledge is closer to that of Aristotle than was Albert's. Bonaventure believed that Augustine had steered a middle course

---

[11] *Summa de creaturis*, II 57. 4 (xxxv. 495).

[12] *De intellectu et intelligibili*, II tr. un., 5 (ix. 510): Lumen quod est actus intellectus agentis, est forma et intellectus possibilis et eius quod intelligitur; see L. A. Kennedy, 'The Nature of the Human Intellect according to St Albert the Great', *Modern Schoolman*, 37 (1960), 127–37, at 126 n. 30.

[13] *De Anima*, III 2. 19 (Cologne edn., vii. 1, p. 205): Et ideo quando recipitur in possibili intellectu, oportet, quod in lumine agentis recipiatur. Cf. Kennedy, 'The Nature of the Human Intellect', 127, 133.

[14] *De intellectu et intelligibili*, II tr. un., 8, 9 (ix. 514–17).

[15] A. Maurer, *Medieval Philosophy*[2] (Toronto, 1982), 159–60.

between Plato, who had wanted to reduce all certitude to ideas, and Aristotle, who emphasized sense too much; so, he says, we should try to combine the *sapientia* of Plato with the *scientia* of Aristotle.[16] This summarizes well Bonaventure's theory of cognition: Aristotle's theory is important and useful, but only at a certain basic level of cognition.

Bonaventure's description of cognition probably interpreted Augustine's doctrine of illumination in the formal and regulative sense. The eternal exemplars are not the objects of our knowledge, nor do they operate through an influence created in our minds; but the eternal exemplars act as movers and regulators of our thought for the purpose of certitude in cognition.[17] Illumination is required for ideas not derivable from sense, such as justice, beauty, charity, and God himself: our knowledge of these depends on divine illumination. Thus Bonaventure speaks of *rationes aeternae* as the source for super-sensory knowledge, and also as the source of certainty for all cognition.[18]

Bonaventure wanted to combine the Aristotelian notions of passive and active intellect with the Augustinian theory of cognition, and developed an attractive and cohesive account. But what he did in elaborating the psychological account was to say that divine illumination is involved in every act of cognition, the process working like this: every corporeal object, by virtue of its light-form, radiates similitudes of itself. These act on the sense organ and on the faculty of sensation, which reacts to judge their contents; then they are received by the common sense and the imagination. The soul, through the combination of active and potential intellect, abstracts the image by separating the universal or spiritual element from the object apprehended by sense.[19]

Bonaventure differed from Aquinas in teaching that the separation of the universal from the phantasm is a judgement requiring the assistance of divine illumination. Thus to make the judgement 'this is a tree' with certitude would seem to require illumination in

---

[16] Bonaventure, *Sermo*, IV. 18 (*Opera Omnia*, v. 572).

[17] *De scientia Christi*, Quaest. 4 (v. 23): ad certitudinalem cognitionem necessario requiritur ratio aeterna ut regulans et ratio motiva.

[18] Ibid. (v. 22): omne quod cognoscitur certitudinaliter, cognoscitur in luce aeternarum rationum.

[19] See *Itinerarum Mentis*, 2. 6 (v. 301), and summary in P. J. McAndrew, 'The Theory of Divine Illumination in St Bonaventura', *New Scholasticism*, 6 (1932), 32–50, at 47.

Bonaventure's theory (even in Augustine the eternal exemplars are needed only at the higher level of perceiving inner meaning). Thus Bonaventure's teaching implies that the intellect has no real truth, even in its natural knowledge, without the influence of divine illumination. Though the value of sense knowledge is admitted by Bonaventure, the connection between certainty and the need for illumination introduces scepticism concerning the results of man's natural powers.

CONSCIENCE AND MORAL KNOWLEDGE

The concept of 'conscience' as moral regulator of behaviour is part of the biblical and theological heritage; when Aquinas treats it in *De veritate* he cites the New Testament, not 'the philosopher'. A further term *synderesis* became part of the discussion, referring to the knowledge of primary moral principles. Whether or not the term itself had an accidental origin owing to a mistranslation,[20] the usage seemed to point to a real distinction between that part of the mind which possessed knowledge of moral principles, and the more specific moral knowledge which varied with individuals. Without some such distinction it would be difficult to maintain both the knowability and reliability of moral principles and the possibility of ignorance and mistakes in individuals.

Albert in his early writings defined conscience as an act, not a power. In other words, conscience was not the source of moral principles, but the actual process of bringing them to bear in a decision to act. *Synderesis* supplies the knowledge, and conscience applies the relevant principles to the situation. There is a kind of syllogistic process whereby conscience derives an imperative for action by the application of universal principle to particular action.[21]

In his *Summa theologiae*, however, Albert changed his position.

---

[20] See J. Rohmer, 'Syndérèse', *DTC* xiv. 2992–6; on the medieval development of the term see Lottin, *Psych. et morale*, ii. 103–349; and M. B. Crowe, 'The Term *Synderesis* and the Scholastics', *Irish Theol. Quart.* 23 (1956), 151–64 and 228–45.

[21] *Summa de creaturis*, II. 72. 1 (xxxv. 599); the treatment in the commentary on the *Sentences* is basically the same.

No longer is conscience an act but a kind of knowledge, a *scientia*.[22] Albert discusses whether these principles are acquired or innate and makes the distinction between general rules derived from innate, principles, and rules derived through experience. The ensemble of innate principles is referred to by Albert as 'natural law'.[23] This is consistent with the implications of a strongly illuminationist theory of cognition and emphasis on the will in action which he maintained in later life.

Bonaventure is at first surprising in connecting *synderesis* with the will, but in many ways his understanding of conscience is more subtle and attractive than Albert's. He defines conscience as a *habitus* or disposition (not an act) which perfects our practical intellect,[24] which could be taken as equivalent to prudence.[25] Bonaventure recognized, as Albert did not, the connection of practical reason with the affective part of the agent. This means that conscience cannot simply be a *scientia*, because the conclusion one comes to about what should be done is reflective of attitudes and dispositions and not just deductive reasoning.

The question whether the knowledge of conscience is innate or not had to be faced. Bonaventure denied the Platonic position, and framed his reply on his doctrine of cognition. Knowing something requires two things: the presence of the knowable thing, and the light by which we judge. That 'light' for the practical intellect can be described as the knowledge of prime moral principles, which is innate in us.[26] Some of the knowledge of conscience is innate, coming from the first directives of nature, or natural law, and some of it is acquired, developed in us by instruction and experience. Examples of primary dictates are that God is, that God is good, that we should honour our parents, and not harm our neighbours.[27]

---

[22] *Summa theologiae*, II 99. 3. 1 (xxxiii. 241); P. Michaud-Quantin, *La Psychologie de l'activité chez Albert le Grand* (Paris, 1966), 239, was not able to explain the reason for the evolution of Albert's views.

[23] *Summa theologiae*, II 99. 3. 2 (xxxiii. 244).

[24] *In II Sent.* 39. 1. 1 (ii. 899): habitus perficiens intellectum nostrum in quantum est practicus.

[25] Similar to J. Pieper's interpretation of Aquinas; see Ch. 1.

[26] *In II Sent.* 39. 1. 2 (ii. 903): primorum principiorum moralium cognitio nobis innata est.

[27] See J. F. Quinn, 'The Moral Philosophy of St. Bonaventure', in R. W. Shahan and F. J. Kovach (eds.), *Bonaventure and Aquinas: Enduring Philosophers* (Norman, Okla., 1976), 35.

Rather than identify *synderesis* with this innate aspect of conscience Bonaventure made it the affective counterpart to conscience. The affections have a natural weight in directing appetite to good, and thus *synderesis* can be described as this fundamental orientation to *bonum honestum*.

The teaching of St Thomas on conscience and *synderesis* combines features of both Bonaventure and Albert. He takes the earlier line of Albert in defining conscience as an act, not a potency or *habitus*. Conscience does not provide the directions but is itself the bringing to bear of the agent's principles in a situation and is the expression of his judgement. Whether the agent considers actions in the past or something to be done, the action of conscience is essentially the application of knowledge.[28] In the *ST* the connection between conscience and judgement is clarified: it is through our conscience that we judge that something is to be done or not done.[29] Conscience is very clearly not the source of any moral knowledge but its application to a particular action and situation.

Readers have looked to the teaching of Aquinas on *synderesis* to find the content of first moral principles. This seems fair, because Thomas, like Albert, said that '*synderesis* is called the law of our understanding, inasmuch as it is the *habitus* containing the precepts of natural law, which are the first principles of human actions.'[30] Thomas has seemed evasive and even disappointing, however, in spelling out just what these principles are. In *De veritate* 16, where he devotes three articles to the subject, he is thin on content; and in the *Summa Theologiae* he seems more interested in reducing the force of *synderesis* to one precept, the famous first principle of practical reason, 'that good is to be done and pursued, and evil avoided' (1-II 94. 2).

The dissatisfaction that scholars have expressed with this first principle reveals a fundamental misunderstanding of the function of *synderesis* for Aquinas, and more deeply of the entire tenor of

---

[28] *De veritate*, 17. 1: Nomen enim conscientiae significat applicationem scientiae ad aliquid.

[29] *ST* I 79. 13: per nostram conscientiam iudicamus aliquid esse faciendum vel non faciendum.

[30] 1-II 94. 1 ad 2: synderesis dicitur lex intellectus nostri inquantum est habitus continens praecepta legis naturalis, quae sunt prima principia operum humanorum.

Thomistic ethics.[31] To be concerned with the process of deriving deontic propositions to guide the moral life is to take the system of Albert, making conscience a *scientia*, with its secondary principles dependent on the truth of the first principles of *synderesis*. The criticisms made about St Thomas might be fairly levelled at Albert's system, but they do not touch Aquinas,[32] since *synderesis* functions differently: not as the source for deriving particular moral principles, but as providing the disposition by which intentions and actions are judged. Thus *synderesis* is not an alien notion which distorts Aristotelian practical reason, nor does it make prudence a legalistic casuistry.[33]

It is important to recognize a stronger and a weaker sense for 'first principles', and that in neither sense do the principles provide the source of knowledge. The study of economics, in McCabe's example, uses the truths of mathematics as principles, but not as '*premisses* from which truths of economics are deduced; they are terms within which, in the light of which (to use Aquinas's own metaphor), the argument is conducted.'[34] This is the weaker sense of 'first principles', meaning the terms of reference or assumptions

---

[31] E. D'Arcy, *Conscience and its Right to Freedom* (London, 1961), 50: 'as it stands in this flat, drab form, such a principle would promise little effect on our moral life.' He (and many others) have pointed out that nothing can be deduced from such a principle. Because 'it is analytic and necessary, telling us nothing about the facts', it will not serve as the major of a syllogism (ibid. 51–2). D'Arcy is right if the principle is considered as the source of norms for a science of action; but Thomas understands it differently, as the first principle of the 'operative' or 'prudential' syllogism; see Ch. 10 below.

[32] P. J. Payer, 'Prudence and the Principles of Natural Law: A Medieval Development', *Speculum*, 54 (1979), 55–70, wrongly links Aquinas with Albert's notion of prudence as the application of a set of principles to particular situations.

[33] We need not follow M. B. Crowe, '*Synderesis* and the Notion of Law in St Thomas', in *L'Homme et son destin d'après les penseurs du moyen âge* (Paris, 1960), 601–9, at 609, who argues that Aquinas minimized *synderesis* in the *ST* in moving from a 'neo-Platonizing' to a more Aristotelian moral philosophy (see O. Brown, *Natural Rectitude and Divine Law in Aquinas* (Toronto, 1981), 175–7); but rather we can accept the estimate of L. Elders, *Autour de saint Thomas d'Aquin* (Paris, 1987), i. 101: 'In introducing the synderesis St Thomas himself was convinced that he remained within the framework of Aristotle's view, but that his doctrinal elaboration allowed him to solve certain problems not adequately dealt with by Aristotle himself.'

[34] H. McCabe, 'Aquinas on Good Sense', *New Blackfriars*, 67 (1987), 419–31, at 425.

needed by a science, often borrowed from another body of knowledge.

The stronger sense refers to principles that every reasoned argument depends on, that must be granted by anyone. The principle of non-contradiction, and the principle that 'the whole is greater than the part', are not the source for the derivation of further knowledge, but, as shown above, are the mind's fixed principles which furnish certitude in judging the truth of ideas apprehended and reasoned. They make it possible to conduct an argument or pursue truth.

Throughout the writings of St Thomas the comparison is made between the first principles of theoretic reason and those of practical reason, the function of which is similar. The self-evident principles 'do good and avoid evil' or 'God must be obeyed' or 'act in accordance with reason' furnish no further direction for action, but are the principles which form the bedrock for the operation of a good conscience. In *De veritate* Thomas writes that 'in human actions, so that there can be some rectitude in them, it is fitting that there be some permanent principle which has immutable correctness against which all actions are tested, so that that permanent principle resists all evil and assents to all that is good.'[35]

Here Thomas incorporates something of the affective view of *synderesis* found in Bonaventure: 'this [permanent principle] is *synderesis*, whose function is to object to evil and to incline towards good.'[36] The cognitive and affective aspects of *synderesis* are summarized by Thomas in the *Summa Theologiae*: 'And so *synderesis* can be said to stimulate one towards good and to object to evil, inasmuch as we proceed by means of first principles to what is to be discovered and then judge the results of enquiry; therefore *synderesis* is not a potency but a natural *habitus*.'[37]

The error involved in the traditional view of *synderesis* is one concerning moral psychology, which is why the comparison of

---

[35] *De veritate*, 16. 2: Unde et in operibus humanis ad hoc quod aliqua rectitudo in eis esse possit oportet esse aliquod principium permanens quod rectitudinem immutabilem habeat, ad quod omnia humana opera examinantur, ita quod illud principium permanens omni malo resistat et omni bono assentiat.

[36] Ibid.: Et haec est synderesis, cuius officium est remurmurare malo, et inclinare ad bonum.

[37] *ST* I 79. 12: Unde et synderesis dicitur instigare ad bonum, et murmurare de malo, inquantum per prima principia procedimus ad inveniendum, et iudicamus inventa. Patet ergo quod synderesis non est potentia, sed habitus naturalis.

Thomas with Albert and Bonaventure is helpful. What was divided between intellect and will by Albert and Bonaventure has been profoundly united by Thomas Aquinas. For Albert, conscience is a set of moral principles derived from the first principles (*synderesis*) whose truth is guaranteed by illumination. The will, if ordered rightly, then decides actions in accordance with conscience. For Bonaventure, conscience is informed by both experience and illumination with principles for action, and the orientation of the will in its subsequent choice is central to right action. For Thomas, the first principle of practical reason, 'Do good and avoid evil', is not tautologous or inert, but combines both intellect and will. Metaphysically it expresses the interchangeability of *verum* and *bonum*; psychologically it represents the point at which intellect and will are invariably united; and theologically it expresses our participation in the being of God.[38]

Thomas was able to describe *synderesis* as a natural *habitus*, while both Albert and Bonaventure had to rely on the notion of illumination to undergird the certainty of moral principles. This use of illumination not only weakens the ability to provide an account of human action of general application to all people, but it implies a separation of intellect and will which is fatal for an adequate moral psychology. If natural law and moral principles are in the intellect by illumination, so as to guarantee their certainty, intellect and will are forced apart. Since illumination and error are mutually exclusive, the will then becomes the pivotal point, either in allowing the intellect to obtain the illumination in the first place, or in deciding not to abide by the direction of the intellect's light.

St Thomas, however, could account for truth in the intellect without illumination, because of the process of conforming the intellect to the thing, the process of judgement. Judgement is performed with more or less accuracy, which allows for the possibility of error in cognition, and the syllogism, both theoretical and practical, supplies the detailed description. Because St Bonaventure did not appropriate Aristotelian logic and the account of intellectual cognition to the same degree, he lacked the flexi-

---

[38] V. J. Bourke, 'The Background of Aquinas' Synderesis Principle', in Gerson, *Graceful Reason* (1983), 345–60, at 355: the first principle was not a new discovery by Thomas Aquinas; 'the real origin of the formula "Do good and avoid evil" is in the Bible.'

bility of the Thomist account of judgement.[39] Without it, he was unable to explain the possibility of error on the one hand, and of certitude on the other, without recourse to divine illumination— its absence (due to faulty disposition of the will) to account for error, and its presence for certitude. Albert interpreted the practical syllogism in a theoretic way, as a means of deriving particular principles for the knowledge of conscience. Thus he lacked the understanding of the practical syllogism as the union of thought and action which Thomas saw in Aristotle's ethics (to be explained in Chapter 10). The resulting separation of intellect and will in both Bonaventure and Albert is revealed in their understanding of free choice.

LIBERUM ARBITRIUM

In his *Summa de homine* (c.1244–8) Albert said that *liberum arbitrium* has something of reason and something of will in it.[40] Echoing previous discussions Albert says that to decide (*arbitrari*) belongs to reason, but the freedom of desiring or not desiring is of the will; therefore *liberum arbitrium* consists of both.

Unfortunately, Albert saw the roles of reason and will as more contradictory than complementary, and set up an opposition between the decree of reason and the appetite of the will.[41] For Albert this was accentuated by his understanding that in Aristotle *prohairesis* (translated as *electio*[42]) was a rational act which seemed to be different from *liberum arbitrium*, a power free to determine itself

[39] For judgement in Bonaventure see Garceau, *Judicium*, 76 ff.; note the estimate of McAndrew, 'The Theory of Divine Illumination', 39: 'It is noteworthy that these Augustinians make no distinction between the reception of the intelligible species and the judgement whereas for St Thomas they are two distinct operations. For him there is no possibility of error in apprehending the essence of the thing because the essence being a simple, indivisible entity is either grasped entirely or not at all. The possibility of error comes with the judgement by which we seek to express the quiddity of the thing. Bonaventura makes no such distinction.'

[40] *Summa de creaturis*, II 70. 2 (xxxv. 575): habet aliquid rationis et aliquid voluntatis; cf. *In II Sent.* 24. 5.

[41] Ibid.; see replies, p. 577.

[42] In the very earliest medieval trans. of the *EN* (the '*Ethica Vetus*') *eligentia* was used for *prohairesis* (e.g. at 1112ᵃ5), but in later versions *electio* came to be the standard word. The different versions have been edited in the *Aristoteles Latinus* series (xxvi. 1–3) by R.-A. Gauthier, (Leiden, 1972–4).

in agreement or not with the judgement given by reason.[43] The opposition between reason and will led Albert to think of *liberum arbitrium* as a special faculty or potency, which would serve to arbitrate between intellect and appetite by performing the real *electio*.[44]

This is hardly a 'solution', since if it belongs to neither reason nor will it is not at all clear on what basis the final choice or arbitration is made—whether rational or affective. Albert's unsatisfactory treatment reflects the tension between Aristotelian choice (understood in too rational a sense by Albert) and the theological tradition of *liberum arbitrium* (understood probably in too voluntaristic a sense), and these are still unresolved by Albert.[45]

Compared to other Franciscans, Bonaventure takes pains to stress the importance of reason in free choice. *Arbitrium* is a *iudicium* which is to discern the just and unjust; but no power can know what is right or wrong, excepting only that which shares in reason.[46] In order to know what is good or evil, what is to be done or avoided, there must be an act of reason preceding the action.[47] The appetite is not moved without thought preceding, because (and here Bonaventure shows his true understanding of Augustine) 'we are never able to love what we do not know.'[48]

Thus Bonaventure affirms the deep connection between reason and will in *liberum arbitrium*: choice cannot occur without each of them functioning. Without reason, there is no reflection, no focus for direction; and without will there would be no movement.[49]

---

[43] *In III Ethic.* 1. 16 (vii. 219): in libero arbitrio electio dicitur non inclinata qua libere accipit quod vult. In prohairesi autem electio est inclinata ad formam rationis diffinientis. See Michaud-Quantin, *La Psych. de l'activité*, 152.

[44] *Summa de creaturis*, II. 70. 2 ad 1–5 (xxxv. 576); cf. *In II Sent.* 24. 5; this was not original with Albert—it was discussed by Hugh of St Cher and became part of the tradition; see Lottin, *Psych. et morale*, i. 98–101.

[45] Michaud-Quantin, *La Psych. de l'activité*, 156: 'Ces difficultés étaient considérables, elles tiennent à l'opposition irréductible entre la volonté d'Aristote, guidée par le choix rationnel qu'a effectué l'agent, et le libre-arbitre, souverain dans sa décision, de la tradition théologique.'

[46] *In II Sent.* 25. 1, a. un., q. 1 (ii. 593): Nulla autem potentia novit, quid iustum et quid iniustum, nisi illa sola, quae est particeps rationis.

[47] Ibid. q. 6 (ii. 605).

[48] Ibid.: nequaquam enim amare possumus quod non cognoscimus.

[49] Ibid. q. 3 (ii. 599): Nam si rationem tantum haberet et non voluntatem . . . posset se super actum suum reflectere, sed non posset movere vel imperare. Si vero appetitum solum haberet et non rationem, posset utique movere et in actum exire . . . non posset utique refrenare, et ita dominium non haberet.

When Bonaventure says that *liberum arbitrium* includes both reason and will, he does not mean that reason gives good advice which the will decides whether or not to follow, in the simple way characteristic of many before him.

Bonaventure improved on Albert's account by rejecting the theory of a diverse potency: 'all acts of the soul are able to be performed through these two potencies, reason and will.'[50] He does not see intellect and will as opposed, but as working together, and their co-ordination and mutual necessity is underlined by the example Bonaventure gives of the one act of writing resulting from the intimate union of the powers of both eye and hand. This explains the deep level at which free choice is a power resulting from the conjunction of the potencies of reason and will.[51]

Bonaventure did not attach liberty to the will only, but to the full act of choice. A person has control, not just with respect to his own action, but with respect to the object as well.[52] That freedom is a function of the variety of objects presented was a central feature of Thomas's position. Bonaventure seems to have seen the essence of the nature of choice and described the operating forces of reason and will in a harmonious way, doing justice both to Aristotle's concept of deliberated desire and Augustine's doctrine of the ordered *voluntas*.

In the final analysis, however, there is a falling short, and in one respect Bonaventure puts the weight on the will after all. This is not because Bonaventure says that action 'begins in the reason and is consummated in the will'[53] (Thomas says much the same in *ST* I-II 13. 1). Bonaventure's view of the actual process of choice was that *optio* or *electio* comes from the *voluntas*, and this is the problem. Reason is to discern, to dictate, to judge, to reflect; but in describing the actual process of choice he says that the definitive judgement is never without will, going on to say 'however much reason deliberates, the definitive judgement is concluded in that place which the will selects.'[54] The reason is important in specify-

[50] *In II Sent.* 25. 1, a. un., q. 2 (ii. 596): omnes actus animae per has potentias, quae sunt cognitiva et affectiva, sive ratio et voluntas, exerceri possunt.

[51] Ibid. q. 3.

[52] Ibid. q. 1.

[53] Ibid. q. 6 (ii. 605): sive facultas, quae dicitur liberum arbitrium, in ratione inchoatur et in voluntate consummatur.

[54] Ibid. ad 3 (ii. 606): Quantumcumque enim ratio deliberet, in eam partem terminatur definitivum iudicium, quam praeoptat voluntas.

ing, even defining the right thing to do; but actually choosing to do this thing, putting it into action, is for Bonaventure a function of the will.

It is at this subtle but crucial point where differences between Thomas Aquinas and Bonaventure emerge: Thomas has a greater interest in and mastery of the details of Aristotle's account of the process of choice; and he also developed an account of cognition along lines different from Bonaventure's theory of illumination which allowed more flexibility for reason. Bonaventure perceived, on the same level as Thomas, the profound interpenetration of reason and will in *liberum arbitrium*; but Thomas knew about the practical syllogism and so could explain how reason chooses.

The superiority of the Thomistic account should not prevent the recognition of the important common ground shared by Bonaventure and Aquinas on the topic of *liberum arbitrium*, which unites them against the Scotist principle of the radical separation of intellect and will. This lends further weight to those who have reacted against the tide of later scholastic voluntarism and have indicated the Thomistic balance of cognition and volition.[55]

A passage in Thomas's commentary on Aristotle's *Peri Hermeneias* deals with the problem of certitude in a way which ties together both theoretical and practical reasoning and provides a summary of his position on free choice. Thomas poses an argument against his position: 'if good is the object of the will it would not seem possible for the will not to desire what appears good to it, just as reason is not able to turn from assenting to what seems true to it; so it seems that choice follows counsel of necessity.'[56] This expresses the Franciscan inability to understand the 'passivity' of an intellectual potency without seeing determinism; and even

---

[55] S. Pinckaers, *Les Sources de la morale chrétienne*, is not the only one to insist on this: Lebacqz, *Libre Arbitre*, 38, says free choice 'ne s'explique que par un étroit concours des deux facultés'; cf. G. Verbeke, 'Le Développement de la vie volitive d'après saint Thomas', *Revue philosophique de Louvain*, 56 (1958), 5–34, at 12; and cf. J. Endres, in the Deutsche Thomas-Aufgabe, xvii B. 521: 'Der befehlende Erkenntnisakt und der wählende Willensakt sind ein und dasselbe'; see also Y. Simon, *Freedom of Choice*, ed. P. Wolff (New York, 1969), 98: 'There is no freedom of the will without the freedom of judgment.'

[56] *In I Peri Herm.*, lect. 14 (23): Cum enim bonum sit obiectum voluntatis, non potest ut videtur ab hoc divertere quin appetat illud quod sibi videtur bonum; sicut nec ratio potest ab hoc divertere quin assentiat ei quod sibi videtur verum; et ita videtur quod electio, consilium consequens, semper ex necessitate proveniat.

Bonaventure, with his Aristotelian account of sensation, would not have been able to answer this argument without appealing to the freedom of the will.

Thomas's answer is faithful to his principles and is profound. He accepts the fundamental similarity between the true and the good, so the link between cognition and practical reasoning holds. In the theoretical field Thomas distinguishes between a truth which is known *per se* (one of the first principles), to which the intellect necessarily assents, and those truths which are derived. Among derived truths there are some which follow from principles and are conclusions of demonstrative reasoning, and others which do not follow of necessity. These can be false even if the principles were true, and these conclusions amount to *opinabilia*.

The case is similar with the 'good'; there is a type of *bonum* which is by definition desirable, namely *felicitas*. But there are many other things which are desirable only for some end (*appetibilia propter finem*). To live and to understand are things we necessarily seek; but not particular goods, which move the appetite or will according to some good considered to be in them.[57] Thus the will is not moved by necessity. The difference between the universal and the particular, so fundamental to Aristotle, is the key to the defence. What is true universally must be assented to; what is good universally must be desired. But since every good in mortal life must be particularized to be desired, and this is the function of practical reasoning, there is full scope for freedom and error.

OPPOSITION TO AQUINAS

Franciscan theologians simply could not accept the notion of the will as a *potentia passiva*.[58] Their criticism showed little sensitivity either to Thomas's analysis or to the philosophical issues involved in the relationship of reason and will. In their eyes if will is a passive potency, and must be 'moved' by an object, then it cannot be free, and so they understood Thomas to be denying the freedom of the will. In their explanation of sin, however, they could propose only the simplistic dichotomy of the rightness of reason against the perversity of will.

[57] *In I Peri Herm.*, lect. 14 (24): Unde moveant appetitum, secundum aliquod bonum consideratum in eis.
[58] Lottin, *Psych. et morale*, i. 243–52.

The context of the debate was much wider than this, however. There was a general reaction against some of the applications of Aristotelian teaching, especially those which seemed to challenge Christian doctrine in the areas of creation, the nature of the soul and its immortality, and man's intellect and knowledge of the world.[59] Having gone through a period of relative openness to new philosophy, many Franciscans began to form a reaction against these new ideas which later crystallized into a neo-Augustinian school. This had not been the case in the 1240s and 1250s, when Bonaventure himself was quite capable of a friendly reading of Aristotle.[60]

At first the conservative reaction developed not against Aristotle's central teaching as such, but against certain proponents of a more radical interpretation. Complicating the picture was the influence of the interpretations of Averroes and Avicenna on theologians in Paris, of whom Siger of Brabant could be seen as a kind of leader in the period after 1265.[61]

Thomas, recalled by his Dominican order to Paris in 1269, took a position in the conflict which many found ambiguous. While he was a champion of the theological party against the Averroists in the matter of the immortality of the soul and the individuality of the intellect, he took what was seen to be an anti-Augustinian position on the relation between intellect and sensory knowledge; and he seemed to side with the extreme wing of Aristotelians on the question of the eternity of the world.[62]

[59] Van Steenberghen, *Introduction*, 333–89.

[60] Id., *La Philosophie au XIIIe siècle* (Louvain, 1966), 235: the attitude of Bonaventure to Aristotle in the *Sentences* 'ne respire ni la défiance, ni l'hostilité, ni la réprobation; elle est faite d'estime, de respect et de sympathie'; cf. J. F. Quinn, *The Historical Constitution of St. Bonaventure's Philosophy* (Toronto, 1973), 859–60.

[61] The use of the term 'Latin Averroism' (see Gilson, *Hist. of Christian Phil.* 387 ff.) may mislead in giving the impression of a definite school of anti-Augustinian or anti-Christian thought; but van Steenberghen, *La Philosophie*, 394 ff., thought it better to think of a radical or 'heterodox' element in the Aristotelianism of certain teachers.

[62] The difference between Bonaventure and Aquinas, even on the doctrines which did divide them (e.g. illumination of the intellect and eternity of the world), should not be exaggerated; see Quinn, *Historical Constitution*, 890: 'St Bonaventure is not an Augustinian theologian opposing Aristotelian philosophy or keeping it out of his theology. It is equally evident that regarding the eternity of the world, he is not an Augustinian opposing St Thomas on theological grounds.'

Though the above questions were the central ones, there was
also concern about determinism and the problem of free will.
Aristotle put an emphasis on voluntary choice in his ethics, but in
some of the Arab-derived teachings there was a form of determinism, especially involving the celestial spheres.[63] Siger of Brabant
(though we have little direct knowledge of his moral teaching in
this period) is known to have taught a less rigorous form of
determinism, and also used Aquinas's *De veritate* as a congenial
source for his teaching.[64] This may well have cast additional
suspicion on Thomas's soundness in the minds of the conservative
theologians. They did not bother to put too fine a point on the
variations within positions they considered inimical to their own,
and thus threatened to include Thomas in their attacks. While
Thomas was careful to distance himself from Siger and his school,
and on some issues led the attack, his teaching on *liberum arbitrium*
with the notion of *potentia passiva* would have seemed idiosyncratic
at best and very different from the dominant brand of Franciscan
voluntarism.

On 10 December 1270 thirteen propositions were condemned
by Étienne Tempier, Bishop of Paris and a former Franciscan
master in theology.[65] The effort does not seem to have been made
to distinguish the varieties of fatalistic astrological determinism
from the proposition linked to Aquinas's teaching by his Franciscan
opponents that the will is a passive potency moved necessarily by
the desirable object.[66] Thomas's teaching was not exactly the same as

---

[63] Aristotelian physics gave a place to the being and causality of celestial bodies
foreign to modern science but standard in medieval thought (cf. Dante); Aquinas
specifically excepts human intelligence and will from such causal influence; see *ST*
I 115. 4 and 1–II 9. 5 and cf. T. Litt, *Les Corps célestes dans l'univers de saint Thomas
d'Aquin* (Louvain, 1963).

[64] F. van Steenberghen, *Maître Siger de Brabant* (Louvain, 1977), 385–6.

[65] Traditional theologians, especially John Pecham, were probably the moving
force behind the process. Tempier went along, but his interest was in the larger
tendencies of the Aristotelian movement rather than the theological subtleties; see
J. Chatillon, 'L'Exercice du pouvoir doctrinal dans la chrétienté du XIIIᵉ siècle: le
cas d'Étienne Tempier', in *Le Pouvoir* (Paris, 1978), 13–45, at 18, 33–4; also J.
Wippel, 'The Condemnations of 1270 and 1277 at Paris', *Journal of Medieval and
Renaissance Studies*, 7 (1977), 169–201, and R. Hissette, 'Étienne Tempier et ses
condamnations', *RTAM* 47 (1980), 231–70.

[66] *Chartularium Universitatis Parisiensis*, eds. H. Denifle and A. Chatelain (Paris,
1891–9), i. 487, Proposition 9: Quod liberum arbitrium est potentia passiva, non
activa, et quod necessitate movetur ab appetibili.

that which was attacked in the condemnation;[67] yet there can be little doubt that Tempier's condemnation must have solidified the position of the Franciscans in their view of the will, and made it much more difficult for Thomas's view to receive a sympathetic consideration.

On some issues it is important not to stress the uniqueness or originality of Thomas, as his contemporaries may have shared similar insights; in the area of the operation of the intellect, however, it is difficult to exaggerate the solitary position Aquinas occupied. Thomas's teaching on cognition, far from winning acceptance, strengthened the Augustinian position of resistance within the faculty of theology at Paris and they responded with a sharpened attack.

The main target for the criticism was the doctrine of the union of soul and body and the related teaching on cognition.[68] There seemed in the doctrine of the potential intellect 'receiving' the phantasm, and the influence of the intelligible species on the intellect, a degree of passivity in the human mind which was simply not acceptable. A spiritual or theological issue seemed to be at stake. Thomas's explanation implied the independence of human cognition without the need for divine illumination, which seemed to advance human power at the expense of divine sovereignty. No more convincing psychological or physiological theories were given; in fact, the very thoroughness of the Aristotelian-Thomist explanation was a major point against it, because it seemed too naturalistic. Even students and defenders of Aquinas 'stepped back in the face of this overwhelming pressure'.[69]

On the question of the will as a passive potency it seems that

---

[67] St Thomas spoke (see Ch. 6 n. 20) not of *liberum arbitrium* but the *appetitus* as a *potentia passiva*, and that it is moved by the *appetibile* but not *necessitate*. These distinctions would have been lost on those who already equated *liberum arbitrium* with *voluntas*.

[68] Z. Kuksewicz, 'Criticisms of Aristotelian Psychology and the Augustinian-Aristotelian Synthesis', *CHLMP*, 623–8, at 623.

[69] Ibid.: this was true of Giles of Rome and Godfrey of Fontaines. Among later Franciscans Bonaventure's mild doctrine of illumination was greatly strengthened and Aristotelian cognition thoroughly expunged. There was a growing fear of the dangers of Aristotelian passivity of the intellect, reflected in Matthew of Aquasparta's conviction that both Thomas and Bonaventure made the soul too passive with respect to material objects; see H. M. Beha, 'Matthew of Aquasparta's Cognition Theory', *Franciscan Studies*, 21 (1961), 1–79, at 9.

neither friend nor foe understood this feature of Aristotelian psychology, which was a technical explanation for the relationship of a rational power to an object, an instance of the general relation between potency and act. The intellect also is a passive potency in relation to its object (*ST* I 79. 2), so no inferiority with respect to the intellect is implied in the will being a passive potency. The intellect does have a certain priority, however, in the order of nature because understanding logically (not necessarily temporally) precedes willing, as mover to moved and active to passive.[70] Behind this is the supremely Augustinian concept that understood good (*bonum intellectum*) moves the will.

The Thomistic account of cognition and volition was rejected because it threatened to reduce the dominance of the soul over the body, which points to the more fundamental metaphysical issues at stake. Thomas's solution to the problem of the relation of the soul to the body was to eliminate the plurality of forms in the soul, and define the soul as the form of the body. The human soul is incomplete without the body, which it needs for sensation and cognition in a way which the Augustinian view of the soul using the body but having its own substantial form would not allow.

On these points of cognition and the soul the contrast between Aquinas and his opponents (nearly everyone else) was real, sharp, and vitally important. The tension between Thomism and Augustinianism was not a simple opposition between Platonic and Aristotelian doctrine, because in certain ways (such as the exaggerated illuminationism) Augustinianism and Platonic thought were being misapplied. In the thought of Aquinas, however, there can be seen a harmonization of Plato and Aristotle, as well as faithfulness to Augustine: 'in Thomas' epistemology, the universal ideals postulated by Plato are fundamentally transformed into creative Ideas in the mind of God, and Aristotle's naturalistic explanation is elaborated into a highly sophisticated psychology of human nature.'[71] In his view of the relation of soul and body, though superficially a rejection of the Platonic tradition of Augustine,

---

[70] *ST* I 82. 3 ad 2: Sed illud quod est prius simpliciter et secundum naturae ordinem, est perfectius: sic enim actus est prior potentia. Et hoc modo intellectus est prior voluntate, sicut motivum mobili, et activum passivo: bonum enim intellectum movet voluntatem.

[71] J. Weisheipl, 'Thomas' Evaluation of Plato and Aristotle', *New Scholasticism*, 48 (1974), 100–24, at 113–14.

Aquinas was providing a metaphysical grounding for the deeper teaching of Augustine. St Augustine delineated human life in history; and Aquinas was trying to show that a human being is 'a wayfarer by *nature* as well as by history . . . if St Thomas made the human a genuine composite, it was not to bury the soul in the body; it was to express, with a deep loyalty and with fuller adequacy, a notion dear to St Augustine: the incarnate soul was a peculiar spirit, a spirit that somehow needed to live in the world of matter and time in order to grow into its destiny.'[72]

The misunderstanding and rejection of the position of Aquinas on soul and body was fatal for later Western philosophy. The refusal to allow the object a determining role in cognition and volition meant the rejection of a realist metaphysics and the setting of the stage for nominalism and voluntarism. Instead of an object activating the mind's power to understand reality by a process of judgements, the intellect simply grasps it; and instead of the value of an object being a function of the ability to understand its attractiveness, the human agent remains indifferent to the object until the will confers value. The successive steps to the dualism of Descartes were small and straightforward.

The recent interest in Aristotle's philosophy of mind, and the determination being shown to dismantle Cartesianism, offer hope that a realist view of the mind and its operations might again be developed. The psychological theory of Thomas Aquinas will offer much of value to the philosophical discussion, but even greater richness for those who want to see a consistent metaphysical treatment thoroughly integrated with profound theological vision and biblical faithfulness.

[72] A. C. Pegis, *At the Origins of the Thomistic Notion of Man* (New York, 1963), 58–9.

PART III
Analysing the Process of Action

8

Stages in Human Action

IN the *prima secundae* of the *Summa Theologiae*, St Thomas deals
with the process of human action as the foundation of a discussion
of the morality of actions and of virtues. The account is Aristotelian in its general structure, beginning with man's desire for the
good, going on to a general account of volition and of the distinction between the voluntary and involuntary, and moving to a more
specific description of deliberation, choice, and action. The reader
familiar with the *Nicomachean Ethics* will notice, however, the
addition of several other stages in Thomas's account; the *Summa*
includes new features in the process: *intentio* (q. 12), *consensus* (q.
15), *usus* (q. 16), and *imperium* (q. 17).

PROBLEMS IN THE CURRENT INTERPRETATION OF AQUINAS

The elements of action were discussed by St Thomas in various
contexts from the commentary on the *Sentences* on, but it is only in
the *ST* that we find a fully integrated presentation of the process of
human action.[1] Twelve steps in the process of action have been
seen in his analysis, and have been set out in systematic fashion as
alternating operations of intellect and will:

Process of human action

Intellect	*Will*
	about the end
1. Apprehension of the end (*apprehensio; simplex intellectus*	2. Wish; willing the end (*velle; simplex voluntas*)
3. Judgement about the end (*judicium circa finem* (or, *iudicium synderesis*)	4. Intention (*intentio*)

[1] See J. Romiti, *De processu evolutivo doctrinae de actu humano completo in operibus Sanctae Thomae Aquinatis* (Milan, 1949).

about means

5. Deliberation (*consilium*)	6. Consent (*consensus*)
7. Practical judgement (*iudicium practicum*)	8. Choice (*electio*)

execution

9. Command (*imperium*)	10. Use; application (*usus; usus activus*)
11. Judgement of the end attained; performance (*usus passivus*)	12. Enjoyment; completion (*fruitio*)[2]

Compared to Aristotle, Thomas seems to have added needless complexity to the structure of action. Further, with the identification of the will as a separate force, and the assigning to it of various stages in the process, Aquinas seems to have made a fundamental change in Aristotle's account. This is especially the case at step 8, where choice, *electio*, is made an act of *voluntas*, while Aristotle's *prohairesis* seems to be an act of reason. Thus one might well conclude that Thomas represents the shift of emphasis in the Christian view of psychology away from reason to will; however, it is the tabular summaries of the commentators which are based on a misunderstanding and have introduced distortion.

Comparison of the various versions of the process of action shows greatest inconsistency at the beginning and end (steps 1–4 and 8–12); but even at the central stages of the process of action, those characteristic of Aristotelian practical reason, we find among

[2] This table is a compilation from various standard accounts; for the English terms see J. A. Oesterle, *Ethics: The Introduction to Moral Science* (Englewood Clifffs, NJ., 1957), 85; V. Bourke, *Ethics: A Textbook in Moral Philosophy* (New York, 1966); and T. Gilby in the Blackfriars edn. of *ST*, xvii. 211 and xviii. 143 (where most of the Latin equivalents are also given). See also A. Gardeil, 'Acte humain', *DTC* i. 339–46, at 343. For fuller discussion see T. Urdanoz, 'Esencia y proceso psicológico del acto libre según santo Tomás', *Estudios filosóficos*, 2 (1953), 291–318; and S. Pinckaers, 'La Structure de l'acte humain suivant s. Thomas', *RT* 55 (1955), 393–412. Pinckaers pointed out the dependence of modern studies on C.-R. Billuart, *Summa Sancti Thomae Hodiernis Academiarum Moribus Accommodata* (Paris, 1876).

Thomist scholars of this century very little clarity. Gilby himself is not consistent, because in the two charts he supplied for the Blackfriars *ST* edition, he has (7) 'discrimination and selection' (where he gives Aristotle's term, *prohairesis*) in the earlier version, and (7) 'decision' in the later one.[3] How does decision differ from 'choice' which he used in both charts? The *New Catholic Encyclopedia* article on human action refers to this seventh stage as 'judgement about choice', which is followed by the eighth, 'choice of means'.[4] This implies that there is some kind of assessment made by the agent's reason of his options, but that the actual 'choice' is made by the will. This standard account is also found in the French neo-Thomist commentators, where decision is associated with the will, and not with the intellect (in contrast to Gilby's second scheme).[5]

In this scheme it is the responsibility of reason to identify the best course of action, but it is the will that actually makes the decision, illustrated by Prümmer in his *Manuale*: a person deliberating about how to recover his health thinks about his options, and he gives his approval to the various medical possibilities; then he discerns the advantages of one particular means; then his choice (act of will) is to choose surgery, for example, from the available options.[6]

Two more recent studies have considered that the problems in the 12-step analysis require more radical revision. Pinckaers has recognized that deliberation should have a conclusion (since Thomas specifically says (*ST* 1-II 14. 6) that deliberation ends at a particular action, that which is in our immediate power to do[7]);

---

[3] See vol. xviii (London, 1966), 143; and vol. xvii (London, 1970), 211.

[4] J. Oesterle, 'Human Act', *NCE* vii. 206–9, at 208.

[5] A. Gardeil in his influential article on human action, *DTC* i. 343, and 'Élection, acte humain', *DTC* iv. 2242–3, described deliberation as 'on recherche les moyens', consent (6) as 'on donne son consentement aux moyens trouvés'; the seventh step is 'on juge quel est le moyen le plus propre', and (8) 'on le choisit' (*electio*). The seventh stage is a judgement of reason that selects one means as the best; then in the eighth the will makes the decision ('on se décide'); cf. Sertillanges, *Philosophie morale de saint Thomas d'Aquin*, 26; H. D. Noble, 'Prudence', *DTC* xiii.1023–76, at 1031; and E. Gilson, *Saint Thomas moraliste*[2] (Paris, 1974), 78 ff.

[6] M. Prümmer, *Manuale Theologiae Moralis secundum principia Sancti Thomae Aquinatis* (Freiburg im Breisgau, 1928), i. 30.

[7] *ST* 1-II 14. 6: Terminus autem inquisitionis est id quod statim est in potestate nostra ut faciamus.

but then this would mean that the practical judgement (step 7) would amount to the same thing as deliberation, and consensus would be little different from choice. Such consideration led Pinckaers to conclude that Aquinas was not successful in his attempt to combine disparate elements from Augustine and the theological tradition with the Aristotelian structure, and to recommend a 'structural' rather than a psychological analysis.[8]

Alan Donagan is clearly sympathetic to the teaching of Thomas, saying that 'Aquinas' analysis of human action is rightly held by his admirers to be a major contribution to philosophy.'[9] But Donagan seriously misrepresents Aquinas by completely rearranging the sequence of stages in human action. In doing this, the complementary relation between reason and will is lost, and thus a major part of the Aristotelian-Thomist conception is distorted. Donagan recognizes that deliberation should end in a conclusion about the best means, but this leads him to include in 'deliberation' the 'judgement' that the means is the best one. While there is some merit in his attempt to reduce the total number of steps, Donagan has chosen the wrong point for reduction.[10]

Two important points of interpretation emerge: first, the importance of distinguishing between *consilium* and *iudicium* as two distinct stages of practical reasoning representing specification and decision; second, the combination of intellect and will in each stage of reasoning. If specification is delayed to *iudicium*, the stages of deliberation and consent become rather vacuous. If deliberation is given the role of specification, as Thomas indicates, then the practical judgement appears to be redundant. The solution to this is to distinguish between specification and choice as two different stages in the psychology of action. Thus even when the agent has specified a particular action as the best means to an end, he still needs to choose to do it. The process of specifying action and the process of deciding are two distinct reasoning processes with different patterns of reasoning.

The distinction Thomas has made in the stages of practical reasoning between deliberation and decision can be seen to correspond to the distinction within cognition between judgement and reasoning (identified in Chapter 5). Thomas articulates this in

[8] Pinckaers, 'La Structure de l'acte humain suivant s. Thomas', 410.

[9] A. Donagan, 'Thomas Aquinas on Human Action', *CHLMP* 642–54, at 652.

[10] Ibid. 653.

articles 3 and 4 of *ST* 2-II 51, where he makes a comparison to the theoretical understanding and the two processes of thought, *inquisitio* and *iudicium*. The dialectic or inquisitive understanding proceeds from common principles; but the demonstrative, which is judicative, proceeds from special principles.[11] Secondly, deliberation and choice both involve reason and will. Choice is not purely an act of will but includes *iudicium* as a constitutive aspect of choice. If choice is equated with *electio*, and *electio* with *voluntas* only, then the difficulties remain. But if choice is understood in the broader sense of *arbitrium*, and the *iudicium* of the practical intellect is understood to be intimately connected with the act of will referred to as *electio*, as Thomas indicates,[12] then this principle (of reason and will) applies also to deliberation. With this analysis (to be spelled out in detail in the following chapters) Thomas's account will seem much more attractive, and the recent reconstructions will not be needed.

This understanding of Thomas can be defended as being also the best interpretation of Aristotle's account of choice. *Prohairesis* in the *EN* is not just an act of intellect, but is a combination of reason and desire.[13] Although there may be a greater emphasis on the rational appetite or will in Thomas because of the Christian theological tradition, there is not the fundamental shift from *intellectus* to *voluntas* as the decision-making faculty which many have assumed to be found in St Thomas: both he and Aristotle teach that human choice is the product of both reason and desire acting together. It is the separation of intellect and will (well represented by the schemata of human action we have been considering), itself the result of a voluntarist view of choice, which has introduced such grave problems for interpreters.

Interest in the process of action seems to have dropped out of theological discussion soon after St Thomas. The results of the success of voluntarism after Scotus are clearly evident in the commentary on the *Summa* by Cajetan (*c.*1510). Here is probably the first summary into twelve steps of Thomas's teaching on the

---

[11] *ST* 2-II 51. 4 ad 2: Unde etiam in speculativis dialectica, quae est inquisitiva, procedit ex communibus: demonstrativa autem, quae est judicativa, procedit ex propriis.

[12] Thomas takes pains to stress the combination of intellect and will in choice at the beginning of his treatment in *ST* 1-II 13. 1.

[13] *EN* 1139^{b}4; cf. Ch. 2 above.

process of human action. The difference from Aquinas, however, is striking: the psychology of action is no longer the interconnection of reason and will, but is conceived as a process of the will: the whole sequence is described as 'habitudo voluntatis ad volitum', and the stages are divided into three orders of *actuum voluntatis*.[14] The whole process of good human action is seen as the perfection of the will towards its object, first towards the end, then to the means, finally to obtaining the end. The principle acts in the process are now *intentio, consensus, electio,* and *usus.*

With the dominance of *voluntas*, gone is the dialectic between reason and desire. In fact, the role of reason has virtually dropped out, having become a mere adjunct of the will. Even *consilium* is seen as something essentially voluntary: studying a problem involves the reason, of course, but Cajetan understood it to be the will deciding to use the reason when it needs its help.[15] There is no mention of a *iudicium rationis* preceding choice (where Thomas mentions this in *ST* 1-II 13. 3 Cajetan is silent): thus choice is purely a matter of *voluntas.*

The distance from Aristotle and St Thomas is immense in Cajetan's account. This is not only because the role of the will has been expanded so disproportionately, but because the entire structure of the process is related to a much more general view of human action. Instead of a picture of the process of making particular decisions and actions, it is an account of moral life in general, with the emphasis on the right general disposition of the will. That Cajetan has completely misunderstood the teaching of Aristotle and St Thomas is clear from his description of *consilium*. It concerns, according to Cajetan, the means (*ea quae sunt ad finem*), but these may be 'for example, the study of theology and moral goodness'.[16] Cajetan was no longer in the same world as Aristotle and Aquinas. His account is not a description of how the agent arrives at a particular action but an account of the moral life in general: the need for the person, in order to live properly, to have his will rightly disposed by making use of the means of grace.

This shift in the context of the discussion of human morality

---

[14] Comm. in *ST* 1-II 16. 4, in Leonine edn., vi. 116–17.

[15] Ibid. 117: Sed quia consilium voluntarium est et a voluntate movetur ratio ad consiliandum.

[16] Ibid.

from particular action to general orientation sheds light on the questions of *beatitudo* and *fruitio*, and the relation of the supernatural end to the natural end of man which has been such a source of misunderstanding and controversy. If human action is seen in Cajetan's terms (which is what has been inherited through the commentators), then the place of an overarching supernatural end becomes vital. But if the context is particular individual action (e.g. eating a meal or mowing the lawn) the relevance of *beatitudo* recedes into the background as the end to which all other ends are ultimately referable but which does not normally enter the psychological process of action.

As far from Thomas's position as he is, Cajetan does not represent the extreme voluntarist viewpoint. Cajetan at least retained the element of *imperium* which follows *electio*, and which Thomas taught was the last act of prudence and clearly an act of reason (1-II 17. 1). It is the executive function of reason putting into effect the decision the agent has made. Cajetan, while he did include a voluntarist element in this, still regarded it as 'essentially an act of reason'.[17] Even this vestige of the role of reason was omitted by later commentators such as Suarez.

Greater faithfulness to Thomas was restored by Billuart in his commentary on the *Summa* published in the mid eighteenth century. He restored the role of reason, especially at stage 7, the *iudicium practicum*, and it is his scheme which has been the basis for modern expositors.[18] Thomist commentators have noted the difference between the emphasis on the intellect and prudence by Thomas and the emphasis on the will in many later treatments. The stage of *imperium* seemed to be the crucial point of difference, and many writers of this century have centred on this as the place to correct the errors of a voluntarist view of human action.[19] *Imperium*, however, as consequent to choice, is not the focal point for the role of reason in action, as the outcome of the choice could only be properly affected by the influence of reason before *electio*. Thus the crucial role of the *iudicium practicum* has not yet been clearly seen.

[17] Comm. in *ST* 1-II 17. 1 (vi. 119): Imperium est elicitive et essentialiter actus rationis, voluntatis vero primordialiter quoad formam. Cajetan adds that it is the principle act of prudence which is an act of reason.

[18] Billuart, 'De actibus humanis', Diss. 3, art. 6, *Summa Sancti Thomae*, ii. 273–4.

[19] See e.g. Noble, 'Prudence', *DTC* xiii. 1050–1, and Deman, 'Le "précepte" de la prudence'.

DEVELOPMENT OF THE THEORY OF ACTION
BEFORE AQUINAS

There was no long tradition of the treatment of the psychological process of action, as this was not of interest to Augustine and was not treated by Peter Lombard. Even after it became a topic for treatment in the thirteenth century it was largely ignored by the Franciscan theologians, including Bonaventure.[20]

The source for this treatment in the Western Church was a translation of John Damascene's *De fide orthodoxa* made by Burgundio of Pisa around 1150. While Damascene was interested in the process of action, the treatment he offered was not original with him; it depended largely on the work of Maximus the Confessor. In two separate works Maximus described a chain of stages in an agent's thinking and willing which resulted in action. His sources were Aristotle and the Stoics, seen through the commentators (especially Nemesius[21]), and his arrangement runs like this:

(1) concept (*logos*);
(2) desire (*boulēsis*);
(3) search (*zētēsis*);
(4) examination (*skepsis*);
(5) deliberation (*bouleusis*);
(6) judgement (*krisis*);
(7) decision (*prohairesis*);
(8) appetition (*hormē*);
(9) use (*chrēsis*);
(10) action ceases (*pauetai*)[22]

Gauthier has pointed to the Stoic influence in the synonyms provided by Maximus: *phantasia* for the first stage, and *sunkatathesis* for the sixth. In addition, the elements of *hormē* and *chrēsis* following decision are basically Stoic concepts.[23]

Compared to Aristotle there is a multiplication to ten different

---

[20] Lottin, *Psych. et morale*, i. 410–11.

[21] R.-A. Gauthier, 'Saint Maxime le Confesseur et la psychologie de l'acte humain', *RTAM* 21 (1954), 51–100, at 57. Burgundio of Pisa made a translation of Nemesius' *De natura hominis* (*Corpus Latinum Commentariorum in Aristotelem Graecorum*, supp. 1, eds. G. Verbeke and J. R. Moncho; Leiden, 1975).

[22] Gauthier, 'Saint Maxime', 82.

[23] Ibid. 64–82.

steps; but these should be taken not as ten chronologically distinct stages but as ten 'aspects' of the process of action. Since Aristotle spoke of a combination of reason and desire in apprehension and in decision, steps 1 and 2 can be seen to be complementary aspects of the stage of apprehension, while 7 and 8 are the intellectual and appetitive aspects of choice (remembering that *prohairesis* is *orektikos nous* according to Aristotle, *EN* 1139^{b}4). Thus much of this more involved treatment, at least in the first steps, can be seen as a spelling out in different terms of what was already implicit in the *EN*; Aristotle emphasized the essential unity of the psychological forces, while Maximus gives the impression of their separation.

It was not Maximus but John Damascene who provided the table of action which was to be influential in the scholastic West. Here is his description of the process in its Latin version:

(1) *bulisis*, which is the will of the end;
(2) *inquisitio*;
(3) *consilium*;
(4) *iudicium*;
(5) *sententia*;
(6) *electio*;
(7) *impetus*;
(8) *usus*;
(9) *cessat*.[24]

Damascene has reduced to one stage the process before counsel by combining reason and will into *bulisis*. His *inquisitio* combines the *zētēsis* and *skepsis* of Maximus, but he adds, at his fifth stage, the *sententia* which is pronounced by the agent in reference to the result of counsel. Note what happens between counsel and choice: following the process of deliberation, which ends in a *iudicium*, a *sententia*, expressive of a dispositional state, is pronounced on this result. Then a choice or decision is made. This well supports the theory of the relationship between deliberation and decision as the distinction between specification and choice, and shows that this interpretation of Aristotle was present in the tradition before the treatment of Thomas Aquinas.

John of Rochelle seems to have been the first Western theologian to bring this analysis of human action into scholastic discus-

---

[24] John Damascene, *De fide orthodoxa*, Latin translation by Burgundio and Cerbanus, ed. E. M. Buytaert (St Bonaventure, NY, 1955), 137.

sion.[25] Though he followed the doctrine of John Damascene, he reduced the steps to six: (1) *consilium*; (2) *iudicium*; (3) *sententia*; (4) *electio*; (5) *impetus*; (6) *usus*. John of Rochelle has dropped the first two and the last from Damascene's list; otherwise he has retained the central steps exactly, with the step from deliberation described as a judgement of what is best; this judgement then being pronounced, there follows an affective disposition on the judgement of counsel, after which the choice is made.

Philip the Chancellor's treatment runs like this: (1) *consiliatio*; (2) *inquisitio*; (3) *iudicium*; (4) *sententia*; (5) *electio*; (6) *exitus ad operationem*; (7) *usus*; (8) *cessat*. It seems that Philip has misunderstood *consiliatio*, but apart from combining *consilium* with *inquisitio*, there is not much difference from Damascene.[26] Alexander of Hales and St Bonaventure were not very interested in developing the account of the process of action, and were content to summarize the flow.[27]

The treatment of Albertus Magnus was more careful, still based on Damascene, but with some additions.[28] He puts at the beginning of the process *apprehensio* and *voluntas*, which restores the separation between *logos* and *boulēsis* in Maximus which Damascene had combined. Then there is (3) *perscrutari*, how to achieve the end, followed by (4) *consilium*: when there are several means one seeks counsel to establish which is best for achieving the goal. After counsel the agent gives (5) *iudicium* about the one he is persuaded is the best course to take; in a situation of differing options he will need to (6) make a preference (*praeoptat et praeligit*). After the actual choice, (7) *imperium rationis*, the mediating action by which the thing is obtained is called *impetus ad opus*. This is followed by (8) *fructus*, which is use with joy, and then by (9) cessation.

Albert's conception of the sequence and nature of the structure of action is remarkable. He treats *apprehensio* and *voluntas* as preliminary, and therefore the action proper begins with *perscrutari*. Albert also realized that *consilium* is necessary only when there are many possibilities. A *iudicium* is then given and the agent selects (*praeoptat*). Following choice, there is an *imperium* and an *impetus ad*

---

[25] Lottin, *Psych. et morale*, i. 401.

[26] Ibid. 406.

[27] Lottin, ibid. 410–11, says of Bonaventure: 'la manière dont il trouble l'ordre original témoigne suffisamment de son incurie sous ce rapport.'

[28] Albertus Magnus, *Summa de creaturis*, II 69. 2 (xxxv. 567–8).

opus; Albert's substitution of *fructus* for *usus* is presumably because when the goal has been reached there is a 'use' with joy, although this seems to be a misunderstanding of Augustine.

For Albert all of these steps are acts of the practical intellect and not of the will[29] (in complete contrast to the later development represented by Cajetan); this is why Albert omitted *voluntas* as part of the initial action itself; why there is no *dispositio* or affective response; and why *electio* itself doesn't figure in the list. There is *praeoptat* and *praeligit* (before choice) and then there is the *imperium rationis post electionem*. Thus choice is not really considered part of the process of action (in terms of practical reason), because of the different category created by Albert for *liberum arbitrium* (as we saw in Chapter 7 above). This required Albert to create two different aspects of choice: there is a free choice which is nothing other than the freedom of doing what one wants, and this 'acceptance' belongs to free choice. There is another *acceptio* which is the choice of one thing over another according to the preference of reason, and this is the act of reason.

Albert seems to have emphasized the role of the practical intellect; but the result is actually a failure to integrate volition or affection within the process of action. He has allowed for desire to be involved in the formulation of a goal, but this occurs before the action begins; the *sententia* after counsel is no longer a *dispositio*, but a *iudicium* of the mind; and at the most crucial place—decision and choice—Albert gives to reason the role of expressing a preference, but then it 'waits' for the real decision to be made by the will, after which it takes over again, commanding the action to be carried out.

Odon Rigaud tried to achieve a neat simplicity by assigning the first half of the series to the operation of reason, and the latter to will. Thus *consiliare, inquirere, disponere*, and *arbitrari* are acts of reason, while *eligere, impetum facere*, and *agere* become acts of the will.[30] This was a spelling out of the split theory of *liberum arbitrium* in which reason proposes while will decides and carries out, using the terms from the theory of the psychology of action. It provides a framework in which to appreciate the stunning solution provided by St Thomas.

[29] Albertus Magnus, *Summa de creaturis*, II 69. 2 ad 11 (xxxv. 568).
[30] Commentary on the *Sentences*, MS Bruges Ville 208, quoted in Lottin, *Psych. et morale*, i. 410.

THOMAS'S THEORY OF THE PROCESS OF ACTION

The process in the account of Aquinas can be reduced to three basic stages: intention, decision, and execution. In its simplicity it is Aristotelian, but with the improvement of a link between decision and action. At the same time, Aquinas knew the Nemesius-Damascene tradition, perceived its insights, and made use of its modifications to Aristotle.[31] But how did Thomas manage to do this? Intention–decision–execution: this seems to bear little resemblance to the nine steps of Damascene or the twelve stages attributed to Aquinas in the Billuart tradition.

The reconciliation was accomplished by Thomas with elegant simplicity and shows him to be consistent and penetrating after all in his interpretation of Aristotle and in his own teaching. The two key principles have been established in discussions above: (1) the distinguishing of specification from decision, with decision as the definite and primary element of human action; and (2) the complementary relationship of reason and will in action.

The first principle allows us to see that the basic 'skeletal' process of action is intention–decision–execution; but also that there are many occasions when the particular action to be done is not clear, and deliberation involving means–end type of reasoning is required. Where this is the case, then the sequence for action becomes: intention–deliberation–decision–execution.

The second principle enables us to see that each stage is made up of a cognitive and appetitive component, or an element of reason and will. A close reading of the questions in this section of the *prima secundae* (e.g. the introduction to *electio* in q. 13) shows just how strongly Thomas emphasized their union: in the act of decision they come together to form a unity, one being the form (*ratio*) and the other the substance (*voluntas*).[32]

Thus if each stage has two components, and we include deliberation, then we have four double steps or eight components:

---

[31] A full comparison of Nemesius, Chrysostom, and Aquinas has been made by E. Dobler, *Nemesius von Emesa und die Psychologie des menschlichen Aktes bei Thomas von Aquin (ST Ia IIae, qq. 6–17): Eine quellenanalytische Studie* (Lucerne, 1950).

[32] *ST* I-II 13. 1: Quandocumque autem duo concurrunt ad aliquid unum constituendum, unum eorum est ut formale respectu alterius. . . . Sic igitur ille actus quo voluntas tendit in aliquid quod proponitur ut bonum, ex eo quod per rationem est ordinatum ad finem, materialiter quidem est voluntatis, formaliter autem rationis.

(1) intention (*apprehensio+intentio*);
(2) deliberation (*consilium+consensus*);
(3) decision (*iudicium+electio*); and
(4) execution (*imperium+usus*).

Each of the four stages is made up of a concurrent input of cognition and volition (see Fig. 2).

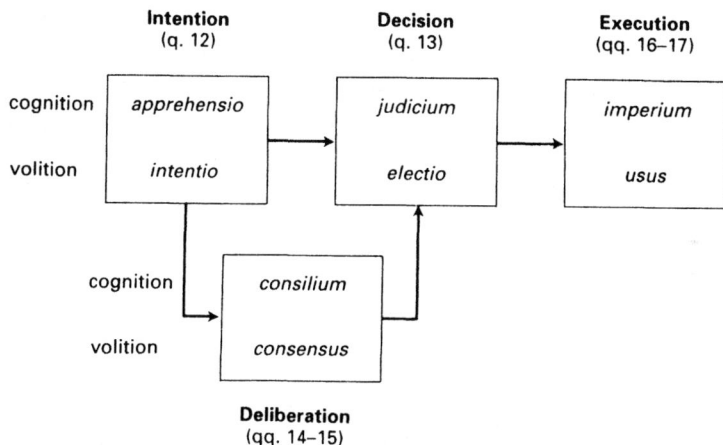

FIGURE 2

Thomas's treatment, which has seemed disordered to previous readers, does follow a definite logical pattern in the *Summa*. Intention is treated in I-II q. 12, with the reason component given special attention in 12. 1 ad 3 and 12. 3 ad 2; then decision is treated in q. 13, with *electio* of the will in 13. 1 and *iudicium* of the reason in 13. 1 ad 1, ad 2, and 13. 3. Then Thomas discusses deliberation, means–end reasoning, as a special stage when required. It is optional, and therefore not an essential or a constitutive part of the process of action. Counsel and consensus, the cognitive and affective aspects of deliberation, are discussed in separate qq. in 14 and 15; *usus* and *imperium*, which make up execution, are also discussed separately, in questions 16 and 17. The treatment in separate questions does not need to indicate that they are chronologically sequential in the process of action, but that Thomas considered that they required more distinct treatment than the stages of intention and decision. In any case, this understanding of Thomas's treatment of stages with double components makes the teaching in the *Summa* coherent, unlike the illogical sequence in the Billuart schema.[33] The natural logic of Thomas's teaching is even clearer to see in the outline in Fig. 2.

Before examination of the stages in detail, however, there are two questions to be dealt with: (1) what about the other four 'acts' in the traditional table of action? and (2) what is the proper terminology for the four stages of action?

In Thomist studies, there can be few better examples of how misunderstanding can become embedded in a tradition—and then make true understanding more difficult—than the distortions in the psychology of action inherited from Cajetan. Starting at the end of the stages, we find that in the teaching of St Thomas there is no distinction made between *usus activus* and *usus passivus* in ST 1-II 16 (or elsewhere), and that this unhelpful complication was simply added to the tradition. *Fruitio* is discussed by Thomas, but in q. 11, which is before the treatment of the sequence of other acts. More fundamentally, it cannot be thought to follow *usus* as a kind of consequence of action, as if enjoyment merely followed naturally. The ordinary distinction between *uti* and *frui*, which is Augustinian, is a contrasting or exclusive one, between enjoying good things for their own sake and seeking good things for the sake of something else.[34] Thus it is appropriate for there to be *uti* in reference to an action which has been conceived in terms of means to an end, and inappropriate to apply the notion of *frui*, especially when the end is remote. Cajetan's conception of *fruitio* may partly be based on a different understanding of Augustine's teaching,[35] and partly, as seen above, on a view of the psychology of action referring to the moral life in general and not to particular actions. In any case, we may note that other scholars have wanted to remove *usus passivus* and *fruitio* from the sequence of action.[36]

[33] See e.g. the disorder in the *ST* references cited in Gardeil, 'Acte humain', *DTC* i. 343.

[34] See O. M. T. O'Donovan, '*Usus* and *Fruitio* in Augustine, *De Doctrina Christiana* I', *Journal of Theol. Studies*2 33 (1982), 361–97, at 366–7.

[35] Augustine was not entirely consistent in his usage, and a text from *De Trinitate* could well have misled later readers; cf. O'Donovan, 365–6.

[36] Gilson, *Saint Thomas moraliste*, 93–5, ends his account of human action with *commander* and *l'usage*; J. Pieper in *Die Wirklichkeit und das Gute* (Munich, 1949), 115, omits *fruitio* and combines *usus passivus* and *activus*; while Donagan, 'Thomas Aquinas on Human Action', *CHLMP* 653, gives only one act after choice.

There is also no need to distinguish four different acts in relation to the 'end' before *consilium* begins. It is much more straight-forward, more sensible, and more faithful to Thomas to combine *apprehensio* with *iudicium circa finem*, and *velle* with *intentio*. Here again, seeing the context of discussion as one of the production of particular actions and not the moral life in general is helpful. The process of action must begin with an attainable object, because one cannot intend an end which is impossible. There can be specula-tive thought about *impossibilia* but certainly no practical reasoning. Therefore a stage to judge the possibility of an end is superfluous (or becomes part of *consilium* as the agent reverts to an end which is desired and possible).

A distinction between four acts concerning the end was not in the tradition before Thomas, either. Only Maximus had *logos* and *boulēsis* before the stage of *inquisitio*, and this was reduced by Damascene to *bulisis*. John of Rochelle and Albert dropped this and began with *perscrutari* or *consilium*. Thus Thomas with his *apprehensio+intentio* is actually restoring this stage to the tradition, and there is no need at all for a further preliminary stage.

Thus the discussion in qq. 8 and 9 of *ST* 1-II is still part of the general account of the relation between desire and action, and the general involvement of reason and will. This is the same kind of discussion as the account of *liberum arbitrium* in *ST* I 83 and of human choice described in general in *De malo* 6 (so not in the actual process of action). Thus Thomas's treatment is quite orderly and consistent: general consideration of good, beatitude as the ultimate end (qq. 1–5); voluntary and involuntary (q. 6); circum-stances (q. 7); the will (q. 8); the way the will is moved (qq. 9, 10); and *fruitio*, the right relation of the will to the end (q. 11). It is only with q. 12 that Thomas begins his special discussion of the actual process of human action.

The second question is about terminology. What names did Thomas give to the stages, and which modern terms should be used? To consider terms for four stages is perhaps begging the question by assuming the interpretation of double acts in each stage. The question is an open one; according to the analysis above, Thomas treated two of the stages, viz. *intentio* and *electio*, each as one stage with two elements, cognition and volition. The other two stages, identified as deliberation and execution, had their elements of reason and will treated in separate *quaestiones*. From

Thomas's treatment in the *Summa*, then, one could argue in favour of the division between acts of intellect and will as presented in the traditional interpretation, or for the unified view advocated here.

At the risk of labouring the point, it is worth while to make as clear and as compelling a case as possible, since this is a new interpretation. It must be agreed that Thomas conceived of human action as an intimate combination of intellect and appetite, because this is essential to every treatment from the commentary on the *Sentences* to the latter parts of the *Summa Theologiae*. Further, Aquinas understood Aristotle's definition of *prohairesis* to be indeed such a combination of intellect and appetite: this is the very first point that Thomas wanted to make in his treatment of *electio* (1-II 13. 1). Thomas carried this fundamental insight further, perhaps as a result of his deep penetration of *liberum arbitrium*, and realized that the entire process of human action depended on the mutual interaction of reason and will. With this principle, he did not find it difficult to assimilate and integrate the separate steps in the Nemesius-Damascene tradition in harmony with the basic process of Aristotelian practical reason.

The interpretation proposed here is that where Aristotle had one term for one stage with two aspects ('noetic' and 'orektic'), Thomas saw that the terms provided by the Damascene tradition could be considered as just more precise labels for these cognitive and appetitive elements. Aristotle saw the process of action as basically desire–deliberation–choice. Thus where Aristotle put *prohairesis*, Thomas saw it as the same stage, but subdivided it into *iudicium* (cognitive) and *electio* (appetitive).[37] Similarly, for the stage of *bouleusis*, Thomas has *consilium* (cognitive) and *consensus* (appetitive); and for the first stage, where he does modify Aristotle, he makes *apprehensio* and *intentio* the cognitive and affective elements respectively. The admitted lack of a stage of execution in Aristotle's account has been seen as a weakness, and it may be that this is the primary Stoic contribution to the philosophy of action, a background reflected in the terms *imperium* and *usus*. What is important to note is that Thomas was able to see these latter elements also as fitting into the cognitive-appetitive scheme, constituting the final stage of action.

An act of reason and will together constitutes one stage; this is

---

[37] It could be argued that Thomas was developing a distinction already in Aristotle, the *krisis* as the cognitive part of *prohairesis*.

more important than the name one assigns to each stage. As long as it is emphasized that both reason and will are involved, then there is no inherent reason why the sequence of stages might not be called *apprehensio-consilium-iudicium-imperium*, noting the corresponding role of the will, just as well as *intentio-consensus-electio-usus*, indicating the corresponding role of reason. But because in Thomist psychology volition is preceded by cognition, and because there is something unfinished at each stage until finalized by the will, there is a preference for the appetitive term as being more inclusive since it presupposes the cognitive. This, I believe, lies behind Thomas's choice of the terms *intentio* and *electio*. The English words used here for the four stages have been selected to be faithful to Thomas, and to convey both cognition and volition without leaning too far in either direction: these are the terms intention, deliberation, decision, and execution.[38]

The treatment in the following chapters corresponds to the order in the *Summa*, with decision coming before deliberation. St Thomas was not being careless; he was indicating that in many of our actions we can decide with certainty and without deliberation (when the situation is identical with one we often encounter, for example). Thus deliberation is subordinate to decision, just as the essence of reasoning is to assist the process of understanding.

---

[38] The clearest confirmation in the *ST* for this 4-stage interpretation occurs in 2-II 153. 5, a remote passage where St Thomas discusses the effects of the vice *luxuria* on the operation of reason and will. 'There are four acts of reason in actions', he says: (1) simplex intelligentia, quae apprehendit aliquem finem ut bonum; (2) consilium de his quae sunt agenda propter finem; (3) iudicium de agendis; (4) praeceptum rationis de agendo.

9

Intention

THERE are different meanings of 'intention': there is the ordinary
usage indicating purpose ('I intend to go to the opera tonight');
there is the legal meaning in connection with *mens rea* (on which
some disagreement exists whether intention is only the knowledge
of the action or indicates desire as well); and there is the philosophical notion of intentionality, which enriches but complicates
the concept for us.[1] The aspect of intention in relation to practical
reason is not one of the clearer points in Aristotle's ethics, and the
tendency to understand his thought (as well as Aquinas's) through
more recent categories has sometimes been a hindrance.

THE ESSENTIAL CHARACTER OF INTENTION

Intention is usually taken to refer to a state of mind, but Thomas
defined it as a tending towards something.[2] This very simple
definition obviously fits in well with his metaphysics of potency
and act, and also makes it possible, at a basic level, to include the
movement of animals as showing a kind of intention. More impor-
tantly, it is a realist account in that it stresses the reality of the object
as motive force and relates intention to that. Intention can be
defined, then, as the aiming of an action towards something.

In general, intention can describe the action of both theoretic
and practical intellect. Intention is part of the process of cognition,
proceeding from apprehension to reasoning, knowledge, and wisdom. In the words of Thomas, that act which first simply apprehends or grasps an object is called the intelligence; then the second
act of the mind, which relates what is to be known or done to

[1] A. Kenny provides a brief summary of the history of intention in ethics in an
appendix to *The Anatomy of the Soul: Historical Essays in the Philosophy of Mind*
(Oxford, 1973), 129–47.

[2] *In II Sent.* 38. 1. 3: Intendere enim dicitur quasi in aliud tendere. In the *ST*
Thomas simply writes *in aliud tendere.*

something else, is called intention.[3] Relating data to known facts and principles is the means of building up knowledge, and relating desired objects to purposes is the key to moral agency. The process of practical reason (in deliberation and judgement) can be seen as a way of clarifying intentions so as to be able to act, 'a device which reveals the order that there is in this chaos'.[4]

In its widest sense intention can refer to all animals, not just humans. According to Aquinas, if one takes the basic aspect of intention as 'aiming at something', nature itself can be said to intend an end, because it is moved to its end by God, as an arrow by an archer. Thus brute animals intend an end to the extent that they are moved by natural instinct towards something.[5] For us, accustomed to think of intention as a mental quality (and to deny it to minors or the mentally handicapped in judicial contexts), the notion that animals exhibit intention in their search for food or mates points out the need to adjust our notion of intention from the description of a mental state to the actual link in the real world between the agent and the object it is moved by or attracted to.

In its proper sense, intention belongs to the will, the rational appetite, and so is restricted to intelligent beings. This is because a rational power and not mere appetite is required to orient the agent to an end. 'Aiming action towards some purpose' would be the more particularized definition applying to rational agents.

A dog enters a room, circles around, then lies down curled up by the fire. The dog 'aims at' or intends a nap. If the circumstances or the dog are well known, a better description may be that he has just eaten, or is worn out from a long walk, or is arthritic, or simply that he naps every day at this time.

With human beings the explanation of action has a similar basis but is not so apparent, even in simple actions, because of the much greater range of purposes which can be served. The description of observable behaviour is inadequate: 'someone comes into a room, sees me lying on a bed and asks "What are you doing?" The answer "lying on a bed" would be received with just irritation; an answer

---

[3] *ST* I 79. 10 ad 3: Quae primo quidem simpliciter aliquid apprehendit: et hic actus dicitur intelligentia. Secundo vero, id quod apprehendit, ordinat ad aliquid aliud cognoscendum vel operandum: et hic vocatur intentio.

[4] G. E. M. Anscombe, *Intention*[2] (Oxford, 1963), 80.

[5] *ST* I-II 12. 1.

like "Resting" or "Doing Yoga" which would be a description of what I am doing in lying on my bed, would be an expression of intention.'[6] Human action involves a purpose, and the total action involves not just a description of the physical posture or movements but the purpose being pursued.

Intention is most characteristic of the will, because pursuing an end by definition belongs to appetite. But the relation to the end is not simply a desire for some end in general, as in a person desiring health. In the case of intention, the purpose or end of an action can be seen as the termination of the process to which the action is ordered, and it is in this way that intention regards the end. We really intend to achieve health when we wish to reach it by means of something else.[7]

If a person claimed a desire for physical fitness, but made no moves to alter her diet or include exercise in her daily schedule, the reality of her intention would be called in question. Intention is not just a desire for a general end, but for an end through some means. Thomistic intention is not just 'planning' to do something some time, but actually tending towards the goal by means of the actions leading to it.

From this it follows that the will requires the intellect. If a relation is set up between goal and action leading to it, then that ordering involves the operation of the intellect. In the commentary on the *Sentences* Thomas wrote that the nature of intention implies a certain order of one thing to another. But the ordering of something to another occurs only through the intellect, whose task it is to establish order.[8] In the *ST* Aquinas compares the relation of cognition and volition to a person using an eye to see something (1-II 12. 1 ad 1). Thus intention in an agent denotes an act of will, but it presupposes (by definition) a structuring by the intellect in relating a means to a purpose.[9]

This implies a difference between intention and desire. You might desire, for example, to be a world champion skier, but

---

[6] Anscombe, *Intention*, 35.

[7] *ST* 1-II 12. 1 ad 4: Non enim solum ex hoc intendere dicimur sanitatem, quia volumus eam: sed quia volumus ad eam per aliquid aliud pervenire.

[8] *In II Sent.* 38. 1. 3: intentio primo et per se actum voluntatis nominat secundum quod in ea est vis intellectus ordinantis.

[9] *ST* 1-II 12. 1 ad 3: Unde hoc nomen *intentio* nominat actum voluntatis, praesupposita ordinatione rationis ordinantis aliquid in finem.

cannot actually intend that without the means to it being possible, any more than you could intend to believe six impossible things before breakfast. Intention is a tending towards some actual thing, and therefore cannot be directed to happiness in general. 'I just want to be happy' does not describe an intention or purpose: it only paraphrases the description of the nature of rational appetite itself, the orientation of the will in general. For an agent to have an intention, the will must be directed to an object.

ACTIONS WITH COMPLEX INTENTION

There are many human actions which are more complicated in intention than the type represented by lying down in order to rest or to meditate. They can be complex in different ways: there may be several purposes involved in a single action, such as going to the beach in order to get a tan, to meet friends, to relax, and to swim. Or a single action may be made up of a kind of hierarchy of actions, so that several subsidiary ends are served by the whole action.

If I intend to do the washing up, for example, this will mean assembling the dirty dishes, washing them with water (usually with detergent), drying them, and putting them away. These steps are intrinsic to the action (whether done by machine or by hand) and don't require a separate intention. Similarly washing up could be one part of the larger task of tidying the kitchen, the one intention for which might also include putting out the garbage, sweeping the floor, and organizing the tins.

St Thomas of course recognized this character of intention and used the central articles of this question (*ST* 1-II q. 12 aa. 2–4) to deal with the relationship between end and means. There can be an end which has the character of an end for the purpose of intention, but is itself a means to a further end. A means may be the end of one motion and the beginning of another. In a series of steps A–B–C, intention can be of either B or C, because though C is the end of the whole series, B is an end with respect to A.[10]

The following article (12. 3) deals with a person intending two ends at the same time. In one way, this may be just a corollary of

---

[10] 1-II 12. 2.

intending one end (B) as related to a further end (C) as above. But there is also a general kind of intention, which can include other ends. The inclusion may be, first, that of constitutive ends. Modifying the illustration of Thomas: a lengthy rest and restricted diet are the implied (and subservient) ends which, following the physician's orders, one must intend when one intends the recovery of health.

A second way is to see other ends which are made possible by a general kind of end: for example, intention for money because of the many possible ends it will serve, without clearly intending those further ends. One may desire money in order to acquire wine or clothes, but these further ends can be seen to be included in the general intention for money (12. 3, and ad 2).

Some care in interpreting this is needed. It might be taken that a general end includes all the steps leading up to it. For example, the action of 'getting an essay handed in on time' can be seen as comprising several different stages: you might telephone your friend to make sure that he does not have a certain book; you get on your bicycle to ride to the library to check out the volume which you need; you miss a committee meeting and stay up half the night to finish writing the essay. Now it is true that all the movements have meaning and purpose in the context of the whole action which can be described as 'getting the essay done on time'; so in this sense they come under the one intention. But the only actions intrinsic to writing essays are thinking and verbal expression by applying pen to paper (or fingers to keyboard, et cetera). Thus the reply 'I was doing an essay' is not an adequate explanation (in itself) for sleepiness or absence from a meeting, because missing appointments and losing sleep are not intrinsic to writing essays in the way that doing the washing up involves getting dishes wet.

The late Herbert von Karajan is reported to have joined the Nazi party in order to further his career as an orchestral conductor. This purpose was undoubtedly better than persecuting Jews or making Germany's military power great again; but the connection between joining the Nazi party and being a great conductor is far from intrinsic. Bruno Walter, Erich Kleiber, and others showed that conducting opportunities existed elsewhere and the choice was not so constricted as von Karajan may have claimed. This is not to say that it could not have been right to stay in Germany;

only that the appeal to a worthy object of intention does not necessarily cover questionable means.

This sets up the distinction in the next article (12. 4) between two different relationships of willing in reference to ends and means. One may consider intention of ends and means *per se*, and in this way there are two separate motions. But in viewing means as for an end (*propter finem*), there is one motion of the will, one intention. According to Thomas, when I say, 'I want medicine for my health,' I indicate one motion of the will, because the reason for the action applies to both the end and the means.[11] This is analogous, says Thomas, to vision, which sees both colour and light, or to the intellect, which in drawing a conclusion from principles is really performing one act of understanding, even though it is possible to consider a separate understanding of each stage in the argument.

The unity and complexity of intention is important. The unity is needed to explain the single direction of the will, and to explain how responsibility and morality attach to the general intention which includes the means. The distinction and separation of intention into ends and means is necessary, too, as it allows for the distinction between *intentio* and *electio*; intention (in this sense) is will for the end, while choice is movement of the will to the means (12. 4 ad 3).

Consider the example of Princip, the man who shot Archduke Ferdinand in Sarajevo, precipitating the First World War.[12] His action can be described in several different stages, some of which must be beyond the scope of intention.

He produced neuron firings
   in his brain
contracted certain muscles
   in his arm and hand

pulled the trigger
fired the gun
shot the Archduke   moved a lot of air molecules

---

[11] I-II 12. 4: Cum enim dico: Volo medicinam propter sanitatem, non designo nisi unum motum voluntatis. Cuius ratio est quia finis ratio est volendi ea quae sunt ad finem.

[12] J. R. Searle, *Intentionality: An Essay in the Philosophy of Mind* (Cambridge, 1983), 99–100, slightly modified.

struck a blow for Serbia
ruined Lord Grey's summer
  season
convinced the Emperor
  Franz Joseph that God
  was punishing the family
angered Wilhelm II
started the First World War

The central action descriptions are closely related. Pulling the
trigger was the means to firing the gun, which was the means to
kill the Archduke, et cetera; and these elements all form the one
action of assassination, and are included in the content of his
intention. 'Princip moved only his finger but his Intentionality
covered the Austro-Hungarian Empire.'[13] But the intention is also
limited to that series: none of the actions in the series which are
above (i.e. the first two), below (the last four), or to the side, can be
considered intentional acts of Princip.

There are three important aspects to note about the nature of
intention as developed along Thomistic lines. First, the means are
included in the intention for the end. Thomas said that simply
willing the end is not intention, but willing the end through the
means. Princip in intending to strike a blow for Serbia also intended the means available to him for that—pulling the trigger of
the gun.

Secondly, intention is not merely a matter of beliefs and desires.
Actions are not explained in terms of anger, aggression, or states of
mind, but in terms of the object intended. This object intended is
the goal of the intention, the achievement of which is the purpose
of the action.[14]

Third, the object and purpose exercise a causality, and action
can really be totally explained only when these are taken into
account. Though final causality remains foreign to most modern
thought, this was bread and butter for Aristotle and St Thomas. No
adequate account of the relation of the human mind to action can

[13] J. R. Searle, *Intentionality: An Essay in the Philosophy of Mind*, 99.

[14] Moral analysis sometimes requires the distinction between object and wider
goal, or between the purpose of an action and the deeper motivation, which are
included in *intentio*; see the discussion of *obiectum* and *finis* and their delicate
relations in *ST* I-II qq. 18–19; cf. Gilby, 'Ends and Objectives', *ST*, Blackfriars
edn., xviii. 176–9.

be given until some description of 'intentional causality'[15] is understood.

The loss of the reality of the object of intention in modern thought has led to unfortunate consequences and misinterpretations of the theory of St Thomas. Attention has been drawn to the tendency, even amongst interpreters of St Thomas, to think of the agent's morality in a subjective way, focusing on the attitude or 'motive' as the most important element of intention.[16] This can be explained by the separation of *finis* and *obiectum* such that the actual object of the action understood in an exterior sense was demoted to an 'accidental value', while what was important was the subjective intention.[17] Separation of the outer world of action from the inner world of intention allows many sincere believers (of any faith) to maintain unjust styles of life even while affirming an overall love for God. The result of the action, even the real nature of the action itself, can be ignored if the moral emphasis is put on the attitude behind the action, or worse, the generally benevolent intention of the agent.

INTENTION AND UNWANTED EFFECTS

Princip, by intending to strike a blow for Serbia also intended to fire his gun at the Archduke; someone who intends to write an essay thereby intends to take the steps necessary to finish it. But what about intending an action which involves steps one doesn't want? Do these elements come under intention?

It is possible to go to the beach and not want to swim, or not want to get a tan (if one goes only when it is cool or not too sunny), or not to make sand-castles, because these are accidental features of going to the beach. But if one did not want to be near a body of water, then one could not intend to go to the beach, because being near water is essential in the action of going to the beach.

If you are planning or intending something, you must intend the

---

[15] Searle, *Intentionality*, chs. 4 and 10.

[16] S. Pinckaers, 'Le Rôle de la fin dans l'action morale selon saint Thomas', *RSPT* 45 (1961), 393–421, at 405: 'On paraît attribuer une primauté dangereuse à l'élément subjectif de l'acte humain, à l'intention déterminée par la fin poursuivie, au détriment de l'élément objectif spécifié par l'objet qu'atteint l'action.'

[17] Ibid. 408 ff.

constitutive means. A lengthy holiday in New Zealand might be a wonderful object to intend, but you must also be prepared to intend to pay the sum required. However, it would be strange for someone to say to you after taking this holiday, 'Why did you want to make yourself poorer by thousands of pounds?' Even though this may well be an accurate description of the results of your trip (from the point of view of your bank), wiping out your savings would hardly be what you were actually aiming at. You were intending an enjoyable trip, and spending the money for it was indeed the only way to achieve it; the elimination of savings comes under your intention only to the extent that it was constitutive of taking the trip.

What of actions which involve an action usually considered immoral, such as killing an innocent person? How can this be justified in terms of means and end? In the holiday example, part of the description of going to New Zealand on holiday might be leaving an ailing parent behind. This might not be relevant; but it might be one of the reasons for going, so as to escape the constant demands. If no provision for substitute care were made, and this were part of the intention, then this would affect its moral quality. Spending money that one has towards a justified object is not wrong; but suppose that one went into debt and avoided other obligations in order to join a friend on this South Pacific holiday. In this circumstance spending thousands would not be right. Then the trip is not described as a pleasant holiday, but as an escape.[18]

In the case of shortening a person's life with the administration of pain-killers, or killing civilians in an attack on terrorists, appropriate description is needed. If there was in fact no other means of providing the required care for the dying person, and no other way of dealing with the armed terrorists (who had to be dealt with), then the action taken is a constitutive means to the right goal, and the consequences unfortunate. The harm resulting from the action (even when foreseen) is properly described as outside of the inten-

---

[18] See J. Finnis, 'Object and Intention in Moral Judgments according to Aquinas', *Thomist*, 55 (1991), 1–27, at 18: 'for moral assessment and judgment, the act is what it is just as it is *per se*, i.e., just as it is intended, i.e., under the description it has in the proposal which the agent adopts by choice—not under some self-deceiving description offered by conscience to conscience to rationalize evil.' On correctly describing acts so as not to disguise their true nature, see E. D'Arcy, *Human Acts: An Essay in their Moral Evaluation* (Oxford, 1963).

tion of the action,[19] although any foreseeable evil likely to result from the act must affect the assessment and choice of action.[20]

In the example given by Aquinas of someone who kills to defend his own life (*ST* 2-II 64. 7), the action has as its intention self-preservation (and not the death of the attacker). The only means available turns out to be the death of the attacker, but this does not mean that a bad action may be chosen by intending a greater good:

the proportionality in question is no more than the proportion of a specific means to a specific end: if stunning one's assailant will suffice for self-defence, one must not shoot him through the heart; that would not be 'proportionate' and the choice to inflict needless harm would be immoral. There is here no trace of any doctrine that it is morally permissible to kill when one considers that the good to be attained by killing outweighs (is proportionately greater than) the harms created overall by killing and the goods to be attained overall by not killing.[21]

Thomas's teaching does not justify a questionable action by appealing to the goodness of the resultant state of affairs. The means–end structuring of intention is restricted to the action itself, not to the further ends which might result.[22] Which results and outcomes are to be judged intended and which are judged side-effects will not always be obvious; yet Finnis is right that the question can in general be settled by considering why one is doing what one is doing, counting as within the proposal one has adopted by choice everything which one wants for its own sake or for the sake of what one wants for its own sake, and describing each and every aspect of the behaviour just as, and to the extent that, it is described in the practical reasoning which identifies its point.[23] Of course one may intend very wide goals, such as the end of tyranny or the pursuit of economic justice; but the vagueness of

[19] J. M. Boyle Jr., '*Praeter Intentionem* in Aquinas', *Thomist*, 42 (1978), 649–54, at 664: 'what is neither ordered to the intended end nor a part of the good which specifies this order does not fall within the intention.'

[20] *ST* 1-II 20. 5; see G. E. M. Anscombe, 'Action, Intention, and "Double Effect"', *PACPA* 56 (1982), 12–25, at 25.

[21] Finnis, *Fundamentals of Ethics*, 85; see Anscombe, 'Action', 24, that *ST* 2-II 64. 7 does not support a 'package' double-effect doctrine, i.e. of assessing a balance of good results over bad.

[22] Someone arguing on behalf of Princip might say that despite the loss of life, the destruction of the German, Austrian, and Russian empires was worth it.

[23] Finnis, 'Object and Intention', 25.

the end and the enormous variety of means (a St Francis or a terrorist could both claim such intentions) point to the need for understanding intermediate goals and providing the correct description of actions, and the absolute necessity of the prudential judgement of the relation of means to end.

10
Decision

DECISION precedes deliberation in the sequence of action in the *Summa*. This seems curious, but it highlights the primary role of choice, basic to all voluntary human action, and the secondary role of deliberation. St Thomas states that when the judgement about an action is clear, then deliberation is not required.[1]

ACTION REQUIRES DECISION

Take a person who is ill and wants his health back quickly. Assuming that he knows from previous experience (or instruction) that this particular medicine is the prescribed treatment for his illness, then his decision is whether to take it or not. The choice is not between different possible treatments (although it might be in other circumstances), but between two alternate courses of action: to take the medicine or not. The thought that goes into the decision may be swift or lengthy, easy or difficult, but it is distinct from the stage of deliberation, the process of reasoning which tries to discover the best action for a given end.

All human actions involve the application of reason in reaching a decision. An action may be fully specified already as the best means to an end, but one must still choose it and decide on it. The point of q. 13 a. 4 is to make the connection between decision and human action: acting for an end involves an intervening or mediating act, a choice of a particular action leading to the end already intended. Thus all human action involves decision.[2]

This point has been ignored or confused by the various commentators. Because deliberation, the consideration and selection of options, has been regarded as the essential aspect of practical reasoning, then in a situation where the decision is clear, that is where there is only one option for a given end, there is presumed

---

[1] *ST* 1-II 14. 4 ad 1: quando iudicium vel sententia manifesta est absque inquisitione, non requiritur consili inquisitio.

[2] 1-II 13. 4: Quia necesse est ut id quod est ad finem, vel sit actio, vel res aliqua, interveniente aliqua actione, per quam facit id quod est ad finem, vel utitur eo. Et per hunc modum electio semper est humanorum actuum.

to be no process of reasoning required. This is the implication of nearly all previous treatments of practical reasoning and the process of action. An example offered in one such account illustrates this:

My boss sends me to a certain town to start a factory, and provides me his car. So I can dispense with establishing the goal, as well as with deliberating about the means of getting there. From 'intention' I can skip directly to 'execution', eliminating all the other steps.[3]

This is fundamentally wrong. To pass directly from *intentio* to *usus* would diminish human action to that of other animals, because they too have a kind of intention and movement to an end (*ST* I-II 12. 5). More to the point, one would not arrive at genuine *usus* without a process of judgement, because *usus* requires the ordering of an act to an end, described in 1-II 16. 2 as an *arbitrium*; it is the setting up and rational awareness of that relationship which makes *usus* part of human action. Voluntary action requires the judgement that one is acting for a certain end and that the action comes under that end.

The employee in the example does not have to consider how to get to the town—the car is provided; and he knows where to go and what he is expected to do. But he still has to decide to go. He is not a robot who moves into action when his boss commands, or presses the keys to the car into his hand. He has to choose to obey his boss, using reason to make a judgement. Now this type of decision will normally be an easy one. If he is a valued employee he will naturally have the policy of obeying directives from his superior and there will probably be no hesitation. But even if the decision is made quickly, spontaneously, habitually, or even 'automatically', that does not mean that there is no choice, or that no act of reason is involved. On the contrary, there would be no human action here if there were not a decision.

Every human action, even the most obvious or straightforward, is subject to a decision involving reason, even if there is little or no consciousness of it. The example of medicine, again, will help to establish this point even more clearly. Health is a basic human good. There are many illnesses with basically one known effective

[3] O. Lottin, 'Psychologie de l'acte humain', *RTAM* 29 (1962), 250–67, at 262: 'Mon patron m'envoie dans telle ville pour y fonder une usine, et il me prête son auto. Je suis donc dispensé de m'assigner un but; dispensé aussi de chercher le moyen d'y arriver. De l'*intentio* je passe directement à l'*usus*, brûlant toutes les autres étapes.'

treatment, and therefore only one means is offered to the desired end. Assuming that one has been prescribed medicine by a physician, there would be little to reason about. Would the agent move from *intentio* to *usus*? He desires to get well, so he swallows the pill. Each act of taking medicine, however, is a voluntary human action, requiring a decision in accordance with a principle. Normally, no great deal of thought is required in order to decide, because neither the end nor the means is called into question, and the decisive action is accomplished virtually automatically, though not dispensed with. Certain circumstances, such as the possibility of side-effects or the high cost of continuing the medication might lead one to reconsider and make a choice for the same end of health but relying perhaps on the natural recovery powers of the body. Even when the means to an end are obvious, however, so that deliberation is not needed, practical reason operates in the decision to act.

THE SYLLOGISTIC STRUCTURE OF DECISION

The complexities of describing practical reasoning are made more difficult by the confusion in understanding Aristotle (observed in Chapter 2). The problem is that there are two separate reasoning processes, one for deliberation and one for decision, and each can be called a 'practical syllogism'.[4] Deliberation and decision differ with respect to their ordering in the process of practical reasoning, their function, and their style of reasoning. While deliberation starts with an end and proceeds to identify a means or series of means to achieve the desired end, decision is a process of reasoning about a particular means or action in relation to actually achieving that end.

To illustrate the difference: a woman has an intention to become physically fit, and deliberation about the means might eliminate a club membership as too costly, bicycling as too dangerous, and jogging as too boring. She then thinks that getting up

---

[4] Most readings of Aristotle treat decision as the conclusion of deliberation, i.e. that deliberation goes on until a decision or choice is made, and that they are part of the same process or stage; the debate then becomes one concerning whether 'means–end' or 'rule–case' reasoning is the better way to describe the process; the teaching of Aristotle is made clearer if we identify 'means–end' reasoning with deliberation and 'rule–case' with decision.

early and walking to work is the best idea. So far there is deliberation (and a specific conclusion), but no action. Now the decision
to act: 'I want to become fit; getting up early to walk is the best
way to start; I'd better set the alarm clock for 6.00. There!'

The syllogistic connection between decision and action obviously came to Thomas from Aristotle, and formed his thinking
from the period of his studies with Albert the Great. In his
commentary on the *Sentences* Thomas understood that the basic
dynamic of human action is to choose *bonum* and avoid *malum*, and
he explicitly cites *EN* VI. 8 as his authority that the agent's reason
uses a syllogism of three propositions, the third being concluded
from the other two.[5] The first proposition is related to the second
as general to particular.

The basic process of the syllogism involves reason making a
judgement from general principles about particular actions. In the
example supplied by Thomas, *synderesis* proposes, 'All evil is to be
avoided'; reason brings in the premiss that adultery is evil, which
may be the product of 'superior' reason which knows that adultery
is prohibited by the law of God, or of 'inferior' reason which
knows that adultery is evil because it is unjust or dishonourable.
The conclusion in either case is the same, i.e. 'This adultery is to
be avoided'; and this conclusion pertains to conscience, which is
the result of the application of the universal or general to the
particular.[6] We may organize this in the following way:

Major: Evil is to be avoided.
Minor: Adultery is evil.
Conclusion: This adultery is to be avoided.

Two points may be noted. First, this reveals something important about the content of *synderesis*: though it is described as the
habitus of the general principles of natural law, the content of the
principles would seem, in the example above, to be very restricted.
Synderesis supplies the premiss 'Evil is to be avoided'. The premiss

---

[5] *In II Sent.* 24. 2. 4: sciendum est igitur quod, sicut in VI *Ethic.*, cap. viii,
Philosophus dicit, ratio in eligendis et fugiendis, quibusdam syllogismis utitur. In
syllogismo autem est triplex consideratio, secundum tres propositiones, ex
quarum duabus tertia concluditur.

[6] Ibid.: Synderesis hanc proponit: omne malum est vitandum; ratio superior
hanc assumit: adulterium est malum, quia lege Dei prohibitum: sive ratio inferior
assumeret illam, quia est malum, quia iniustum, sive inhonestum; conclusio
autem, quae est adulterium hoc esse vitandum, ad conscientiam pertinet.

'Adultery is evil' is not from *synderesis* or natural law but from reason (aided or unaided by revelation). Though Thomas would appear to hold that it is 'natural', in a way, for people to conclude that adultery is evil, he does not ascribe that premiss to *synderesis*.

Second, Thomas has made this form of reasoning too concise and therefore engenders some confusion. The conclusion states 'this (*hoc*) adultery is to be avoided', but the minor premiss says only 'adultery is evil'. There is thus a missing step, the one which says 'This is adultery'. However obvious it may seem, this is a crucial step, since it makes the difference between speculative and practical reasoning, between moral knowledge and action. The logical conclusion of the syllogism given above should be 'Adultery should be avoided', which may or may not be decisive in relation to the action contemplated, because it makes all the difference in the world whether the agent recognizes or admits that the action is adultery. The syllogism that Thomas is really using would run like this:

Evil is to be avoided.
This act is evil because it is adultery.
This act of adultery is to be avoided.

What is crucial is the recognition that the particular action being considered falls under the principle being used. This is what constitutes the judgement of decision. Thomas was interested to show (in the discussion here) that conscience pertains to the conclusion, the judgement about the particular case, and not to the first two steps dealing with moral principles. Thus the act of conscience is the conclusion of a syllogism of action, the result of deciding what to do.

Thomas took the conclusion of this syllogism as the 'choice' of the agent in the full sense, uniting cognition and volition. That is, the conclusion of the syllogism is not merely the judgement of reason, about which the will makes a separate choice, but is the judgement which expresses the combination of the agent's intellect and will. This is explained by Thomas in relation to *liberum arbitrium*. Free choice involves a judgement, which cannot be a matter of the will alone ('quia per se voluntatis non est iudicare'). It is one process, and one conclusion, expressing the judgement of both potencies; and though the conclusion unites them, we can see the conclusion or decision in its two aspects: the conclusion is of some particular action to be done; conscience is the conclusion in its cognitive aspect, while choice (*electio*) is the appetitive conclusion.[7]

In the *De veritate*, St Thomas discussed the syllogism of decision in the same context of conscience, with a similar structure of premisses: 'through conscience the *notitia* of *synderesis* and of superior and inferior reason is applied to the examining of the particular action.'[8] In the example provided, the premiss of *synderesis* is: 'Nothing prohibited by the law of God is to be done'; next, from superior reason (aided by revelation): 'Lying with this woman is prohibited by the law of God'; then there arises the application of conscience in the conclusion: 'This sexual union must be avoided.'[9] The structure of the syllogism is similar to that presented in the commentary on the *Sentences*, along with the conflation of the reasoning about what is prohibited with the recognition of the status of the particular action. In this syllogism the conflation occurs in the second premiss rather than in the conclusion: strictly speaking, the law of God is not worded to prohibit sexual union with any particular person—it rules out adultery and fornication in general. The agent (who may be married and allowed sexual union with a partner) must correctly recognize the nature of the particular action contemplated.

Thomas Aquinas clarified the function of the practical syllogism from a reading of Aristotle's *De Anima* III. 11.[10] Thomas understood Aristotle's explanation of the difference of the principle of action in animals from that in humans: animals are drawn to a desirable object, which is the motive force for action; in humans it is something 'rational', in other animals it is 'sensible' only.[11] This is

---

[7] *In II Sent.* 24. 2. 4 ad 2: unde tam conscientia quam electio, conclusio quaedam est particularis agendi, sed conscientia conclusio cognitiva tantum, electio conclusio affectiva.

[8] *De veritate*, 17. 2: per conscientiam applicatur notitia synderesis et rationis superioris et inferioris ad actum particularem examinandum.

[9] Ibid.: ut si ex iudicio synderesis proferatur 'nihil prohibitum lege Dei est faciendum', et ex superioris rationis notitia assumatur concubitum cum ista muliere esse contra legem Dei, fiet applicatio conscientiae concludendo ab hoc concubitu esse abstinendum.

[10] Compare the crucial role of the passage 434^{a}16–21 for Allan, 'The Practical Syllogism', 325–6, who identified the rule–case or universal–particular form of practical reasoning with the psychological explanation of human action.

[11] *In III De Anima*, 433^{b}27, 836: appetitivum non est sine phantasia, quae vel est rationalis vel sensibilis. Sensibili autem phantasia alia animalia ab homine participant, non autem phantasia rationali.

the basis for the argument of freedom—that animals are determined to follow what appears to them as desirable, while human beings are able to deliberate and choose, which is the function of reason.[12] In such deliberation a kind of rule or measure is used in thinking about what is best to do: 'Thus reason when deliberating is able to select one attractive thing from many by comparing them, preferring one to another, using a third as a standard.'[13] This reasoning process is a description of deliberation or *consilium*, selecting the best means to accomplish a desired end.

This selection process does not have the motive force for action, however. That requires the process of decision, the rule–case syllogism which Aristotle describes a few lines later at 434ª16. Aristotle had described the motion towards action as originating not from the first premiss, but from the combination of the first (universal) and second (particular) premisses. Thomas developed this by stating that practical reason is partly general and partly particular; the general proposition states something like 'Such a person should do such and such', for example 'A son should honour his parents'; particular reason says that 'This indeed is such, and I am such a person', e.g. that 'I am a son'; 'I ought now to show respect to my parents.'[14]

The example supplied by Thomas is instructive, and shows that he had refined the concept of the practical syllogism as the psychological explanation for action, and was no longer confusing it with the deductions of moral science as he had tended to do in his earlier works. The middle premiss is the key element here. It is not a more particular aspect of a general rule (as 'Adultery is evil' gives an instance of something evil), but the recognition by the agent of

[12] *In III De Anima*, 434ª5, 840: quia considerare utrum hoc sit agendum aut hoc, quod est deliberare, est opus rationis.

[13] Ibid. 841: Unde manifestum est quod ratio deliberans potest ex pluribus phantasmatibus unum facere, scilicet ex tribus quorum unum praeeligitur alteri, et tertium est quasi mensura qua praeeligitur.

[14] Ibid. 434ª16, 845: Ratio autem practica quaedam est universalis et quaedam particularis (universalis quidem sicut quae dicit quod oportet talem tale agere, sicut quod oportet filium honorare parentem; ratio autem particularis, quod hoc quidem tale et ego talis, puta quod ego filius[;] hunc honorem nunc debeo exhibere parenti).

Note: the semicolon has been inserted because the lack of punctuation in the Leonine edition obscures the difference between the minor premiss and the conclusion.

the action (in those circumstances) as an instance when the general principle applies: 'I am the person (to whom this principle applies); this action is that kind of action (to which the principle applies).'

It is this recognition of the application of the general principle in the particular situation that generates action, and results from the combination of the universal and particular in the syllogism to generate the conclusion. In Thomas's exposition of Aristotle the universal premiss is the 'prime and motionless cause' and the particular premiss the 'proximate cause, applied in some way to an action'.[15] The theory of the syllogism is clearly meant to be an explanation of all voluntary action: 'For actions and movements occur in particular instances; thus in order for an action to follow, one needs to have the general proposition applied to the particular circumstances.'[16]

In this commentary, Thomas has explained the dynamic of voluntary human action, which involves application of general principle to particular situation, resulting in decision to act; and the syllogism is the analysis of that application. Thus the practical syllogism is a psychological account of human decision. Aristotle recognized the special qualities of this unusual type of syllogism which puts motive force into action. Merely knowing the universal principle in itself—that one should do such and such—has no force; but combined with the recognition of its application to the agent, there is motive force and then action.

The terms that Thomas used are noteworthy: he spoke not of *synderesis* and higher or lower reason, but of *ratio practica* which is both general and particular. The general premiss is thus no longer necessarily tied to a principle of natural law; it is an operative principle, or general premiss for action. The character of the second premiss has shifted from a datum of knowledge (derived from revelation or from natural reason) to the perception of the circumstances, a kind of recognition of the here-and-now applicability of the general rule. This was present to some extent in the syllogisms as given in the commentary on the *Sentences* and in the *De veritate*, but the presence of the feature of rule deduction in those works obscured the function of the syllogism as a psychologi-

---

[15] *In III De Anima*, 434ª16, 846: illa quae est universalis movet ut causa prima et quiescens, particularis autem ut causa proxima et quodam modo motui applicata.

[16] Ibid.: Nam operationes et motus in particularibus sunt, unde oportet, ad hoc quod motus sequatur, quod opinio universalis ad particularia applicetur.

cal account of action. The more careful reading of Aristotle and his own further reflection represented in the commentary on the *De Anima* enabled Thomas to clarify the nature and function of the syllogism of action.

THE OPERATIVE SYLLOGISM

Though Thomas apparently never wrote a commentary on *De Motu Animalium* (as Albert did), he revealed fresh insights into practical reasoning in his commentaries on the *De Anima* and on the *Nicomachean Ethics*. Although some questions remain about chronology, the commentary on *EN* was the product of his later period, after 1260, perhaps preceding the *De Anima* commentary in its first version, and contemporary with the *Summa Theologiae* in its revised form.[17] Though some scholars have not had a high opinion of it,[18] it can be argued, at least from the evidence put forward here on the psychology of action, that Thomas's penetration of Aristotle was profound, and his commentary successfully clarified certain obscure passages in the *EN*.

An important point established by Aristotle (*EN* 1142ª25) is that *phronēsis* deals with the particular, because actions are particulars, and this is the object of a kind of perception. Thomas developed this point: science is of universals, prudence of the particular, because action is a particular.[19] The kind of perception involved in prudence is not like that by which we perceive the sensible

[17] If we accept the dating of the commentary on *EN* to *c*.1271 (see J. Weisheipl, *Friar Thomas d'Aquino: His Life, Thought, and Works*[2] (Washington, DC, 1983), 380), then the study of the *De Anima*, which seems to be from about 1268, would precede the *EN*, and would represent a breakthrough in insight; but see V. Bourke, 'The *Nicomachean Ethics* and Thomas Aquinas', in *St Thomas Aquinas, 1274–1974: Commemorative Studies* (Toronto, 1974), i. 239–59, who favoured the traditional dating of the *EN* commentary to the earlier 1260s. In the end, however, the relative ordering of the works is not so important as the recognition of the development of the theory of practical reasoning to be seen in the whole last phase of Thomas's teaching and writing.

[18] Gauthier and Jolif, *L'Éthique à Nicomaque*, i. 131, do not rate Thomas's commentary very highly; and V. Bourke, 'The *Nicomachean Ethics*', i. 255, remarks that 'one does not get the impression that it is a well developed and mature piece of work'; for a more positive view see L. Elders, 'St Thomas Aquinas' Commentary on the *Nicomachean Ethics*', *Autour de saint Thomas d'Aquin*, i. 77–122.

[19] *In VI Ethic.* (1142ª23), lect. 1213: Scientia enim est universalium . . . prudentia autem est extremi, id est singularis, quia est operabilis, quod est singulare.

qualities of objects such as colour, sound, et cetera, but an 'interior sense' such as in perceiving a geometric figure to be a triangle. It is to this sense, says Aquinas, that prudence belongs, 'by which particular reasoning is perfected for judging rightly about the particular tendencies of actions.'[20] Animals which have a good natural judgement can be called prudent. But there is another kind of perception, able to discern differences, and this belongs to the intellect. Prudence involves both the universal (which is for the intellect) and the particular (which is a kind of perception). It is the combination of the two that underlies the process of practical reasoning in deciding.

In *EN* VI. 12 Aristotle considered more specifically the process of choice. He described the operation of the mind in practical reason as involving two levels, universal and particular, and this passage ($1143^{a}35-1143^{b}11$) has been a source of some difficulty.[21] Thomas's commentary is a helpful explanation of Aristotle on this: there is a twofold understanding (*duplex intellectus*) involved: one concerns immovable and first principles; but the intellect in practical reasoning is of the other kind of term, namely the singular and contingent, and is of the other proposition, i.e. not the universal which is like the major, but the singular which is the minor in the operative syllogism.[22]

This passage is significant for the greater clarity Thomas achieved, indicated by the term 'operative syllogism'. Thomas identified the general proposition (first premiss) with the understanding based on demonstrations, and the minor proposition (second premiss) with the action of the mind involved in the perception of the singular. But perception of the singular is intimately related with the understanding of the general principle, because the principle is a product of the observation of singulars ('quia ex singularibus accipitur universale'). Thus in perceiving the singular as the middle term, as the particular of a universal principle, the agent perceives in it the general principle. One perceives

---

[20] *In VI Ethic.* ($1142^{a}23$), lect. 1215: Et ad istum sensum, id est interiorem, magis pertinet prudentia, per quam perficitur ratio particularis ad recte aestimandum de singularibus intentionibus operabilium.

[21] For the problems see Gauthier and Jolif, *L'Éthique à Nicomaque*, ii. 536 ff.

[22] *In VI Ethic.* ($1143^{a}35$), lect. 1247: sed intellectus qui est in practicis est alterius modi extremi, scilicet singularis et contingentis et alterius propositionis, id est non universalis quae est quasi major, sed singularis quae est minor in syllogismo operativo.

the particular not as a particular in isolation, but as an instance of a general principle. Thus, in Thomas's example, a herb is recognized for curative properties—it is not chosen as a plant attractive in itself (which may be bitter to taste and non-nourishing), but it is taken because it is productive of health. Thus prudence involves that 'interior sense' and not just exterior perception.[23] Using this example of a medicinal herb, what Thomas is saying could be set forth in this way:

> Major premiss: I want to get well.
> Minor premiss: This herb will help me get well.
> Conclusion: I want to take this herb.

The knowledge that this particular plant is indeed the right kind of herb is necessary, but for the purposes of action there is required a special kind of perception that the particular action is an instance of a general practical principle, in this case, to stay well. The person who knows botany, and thus recognizes the plant, but who feels no need to pluck it and grind its leaves, would not use this syllogism of action, because, although knowing the plant and its qualities, he would not join the particular perception with the general principle of desire for health. That combination of universal and particular generating the particular conclusion is the syllogism of action, or operative syllogism.

Aristotle at 1147ª25 ff. brings out more clearly the structure of the syllogism as the psychological explanation of action. He says: 'The one opinion is universal, the other is concerned with the particular facts and here we come to something within the sphere of perception; when a single opinion results from the two, the soul must in one type of case affirm the conclusion, while in the case of opinion concerned with production it must immediately act.'[24] Here the decision to act as the linking of universal and particular is made prominent.

Thomas grasped well the account of action here. In the agent's practical reasoning there is a double proposition: one universal, e.g.

---

[23] *In VI Ethic.* (1143a35), lect. 1249: quia singularia proprie cognoscuntur per sensum, oportet quod homo horum singularium quae dicimus esse principia et extrema, habeat sensum non solum exteriorem, sed etiam interiorem, cuius supra dixit esse prudentiam, scilicet vim cogitativam sive aestimativam quae dicitur ratio particularis.

[24] *EN* 1147ª26–29, trans. W. D. Ross.

anything base must be avoided; the other proposition is a singular concerning those things which are recognized by perception; thus e.g. 'this is base'. Since there is one reasoning process (*ratio*) generated from these two propositions, the conclusion necessarily follows.[25] This basic pattern can be put in syllogistic form:

> Major: Avoid anything bad.
> Minor: This is bad.
> Conclusion: Avoid this.

As Thomas says, the conclusion necessarily follows, so this shows how the conclusion of a reasoning process has directive and motivating force for action. The key to prudent action (using the syllogistic pattern) is in the accurate perception of the quality of actions. Perception and judgement are central to action, and wisdom in this is a product of age and of experience.

THE SUMMA THEOLOGIAE

The teaching of St Thomas in the *ST* on the decision-making process is consistent and clear. At I 86. 1 Thomas formulates the theory of the practical syllogism: 'The choice of a particular action is like the conclusion of a syllogism of the practical intellect, as Aristotle says in *EN* VII; however, a particular cannot be deduced directly from the universal, without another singular being taken as a middle term. Thus the universal reasoning of the practical intellect does not move unless there is, as a middle term, a particular apprehension of the sensitive part' (referring here to *De Anima* III).[26]

The connection between intellect and action is summarized here: a general principle; a perception of the particular circumstances as an instance of that principle; the judgement of the two

[25] *In VI Ethic.* (1147ª24), lect. 1345: oportet scire quod in eius processu est duplex opinio: una quidem universalis, puta: 'omne inhonestum est fugiendum'; alia autem est singularis circa ea quae proprie per sensum cognoscuntur, puta: 'hic actus est inhonestus'. Cum autem ex his duabus opinionibus fiat una ratio, necesse est quod sequatur conclusio.

[26] *ST* I 86. 1 ad 2: Dicendum quod electio particularis operabilis est quasi conclusio syllogismi intellectus practici, ut dicitur in vii *Ethic.* Ex universali autem propositione directe non potest conludi singularis, nisi mediante aliqua singulari propositione assumpta. Unde universalis ratio intellectus practici non movet nisi mediante particulari apprehensione sensitivae partis, ut dicitur in iii *De Anima*.

being performed, a particular conclusion is generated. This three-
part process of general proposition–particular apprehension–particular conclusion is in the form of a syllogism.

   The passage at *ST* 1-II 13. 3 merits further attention in the
context of decision. 'Choice follows on the *sententia* or *iudicium*,
which is like the conclusion of an operative syllogism.²⁷ Thus what
falls under choice is like the conclusion in a practical syllogism.'
Thomas goes on to show that what choice is about is the means,
not the end, which stands as the first term, not the conclusion of
the syllogism. Noteworthy here is: first, the clear connection
between choice (involved in all voluntary action) and the structure
of the syllogism, which thus becomes the ordinary model for all
human action; and, second, the use of the term 'operative syllogism', the first time in the *ST*.

   'Operative syllogism' is also used in *ST* 1-II 76. 1; Thomas is
quite clear on the process of action, and describes the motive force
well: reason is directive of human action in two respects, universal
and particular. 'Thinking about what to do (*conferens*, not *consilians*)
one uses a kind of syllogism, whose conclusion is a judgement or a
choice or an action. Since actions occur in particulars, the conclusion of an operative syllogism is particular; and a particular proposition is not concluded from a universal without another singular
proposition as a middle.'²⁸ Thomas more clearly brings out the
essential process of the operative syllogism as an act of judgement
of the intellect, as bringing together the general principle and the
particular instance and generating the conclusion which has motive
force for action. In this passage, Thomas accepts the description of
the conclusion of the syllogism as an action (*operatio*) or the
decision to act.

   In the section on prudence Thomas devoted question 2-II 49. 2
to the role of intellect. 'The character of prudence is to stop at the
particular action to be done, to which it applies general knowledge. The particular conclusion is deduced (*syllogizatur*) from a

²⁷ 1-II 13. 3: electio consequitur sententiam vel iudicium, quod est sicut
conclusio syllogismi operativi.
²⁸ 1-II 76. 1: Considerandum est autem quod ratio secundum duplicem scientiam est humanorum actuum directiva: scilicet secundum scientiam universalem,
et particularem. Conferens enim de agendis, utitur quodam syllogismo, cuius
conclusio est iudicium seu electio vel operatio. Actiones autem in singularibus
sunt. Unde conclusio syllogismi operativi est singularis. Singularis autem propo-
sitio non concluditur ex universali nisi mediante aliqua propositione singulari.

general and a particular proposition. Thus the nature of prudence derives from a twofold understanding (*ex duplici intellectu*).'[29] Thomas explains the Aristotelian view of the combination of universal and particular: 'one type of understanding is of general principles; the other, as Aristotle says in *EN* VI, is of the prime singular or the first contingent action to be done, namely the minor proposition, which must be the singular in the syllogism of prudence.'[30] With characteristic flexibility, Thomas uses the term *syllogismus prudentiae*, but it is clear that his view of the structure and purpose of this process of reasoning is the same as of the operative syllogism.

Thus when Thomas qualifies the operative syllogism by calling it a 'kind of' or 'quasi syllogism',[31] this is not because it lacks the form of a proper syllogism; it is because the content of the syllogism affects the certainty of the conclusion—both the principles being used (all but the very first principles, that is) and the singular actions being judged are not necessary truths but deal with the contingent matters of life.[32] But the form of the syllogism is the same in theoretic as in practical judgements and, in regard to form only, just as productive of truth and certainty. In the context of practical reasoning (understood psychologically) it is 'decisiveness', and looked at morally, 'correctness'. This is important in understanding the place of the practical judgement in Aquinas's psychology of action and his explanation of the process of decision and the possibility of error.

THE UNION OF INTELLECT AND WILL IN DECISION

The view of the syllogism of action presented here differs from the traditional interpretation of Thomas Aquinas. The nature of the difference stems from the argument that the powers of intellect and

---

[29] 2-II 49. 2 ad 1: ratio prudentiae terminatur, sicut ad conclusionem quandam, ad particulare operabile, ad quod applicat universalem cognitionem . . . Conclusio autem singularis syllogizatur ex universali et singulari propositione. Unde oportet quod ratio prudentiae ex duplici intellectu procedat.

[30] Ibid.: Quorum unus est qui est cognoscitivus universalium . . . Alius autem intellectus est qui, ut dicitur in vi *Ethic.*, est cognoscitivus extremi, id est alicuius primi singularis et contingentis operabilis, propositionis scilicet minoris, quam oportet esse singularem in syllogismo prudentiae.

[31] Cf. *De veritate*, 17. 2; *De malo*, 3. 9 ad 7.

[32] On the lack of certitude because of the contingencies of life see *ST* 1-II 94. 4.

will in the process of action are meant to function together, not in series. In the common view the practical syllogism would belong to the intellect, which would reach a conclusion; this would then be accepted or rejected by the will. In such a view the operative syllogism is not the decision or choice itself; it is preparatory, furnishing the grounds of the decision which is actually made by the will. According to this erroneous interpretation, when the agent reaches the conclusion 'I must not commit this act of fornication', this expresses the judgement of his intellect but not his actual decision to act.[33] On this interpretation, however, the syllogism becomes tautologous: it makes little sense as a piece of theoretic reasoning, nor is there directive force to it (which is subsequently supplied by will).

Thomas's structure of practical reasoning is best understood when intellect and will are co-ordinated. The interdependence of reason and will is in fact the first and essential point that Thomas wanted to make about *electio* (*ST* 1-II 13. 1): that it pertains to both reason and will, quoting *EN* 1139^{b}4. The two potencies unite to form one principle, and the pattern is like the relationship of form and matter: an act which is essentially of one potency receives its form and species from the other. For example: when someone performs an act of fortitude for the love of God, it is materially an act of fortitude, formally one of love.[34] This is similar, in Thomas's view, to the relation of reason and will in decision. Reason in some way precedes the will and specifies its act. The will tends to its object, following the specification of the reason; or the appetitive force receives its direction from the apprehensive power.[35]

---

[33] Merkelbach, *Summa theologiae moralis*, i. 189, used the example of the syllogism dealing with fornication. The conclusion of continence, according to his reading, is: 'Ergo mihi hic et nunc illicitus est cum illa concubitus.' The judgement has been particularized to specify this action; but it does not express the decision of the agent—only a particularized instance of a rule which he then must decide to obey or disobey.

[34] *ST* 1-II 13. 1: Est autem considerandum in actibus animae, quod actus qui est essentialiter unius potentiae vel habitus, recipit formam et speciem a superiori potentia vel habitu, secundum quod ordinatur inferius a superiori: si enim aliquis actum fortitudinis exerceat propter Dei amorem, actus quidem ille materialiter est fortitudinis, formaliter vero caritatis.

[35] Ibid.: Manifestum est autem quod ratio quodammodo voluntatem praecedit, et ordinat actum eius: inquantum scilicet voluntas in suum obiectum tendit secundum ordinem rationis, eo quod vis apprehensiva appetitivae suum obiectum repraesentat.

162   *Analysing the Process of Action*

Thus Thomas can sum it up by saying that choice is materially of the will, but formally of the reason.[36]

The material/formal description in 13. 1 makes it very clear that for Thomas reason and will act together. The will operates in the act of reasoning, and reason operates in the movements of the will. Underlying the cognitive power which makes a judgement is the motivation of the appetite seeking what is good; and involved in the tendencies of the will toward particular goods is the specifying operation of the intellect.

Each premiss is then expressive of both faculties, the operation of the syllogism is the result of both, and the conclusion is not just an 'intellectual' conclusion but is expressive of the will of the agent as well. This is the correct way in which to understand the clear insistence of Aquinas on the intellect as specification and the will as exercise. The specific terms, the precise formulation of the premisses and conclusion, is of course, a matter of the intellect; but the selection of the premisses and the process of the syllogism itself involve a dynamic movement of the will, such that the use of the operative syllogism expresses the agent's will or rational desire.

This implies that an agent's general premisses are ones which express his desires, or are acceptable to or affirmed by his will. The principle 'one must not harm the innocent', for example, is not merely an intellectual principle, but expresses the will, the rational desire of the agent; or, rather, for it to function as an operative principle (for a syllogism of action), the agent must have his will behind it, and affirm it. This is what is meant by saying that someone 'holds' a principle: it can function as a premiss in a syllogism of action, leading to a decision and an action.

The complete union of intellect and will is represented in the first principle of practical reason: do good and avoid evil. This is the first step in the process of specification—it discriminates between positive and negative, attractive and unattractive, good and bad (in the most general sense). This first step in specification is also fully descriptive of the basic orientation of the will: to be drawn towards the attractive, and to shun the unattractive. As a principle, in its generality, it is a principle with which the will is by

[36] Aquinas can even appear a voluntarist (if one takes phrases out of context) when he says 'electio substantialiter non est actus rationis sed voluntatis'; but that appearance is well qualified by reference to the will's need to be ordered by the intellect.

definition in complete agreement.[37] At this fundamental level, the ideal pattern of practical reasoning would be:

Major:	Do good and avoid evil.
Minor:	This is good.
Conclusion:	Do this.

The first principle of practical reason remains the basic ground of all voluntary action, and all other principles may be taken as specifications of that principle. In order to become operative principles, that is, available to the agent as general premisses for a syllogism of action, they need to be accepted by the will as descriptive of the person's orientation. Thus the premiss 'one should obey God' operates as a general operating premiss for a Christian or other theist, but not for an atheist.

The will is also involved in the minor premiss of the operative syllogism. The perception of the circumstances is a judgement of intellect ('I am a son', 'This act is adultery', 'This will give me pleasure', and so on), but the selection of the minor premiss is the result of the will, the way the agent wants to see the situation. The operative syllogism works by simultaneously conjoining the major and minor; from the general premisses by which an agent defines or shapes his life, he selects one to fit his perception of the circumstances. Thus there is an openness about the selection of both premisses, and the evaluation of the circumstances will lead to the dominance of a certain line of thinking about the action. In other words, the agent chooses to see what action is called for in a situation, and evaluates the action within a structure of, for example, responsibility or pleasure. This is the real test, not only of the will of the agent but of his entire character: so to keep various inclinations under control as to allow himself to be able to see the situation properly and judge correctly. To a large extent, the agent is able to see a situation in the way he wants to (which forms a major part of Thomas's explanation and defence of free agency); and this means that the combination of major and minor premisses

[37] The argument of Grisez, 'The First Principle of Practical Reason', that 'do good and avoid evil' is merely 'descriptive' is thus defective, for it does not recognize the need for the will's acceptance of the operation of the practical intellect. While we may approve his desire to avoid a legalistic emphasis, Grisez still operates with a model of practical reasoning which splits the function of intellect and will.

for judging an action in a situation is an expression of the agent's desire to see it in a certain way as well as the result of his rational appraisal.

The universal and particular premisses together yield a conclusion, which is the decision to act, which also expresses the agent's reason and will: it is a judgement of the best particular means to a desired end. The conclusion is in accordance with the principle for action which he adheres to; the principle used for judging the action, and the concomitant way of perceiving the quality of the action, are both products of the agent's will and thus of his character.

I I

Deliberation

DELIBERATION is perhaps the easiest of the different stages of action to grasp, as to its function; yet its relationship to the rest of the process of action has not been well understood. This is partly due to a misunderstanding of the *Ethica Nicomachea* itself, because Aristotle takes pains to indicate the close link between deliberation and the rational nature of human action; and this is misleading if one goes on to deduce that deliberation is necessary for rational action. Further, if deliberation is restricted to a consideration only of means and not of ends, and prudence to excellence in deliberation, as is often done, then both Aristotle and Aquinas will be misunderstood on the scope of practical reason.[1] For Aquinas, prudence is more a matter of wise judgement, and even more of right execution, than of good deliberation.

THE NATURE OF DELIBERATION

For Aquinas, deliberation, as a stage in practical reason, is not even a necessary part of human action. It is choice or decision that provides the essential link between intention and action. The rational structure of action (a means related to an end) is seen and desired in intention, and approved and chosen in decision. A great many ordinary actions are intended, chosen, and executed (and are fully voluntary), without deliberation.

There are many cases, of course, where there is uncertainty connected with the contingencies of life: it is not clear what decision is the best one to make, and so the action cannot proceed without further thought. At the very outset of his discussion of

---

[1] The problem in practical reason seen by T. H. Irwin, 'The Scope of Deliberation: A Conflict in Aquinas', *Review of Metaphysics*, 44 (1990), 21–42, seems based on both of these misapprehensions. On ends and means in Aristotelian practical reason see Ch. 2 n. 6; on the role of deliberation see Urmson, *Aristotle's Ethics*, 81: 'it is a superficial, but surprisingly common, mistake to suppose that the scope of practical wisdom is limited to excellence in deliberation.'

deliberation Thomas says that in doubtful and uncertain matters, the mind does not bring forth a judgement without a kind of investigation, which we call 'counsel'.[2] Deliberation is often necessary to clarify certain actions, but it is not the factor which makes voluntary actions rational.

In the *Summa Theologiae* Aquinas shows that the intellect functions with the will at each stage, that rationality is built into intention with the means–end structuring, that choice is based on the judgement of the intellect as well as the will, and that execution is a matter of intellect and will. Rational action and practical reason do not require a stage of deliberation in order to be rational. When there is intention expressed in chosen action it is rational and voluntary at the same time. An ordinary day with rising, eating, uneventful routine work, meeting friends, no difficult decisions to make, may have very little to deliberate about. But all of these voluntary actions are fully rational.

When the judgement or sentence is obvious without investigation, says Thomas (14. 4 ad 1), then the inquiry of deliberation is not required. These actions are still done with reason (*ratione aguntur*) although deliberation is not needed (ad 2). Thus if there is one thing to be done, and one way to do it, no counsel is needed (ad 3). If there is one task but diverse ways of doing it, then there is need for deliberation.

According to 14. 4, there is no uncertainty (and therefore no deliberation) in two types of cases. First, when there are set means for accomplishing certain set ends, as in certain actions which have characteristic ways of operating. Thomas's example is from Aristotle: when we write we do not deliberate about how to write the letters, because this is already determined. The example may be broadened to include many kinds of techniques and quasi-mechanical operations which are designed to be done in one way for efficient performance. In learning to drive a car one tries to learn the one best way of operating the shifts and pedals, and to make it habitual so as not to have to be deliberating what to do when driving.

Secondly, there is also no need to deliberate about trivial matters, or about those in which the ultimate outcome is not much

---

[2] *ST* i-II 14. 1: In rebus autem dubiis et incertis ratio non profert iudicium absque inquisitione praecedente. Et ideo necessaria est inquisitio rationis ante iudicium de eligendis: et haec inquisitio consilium vocatur.

affected by how it is done. Thus, even if there are diverse ways of doing something, we do not need to deliberate much if the methods will produce largely the same result. If taking the bus or train are roughly equivalent in time, cost, convenience, and so on, one should just decide on one without losing time in deliberation.

Practical reason must also be 'practical' in the sense that it is oriented to action, to getting something done, and not to perfection of understanding. It is in this respect that Kenny has identified the logic of 'satisfactoriness': that reasoning from an end to be achieved down to a means where one might begin is not an ironclad procedure;[3] there may well be a number of patterns of action which might accomplish the same goal, and it is after deliberation has identified these possibilities that the agent makes a decision.

It is not that there is no concern for truth; but in the kind of knowledge dealing with particular contingencies of life, Aquinas says that the character of the knowledge we want is not like the knowledge of universal and necessary truth, but is pursued according to what is useful for action.[4]

The decisive stage that judges the quality of the action is the one central to practical reason, where the agent makes his choice whether the action is indeed the one to do. For both speculative and practical reasoning, truth, the correspondence of understanding to reality, is affirmed in judgement, not in investigation.

DISTINGUISHING DELIBERATION AND DECISION

It is important to follow Thomas here, because the proper character of both deliberation and decision and their independence as separate stages of reasoning hinge on the point that deliberation comes to its own conclusions. The common way of understanding counsel and choice, consistent with a (faulty) voluntarist view of human action, is that counsel is a process of reason which inves-

---

[3] A. Kenny, 'Practical Inference', *Analysis*, 26 (1965–6), 65–75; and *Will, Freedom, and Power*, 80 ff.

[4] *ST* 1-II 14. 3: *inquisitio consilii proprie pertinet ad contingentia singularia. Cognitio autem veritatis in talibus non habet aliquid magnum, ut per se sit appetibilis, sicut cognitio universalium et necessariorum: sed appetitur secundum quod est utilis ad operationem.*

tigates various possibilities: it is a stage of research, after which there is an affective response (*consensus*), followed by a judgement which indicates the best option from a rational point of view; then the will, in the act of election, makes the real choice. But this is false to Thomas's most profound convictions and to his clear presentation of the nature of free choice and the process of action. It is also manifestly contrary to the teaching of Thomas in *ST* 1-II 14. 6. In the stage of *consilium* the agent investigates and compares the possibilities, but also reaches a conclusion and makes a kind of judgement about where to start. This is the nature of the process of *inquisitio* itself: to begin at an end, and then finish at that particular point where one can begin to act. There is a terminus to *consilium* which is a particular action.

Thus the function of deliberation is to specify the means to a desired end. Sometimes one means or chain of means will clearly emerge; in other cases, deliberation will produce two or more possible lines of approach to the end, and will leave the final decision to the stage of choice, but the deliberation will have identified the particular actions at which to begin.

In 1-II 15. 3 Thomas gives a helpful summary of the first two stages of the process of action: *apprehensio finis* and the *appetitus finis* (which constitute intention); then the *consilium* and *appetitus* of the means (deliberation). This difference between end and means corresponds to the difference between *voluntas* in general (or *intentio*) and *consensus*, which is the more particular application of the will to the means or action which has been judged by deliberation.[5] This clearly indicates that deliberation arrives at a conclusion, and that consensus is to be understood as the appetitive counterpart to the *inquisitio* of reason in deliberation.

The distinction between *consensus* and election (as the volitional part of choice) is explained by Thomas in 15. 3 ad 3. If there is only one means to an end, then *consensus* and election would not really differ—they would be an appetitive movement to the same object. Alternatively, in certain cases where *consilium* is not required at all, *consensus* is included in election. In other cases where deliberation results in several means being identified, there may be a kind of preliminary selection of the most attractive ('quorum dum quodlibet placet'). The character of *consensus* is then an initial prefer-

---

[5] 1-II 15. 3: motus appetitivus applicatur ad id quod ex consilio iudicatum est.

ence, while the quality of *electio* is a more decisive choice in preference to other options[6], and is also the decision to act.

INTELLECT AND WILL IN DELIBERATION

In 14. 1 ad 1 Thomas makes it quite clear that the stage of counsel is composite. Just as choice, which may be considered an act of will, includes reason as the principle of order, so counsel, which may be considered essentially an act of reason, has an element of will. Its substance, its matter and its motive, are aspects of the will, because counsel concerns those things which one wants to do.[7]

Some explicit teaching of Aquinas here underscores the validity of maintaining the principle of the combination of reason and will. 'When the acts of two potencies are interrelated with each other, something of the other is found in each, and thus each act could be named from either potency.'[8] At the end of this reply, Thomas quotes Damascene that *consilium* is *appetitus inquisitivus*, and shows that counsel pertains to both the will and to enquiring reason. Therefore *consilium* may be taken to include both, and we could use the terms *inquisitio* and *consensus* for the cognitive and appetitive components. Thomas, however, also uses *consilium* more narrowly for the cognitive function, which is indicated by its pairing with *consensus* in the titles of these successive questions; therefore deliberation seems the better overall term for this stage.

The appetitive aspect of deliberation is *consensus*. This can be defined as the application of the appetitive power to a thing, and there is a certain quality of affection involved, since being joined or adhering to something seems to be part of the connotation of *consensus* (15. 1). The reason we do not attribute consent to animals (15. 2) is that although they have appetite, their inclination is from a natural instinct and so is not under their control in the same way as that of human beings. Consent belongs to rational nature, which has the ability to apply or not apply its appetitive motion.

[6] 1-II 15. 3 ad 3: ut consensus dicatur secundum quod placet ad agendum; electio autem, secundum quod praefertur his quae non placent.

[7] 1-II 14. 1 ad 1: Unde et in actu voluntatis, quae est electio, apparet aliquid rationis, scilicet ordo; et in consilio, quod est actus rationis, apparet aliquid voluntatis sicut materia, quia consilium est de his quae homo vult facere.

[8] Ibid.: quando actus duarum potentiarum ad invicem ordinantur, in utroque est aliquid quod est alterius potentiae: et ideo uterque actus ab utraque potentia denominari potest.

Deliberation presupposes the involvement of the will in intention, the desire for a certain end. When the means to the end is not clear, deliberation is involved to identify the particular steps to achieve it. *Consensus* is the volitional acceptance of this process and can thus be defined as the application of the appetitive movement to the conclusion of deliberation.[9]

This does not mean that *consensus* is equivalent to choice, however. Consent is the appetitive approval given to the means identified by deliberation; but without a decision, there is still an openness about the possibilities which implies that one can consent to more than one means. This can often make choice more difficult, as one might find, for example, three options from a menu equally appealing. In this kind of case Thomas would say that the nature of the choice is trivial—just decide on one. But if the situation is one of choosing a vocation, then it is altogether possible to consent, for example, to the idea of entering a career in journalism, or government service, or business. Having an interest and ability in all three areas may well make a decision difficult; and since it is not trivial, it should be resolved by further deliberation about values and goals and circumstances.

THE PROCESS OF DELIBERATION

Suppose that there has already been intention for some definite thing, identified as good, but lack of clarity about the means to achieve it. So deliberation begins with the end to be achieved and works back from that to figure out what should be done first. This is a distinctive feature about practical reasoning and final causality, that what is first in the intention (the goal) is the last thing achieved in execution; while the first action in the process of execution is the final step in deliberation.

For example, you want to attend a tennis match and plan to take your friend (this plan might itself represent the conclusion of previous deliberation about what to do on the weekend). You need to decide how to get there, where to meet, what kind of tickets to get, and so on. You realize that the first thing to do is to find out if good tickets are available. So you pick up the telephone to ring the stadium. The idea of watching tennis and spending time

[9] I-II 15. 3: Et ideo applicatio appetitivi motus ad determinationem consilii proprie est consensus.

with a friend were the goals which started the process; but actually watching the match will be the last thing accomplished in a chain of actions which begins with a telephone call to the stadium, followed by a call to your friend, picking up the tickets, and so on.

When it is said that deliberation is only about means and not about ends, what is meant is that deliberation always begins at the end which is taken as given. But because no end is ultimately fixed (except beatitude) the potential scope of deliberation is necessarily vast. By recognizing lack of clarity, or difficulty in accomplishing one's intention, one might begin to have doubts about the end; then that end itself can become the object of deliberation subordinated to a higher end (14. 2 ad 2). An end fixed for one line of deliberation becomes just a possible means to a more general purpose.

You might, for example, spend an afternoon comparing one car to another, trying to decide which one is best, deliberating about the merits of each. Over a cup of coffee, perhaps a friend asks, 'Do you really want to buy a car?' You then start to think that by renting an apartment closer to your office you might be able to walk to work and rent a car on those occasions when you need one. 'Getting a car' was the fixed end (or purpose) for a lengthy process of deliberation; but it then became only one of the possible means to be considered, subordinated to the higher intention of 'getting to work' (or even just 'getting around'). Thomas notes that this process does not carry on indefinitely; although one might deliberate about what kind of job to have, working itself, like friendship or knowledge, is a basic end, and there is no deliberation about it.[10]

That deliberation, the process of reasoning from end to means, is not essential to rational action is shown by the difference between the reasoning process of man compared to the characteristic of God's mind. God uses his intellect and will to decide and act,[11] but since we cannot ascribe uncertainty to God he has no need for counsel and does not deliberate.[12] Human beings, however, do face uncertainties and must use their reasoning in order to discover

---

[10] 1-II 14. 2 ad 2; cf. 1-II 1. 1 ad 2; but even such primary ends as loyalty to family or country, preservation of physical life, etc., may need to be judged under a higher love for God.

[11] On *liberum arbitrium* in God, see *ST* I 19. 10.

[12] 1-II 14. 1 ad 2.

what to do; they do this by first thinking of the desired effect, which is prior in intention, and then by reasoning 'back to the cause which is actually prior in order of action' (14. 5). God always understands the relation between effects and causes[13]; for humans, while sometimes it is clear what the cause needs to be to produce the desired effect, often a reasoning process from *a* to *b* to *c* is required to establish the linkage.

Since deliberation is related not to choice (means–end reasoning is different from the operative syllogism) but to the need to resolve doubt or uncertainty,[14] it is interesting to note what Aquinas said about free choice in the person of Jesus Christ. Since ignorance cannot be ascribed to Christ (*ST* III 15. 3), therefore he had no doubt, and no need to calculate or deliberate. This does not at all mean that he did not have free choice, because if an action is judged as something to be done without preceding doubt or inquiry, this is sufficient for choice.[15] Whatever we may think about the humanity of Christ in the doctrine of St Thomas, this points up the need to eliminate from the theory of practical reasoning the common notion that it is deliberation that makes it rational.

DELIBERATION AND THE NEED FOR GUIDANCE

For Thomas the principles of human action are knowledge of the truth and desire for the good. Desire is the motivation, reason interprets and specifies reality. There is no need for obligation to be added as a motivational force, and in many cases rules are not needed for instruction either. If the central stage of practical reason is the judgement of a particular action as an instance of doing good here and now (the basic character of decision), then many if not most of our actions do not require any additional rules. We write letters, greet friends, prepare meals, hug our children, and perform many other moral actions (all properly human actions are moral)

[13] God does not need to reason from end to means because his intelligence understands all causes and effects simultaneously; I 14. 7: cum Deus effectus suos in seipso videat sicut in causa, eius cognitio non est discursiva.

[14] III 18. 4 ad 2: Et sic patet quod dubitatio, sive inquisitio, non per se pertinet ad electionem, sed solum secundum quod est in natura ignorante.

[15] Ibid.: Et ideo, si aliquid iudicetur ut agendum absque dubitatione et inquisitione praecedente, hoc sufficit ad electionem.

simply by perceiving and judging them to be the right things to do at the time. Intention, choice, and execution form the basic and common pattern for human action.

There are also cases when it is not clear what is right and good to do, and then deliberation about what is the best thing to do is needed. It is for this reason, that is, to clarify what is true and good, that we need law.

The human mind differs from the divine in several important ways: first, by its finiteness and dependence on experience and reasoning for knowledge. Thus even in a perfect (unfallen) state mankind would still require principles and rules for guidance, summaries of previous persons' experience. But, secondly, because of the fall the effect of sin was to bring disorder to the human psyche—the reason no longer properly ordered to the truth, and the rational and sensitive appetites no longer properly oriented (*ST* 1-II 85. 3). Thus no longer can a human person be relied on always to have proper goals and choose appropriate means. Though in many cases a person can and does perceive the right relation of ends and means (within certain spheres), there is a wounding (*vulnus*) in human nature because the reason, will, and passions are disordered, especially with respect to the ultimate end.

Law is meant to remedy this defect in understanding the right relation of means to ends in human action.[16] This implies that law directly enters into practical reasoning at the stage of counsel or deliberation, remembering that deliberation is necessary only when the course of action is uncertain. Therefore in the process of specifying what is the best action (deliberation), one may need to consult the relevant laws. 'Something laid down in law, although it does not come from the agent seeking counsel, is nevertheless directive of his action, because that is one reason for doing something, namely the mandate of the law.'[17] This suggests that the function of law in practical reason is not to establish a set of duties or obligations (the motivation must be desire for the good), but to

[16] This explains why the section on law in the *Summa* is not included in human action or the virtues, but follows immediately after the section on the effects of sin.

[17] 1-II 14. 3 ad 2: id quod est lege positum, quamvis non sit ex operatione quaerentis consilium, tamen est directivum eius ad operandum: quia ista est una ratio aliquid operandi, mandatum legis. Note: this appears to be the only reference to law in the entire section on human action, 1-II qq. 6–17.

provide a way to eliminate or 'filter out' means to ends which are not suitable, and to reinforce this (with sanctions if need be) if the desire for some end might be strong enough to tempt us to choose improper means.

For example, you might be constructing a swimming-pool in your back garden. To save money, you speak to the contractor about the possibility of deferring the construction of a fence until the following year; but he informs you that you have no choice here—the law requires a pool to have an adequate protective fence. Ignorance of the law does not excuse a person where he or she should have taken the steps to enquire about the relevant regulations.

Thus the function of law is an aid to the uncertainty of the mind in the quest for the *bonum intellectum*; when the agent does not know the right relation of means to end, then law may become part of the counsel or inquisition which takes place in uncertain situations before the mind can decide.

This relation of law and practical reason also corresponds to the gift of the Holy Spirit in the mind of the Christian. The gift which corresponds to prudence is not addressed, as one might expect (cf. 2–II 52. 2 arg. 1), to the stage of decision or execution, but to the stage of counsel. It is at this stage of deliberating, in a time of uncertainty, that the agent is 'open', when he can be 'moved by the Spirit'. Once he is deciding and executing according to his train of reasoning, he is the one doing the moving, and no longer open in the process of action to new information from outside.[18]

Fortunately many daily actions can clearly be chosen without doubting that they are the right ones to be performed; they are the obvious means to good ends, and may be decided on with confidence. When there is uncertainty or inner conflict, then deliberation is helpful in clarifying the best means, both for efficacy in pursuing desired ends, and for evaluating their moral quality.

---

[18] 2–II 52. 2 ad 1: iudicare et praecipere non est moti, sed moventis. Et quia in donis Spiritus Sancti mens humana non se habet ut movens, sed magis ut mota . . . non fuit conveniens quod donum correspondens prudentiae praeceptum diceretur vel iudicium, sed consilium.

12

Execution

THE final stage in the psychological process of action is execution. It follows decision, and is the actual carrying out of the decision into action. Execution includes both cognitive and appetitive components, to which Aquinas gave the terms *imperium* and *usus*. While the teaching of Thomas on this stage is consistent and clear, there has been much misunderstanding about this.

A PROBLEM IN INTERPRETATION

In some recent studies the stage following decision or choice has been seen as a mistake on the part of St Thomas. Alan Donagan in his summary of the Thomistic theory of action sees this part as an innovation, even an 'excrescence'.[1] One of the reasons for this judgement is that there is very little in Aristotle's theory of action on this stage. In Aristotle's account of practical reasoning the conclusion of deliberation is choice, and *prohairesis* generates the action. The action is meant to stem directly from the decision.

Perhaps the more important factor has been the misunderstanding characteristic of a theory of action emphasizing the will which dominated much of the later scholastic tradition. Suarez, for example, disagreed with Aquinas and transferred *imperium* to the will from the intellect.[2] While this does reflect an important shift to a voluntarist view of the basis of law, the primary fact to note is that Suarez disagreed with Aquinas on the grounds that an intellectual *imperium* would not have the necessary motivation for action; and if one thought it had, then, according to Suarez, this threatened the freedom of the will.[3] It is the loss of a teleological motivation in nature and the split between intellect and will which govern this position. The moral theories of Scotus and Ockham had conquered, even in the commentaries on the *Summa Theologiae*.

[1] Donagan, 'Thomas Aquinas on Human Action', *CHLMP* 652: 'This seems to be one of those sheer blunders into which even the greatest philosophers fall.'
[2] Suarez, commentary on *ST* 1-II, 'De usu et imperio', 2. 9. 3 (iv. 269).
[3] See *Disputationes Metaph.* 19. 6. 10 (xxv. 722–3).

Readers of St Thomas could not help but notice that *imperium* following choice was clearly designated an act of reason and not of the will; this was recognized by certain commentators, notably Cajetan and John of St Thomas. Since the twelve-step scheme established by Billuart in the eighteenth century featured an intellectual *imperium*, that stage seemed the keystone for re-establishing the doctrine of prudence and the place of reason in morality.[4]

Père Gauthier has strongly resisted this line of interpretation and argued that Thomas was misled by the tradition he inherited into adding unnecessary steps to Aristotle's theory of action. Gauthier concluded that this insertion of an additional stage was 'une fatale méprise' because it gave this stage, after *electio*, a determining role in the course of action which undermines the integrity of decision; he recommended that *imperium* be assimilated with the *iudicium electionis* and *usus* with *electio*.[5] By doing this Gauthier seems to be restoring Thomas's account to the Aristotelian model, which concludes with *prohairesis*.

Gauthier is correct in one respect. *Imperium* in the sense understood by the commentators, as a precept or command providing the final specification of the act, makes nonsense of a theory of action. If the agent has made a decision, then it can be changed only by making another decision. Effective 'command' cannot rectify erroneous choice.[6]

On the other hand, arguments against a stage of execution ignore or discard some very clear and central teaching of Aquinas. Prudence is clearly divided into the three acts of counselling, judging, and commanding (*ST* 2-II 47. 8). If commanding is assimilated to judging, this calls into question the entire scheme of Thomas, who says that commanding is not only a distinct part of prudence but is the 'principal act'.

[4] Deman, 'Le "précepte" de la prudence'.

[5] Gauthier, 'Saint Maxime le Confesseur', 88.

[6] Because Deman was not clear about the exact role of reason in choice, he made false claims for the final preceptive stage of practical reasoning, and opponents remained unconvinced about the importance of *imperium*.

Lottin, in 'Psychologie de l'acte humaine', 260–2, was a fence-sitter in the controversy between Deman and Gauthier: he thought that one might consider *imperium* in two senses—as part of the *iudicium electionis* (Gauthier's view) and in an executive sense, conceding something to Deman. See the summary by P. Morisset, 'Prudence et fin selon saint Thomas'.

TREATMENT BY ARISTOTLE AND THE STOICS

There is a weakness in Aristotle's philosophy of action precisely at the stage of the connection of decision with action itself. In some explanations of the practical syllogism Aristotle gives the impression that once the conclusion of the syllogism is reached there is nothing more to be explained. In the *EN* he says 'when two premisses are combined into one, the soul is thereupon bound to affirm the conclusion, and if the premisses involve action, the soul is bound to perform this act at once' (1147a26–8). In the *De Motu Animalium* (701a17–25) Aristotle gives this example of practical reasoning:

I need a covering, a coat is a covering. I need a coat. What I need I ought to make, I need a coat: I must make a coat. And the conclusion the 'I must make a coat' is an action. And the action goes back to a starting-point. If there is to be a coat, there must first be this, and if this then this—and straightway he does this. Now that the action is the conclusion is clear.

Though Aristotle's theory of practical reasoning was a brilliant contribution to ethical theory the connection between the conclusion of thought and the action itself is not clear. This lacuna or ambiguity is reflected in the debate among Aristotelian scholars about whether the conclusion of a practical syllogism is an action or not.[7] Gauthier considered Aristotle's account defective on this score and asserted that the will was the missing element (see Ch. 2). From this point of view, with choice identified with the will, no further psychological step is required after the choice of the will to do something.

It is not clear why Aristotle could not (or thought it unnecessary to) explain the connection between reasoning and actual bodily movement. Some attempt was made in *De Motu Animalium* at 702a18: 'For the affections suitably prepare the organic parts, desire the affections, and *phantasia* the desire; and *phantasia* comes about either through thought or through sense-perception.' Aristotle has a few passages dealing with the concept of *pneuma* as a connecting factor between thought and bodily movement, but the account is

---

[7] See Kenny, *Aristotle's Theory of the Will*, 142–3; Gauthier and Jolif, *L'Éthique à Nicomaque*, ii. 202.

too sketchy to be very helpful.[8] In any case Aquinas did not make use of this treatment by Aristotle.

The Stoic philosophers developed and changed Aristotle's theories. They were keenly interested in ethics and the psychology of action, but in their more materialist view of the soul (which in some ways resembles modern behaviourism) they moved away from the emphasis on rational choice found in Aristotle.[9] They used some of the same terms and concepts, but emphasized instincts and drives as causes for action, with a reduction of interest in the practical syllogism. The Stoics developed the notion of *pneuma* as the connecting link between thought and action, and because their theory of the soul was a material one 'the question of the psycho-physical link was much easier to handle for the Stoics'.[10]

USUS: THE COMPLETION OF THE ACT

The source for the term *usus*, as well as some of the content of the teaching, comes ultimately from the Stoic ethical terminology and from St Augustine. This is reflected in the fact that in the four articles of *ST* I-II q. 16 Aquinas quotes John Damascene and Augustine; and it is the only question in the section on human action without a citation of Aristotle.

The Stoic theory of Epictetus (second century AD) had an account of *chrēsis*, a rational faculty which decides. Cicero translated this as *usus*, and when we come to Maximus the Confessor the term refers to the action itself, with a moral evaluation.[11]

In St Augustine's teaching *usus* is given both a psychological and a moral dimension. It is used to indicate the object of the will in action;[12] but it is also used in an evaluative sense in distinction to *fruitio*: *frui* is the attitude of the will to those things which we love for their own sake, while *uti* is used for other objects. Thus God himself is the only proper object of *fruitio*.[13] This teaching of

[8] See Nussbaum, 'The *Sumphuton Pneuma* and the *De Motu Animalium*'s account of Soul and Body', in *Aristotle's De Motu Animalium*, 143–64.

[9] A. Preus, 'Intention and Impulse in Aristotle and the Stoics', *Apeiron*, 15 (1981), 48–58, at 56: 'Stoic materialism was so attractive in antiquity that it became synthesized with the Aristotelian theory of action.'

[10] B. Inwood, *Ethics and Human Action in Early Stoicism* (Oxford, 1985), 51.

[11] Gauthier, 'Saint Maxime', 77.

[12] *De Trinitate*, x. 11. 17: uti est enim assumere aliquid in facultatem voluntatis.

[13] *De doctrina christiana*, i. 33. 37.

Augustine was very well known; perhaps just because it formed the very opening discussion in the *Sentences* of Peter Lombard, and was what budding theologians first sank their teeth into, the notion was not maintained very clearly.

In his own commentary on the *Sentences* Aquinas distinguished three different meanings of the word *usus*: (1) an operation in general, in which the use of something can be good or bad (he quotes Augustine's *De Trinitate*); or (2) frequency of operation, and thus equivalent to *consuetudo*; or (3) to use means which are ordered to some end. This is the proper meaning, and he defines *usus* as 'the execution of that which is ordered to an end'.[14] By emphasizing the means–end structuring of execution Thomas has changed the Stoic flavour of the concept and made it thoroughly Aristotelian.

The end of the psychological process is *usus*, treated in *ST* 1-II 16. The key word in the treatment is *applicatio*: the application of something to another operation is *usus*. To ride on horseback is to use a horse. To beat on a drum involves the 'application' of a stick. To move into action is to apply the interior principles of acting, the psychological powers, on the bodily members, which is analogous to using the intellect for understanding, or the eye for seeing. This concept of *applicatio* is clearly a movement: something already determined moves from interiority in the psyche into exterior action.

Usus is a matter of the will, because it involves movement. Because the will wants to accomplish its movement toward the activation of a good, the process does not stop at *electio*. In 16. 4, Thomas says that for the will to tend to something proportionate to some end (which is *electio*) is to will only imperfectly; the will also wants to have the end in fact—to accomplish it, and thus be complete (*perfecte*). It is this further dimension of completion, of application of the particular action decided on to the functions of mind and body which will perform it, which explains the character of *usus* and is clearly based on the movement of nature toward perfect act which is the basis of the metaphysics of action.

One cannot proceed directly to *usus* from *electio*, however (let alone from *intentio*[15]). The application of specified action to perfor-

---

[14] *In I Sent.* 1. 1. 2: uti autem nominat executionem eius quod ad finem ordinatum est.

[15] As Lottin suggested; see Ch. 10 n. 3.

mance must have a cognitive element. That is why *usus* cannot properly be attributed to animals (16. 2), because *applicatio* involves an *arbitrium*, a judgement of the relationship, and this occurs only where there is reason. Animals do things through their members by instinct; thus they cannot properly be said to use things, as they do not know the relationship of their powers and members to their actions (16. 2 ad 2). Birds can build nests, but only human beings use tools.

IMPERIUM: THE COGNITIVE ASPECT OF EXECUTION

According to Gauthier, the term *imperium* inherited by St Thomas from Albert the Great rested on a series of mistakes.[16] The notion of *imperium* in the Western tradition can be traced to Maximus the Confessor, who introduced the Stoic concept of *hormē* following choice. At first this stage in the theory was known as *impetus*, but it was further confused by William of Auxerre who changed this to *imperium*. Aquinas, however, was able to clarify a confused tradition and make a genuine enrichment to the psychology of action.

In the first article on *usus* Thomas says that 'to use' is primarily a matter of the will, as prime mover, but involving the direction of reason.[17] This activity of reason as director Thomas calls *imperium*. The word is possibly misleading if taken out of psychological context. When the process of action is mistakenly understood as alternating acts of reason and will, the implication is that reason gives a 'command' which the will must carry out. The element of intellectual determinism implied by this has been resisted and is perhaps the chief reason why there has been suspicion of this stage.

When the operation of intellect and will are understood concurrently, then the question of determinism no longer arises, and the nature of this stage is better appreciated. The stage of execution translates an agent's decision into actual bodily movements, and the intellect must still be involved in this. There is no question of new information at this stage; it is the action of the intellect following through with what has already been decided and chosen by the will.

The word *imperium* should perhaps be understood in the sense of

[16] Gauthier, 'Saint Maxime', 85.

[17] *ST* I-II 16. 1: uti primo et principaliter est voluntatis, tanquam primi moventis; rationis autem tanquam dirigentis.

governing or directing, rather than the giving of a command.[18] In this case the English word 'command' could be taken in the sense of governing authority, as in the phrase 'taking command' or 'commanding officer'. In the stage of execution the intellect has command in the sense of 'oversight' or 'seeing something through', and not so much in the sense of issuing mandates for the will to follow (especially to be avoided here is any Kantian notion of an agent acting in obedience to self-generated moral dictates).

On the other hand the language of command is a valid way of describing the connections between mind and body and between decision and action; the mind 'commanding' the body expresses the force of the agent's decision. This use of 'imperatival language' to express the motivating power of rational desire is present to some extent in Aristotle (in the *De Motu Animalium*, for example), and was developed more fully by the Stoics.[19] In this context the insistence by Aquinas on the intellectual character of *imperium* can be seen as the recognition of the dangers of the Stoic account and of the need to maintain the rational ordering of desire.

The word characteristic of the intellect in execution is *ordo*: *imperium* is said to set in order (*ordinat*, 17. 1), which is a characteristic of reason (17. 2), and its act is said to be of *rationis ordinantis* (17. 5). Thomas's usage is restricted to the idea of properly relating one thing to another, and not 'order' in the sense of giving a mandate, unless this is understood as a verbal expression for the governing link between mind and body. In relation to *usus* the intellect, as it were, sets the bodily powers in order, while the will moves them into action.

In 17. 5, Thomas says that since reason is able to judge what is good to desire, so it is also able to set things in order by commanding what the agent wants ('potest ordinare imperando quod homo velit'). Though the terms could be misleading, it is clear that the function of the *imperium* is to be the rational link between *electio* and *usus*: to 'make sure' that the specific action chosen by the agent (and none other) is what is indeed carried out. Though the particular action has been fully specified at the stage of decision, the role of reason still has its specifying function, as it ensures that the same specificity is retained in the process of actualizing a mental decision

[18] In his version of the table of 12 steps in action, Finnis, 'Object and Intention', 4, puts 'Direction' for step 9 (*imperium/praeceptum*).

[19] Inwood, *Ethics and Human Action*, 16–17.

in bodily action. Changing circumstances might alter the way a decision is carried out.

If you have decided to write a letter to your father, you sit down to write it. So far so good. You play with the pen as you fill it, you doodle, you write a paragraph or two and get distracted. Eventually you finish it, but not as promptly or expansively as you might have done it; this may be partly due to the will, but also partly due to lack of concentration or uncertainty about what to write, the poor operation of cognition in action.

The qualities needed for good execution are awareness, firmness, and flexibility, and cognition must continue to be a part of bodily action. You may decide to go for a walk. The will then initiates the bodily movements. But in the act of walking cognition must be active, not only to see where one is walking (and provide direction), but to maintain the activity of walking. The decision 'walking is good—so I will do it' must in a sense be continuously reaffirmed, not as a conscious decision, but as a mode of action open for reassessment, as when a rest is called for, or a brief stop is made to chat with a friend, and so on.

It can now be appreciated that the difficulties that scholars have had with *imperium* stem largely from the faulty model in which intellect and will are assigned separate stages, and not from Thomas's actual teaching. His description of the stage of execution closely follows his principles: since cognition and volition operate together, freedom is connected with both (17. 1 ad 2); the general function of intellect is *ordinare* and that of the will is *movere*, reflected in Thomas's explanations of *imperium* and *usus*; and the metaphysical priority of cognition means that *imperium* logically precedes *usus*.[20] When Aquinas says that 'sometimes' (*aliquando*) the ordering is prior in time to the application to movement, he indicates their normal conjunction.

Thomas Aquinas was not really dependent on Stoicism for his analysis of this executive stage of human action, even though the terms he inherited came from this tradition. He was able to see the value in the explicit link to action, but wanted to maintain the rational element in the stage of execution, using the word *imperium* in preference to *impetus*. Thomas's redeployment of the termino-

---

[20] *ST* 1-II 17. 3: Imperium autem non est simul cum actu eius cui imperatur: sed naturaliter prius est imperium quam imperio obediatur, et aliquando etiam est prius tempore. Unde manifestum est quod imperium est prius quam usus.

logy is an example of how a moral philosopher may make use of the discoveries and insights of somewhat alien systems in order to clarify his own presentation.

In summary, note that the means–end structuring is a feature in each stage of the process of action from intention to execution. The agent in deliberation formulates this structure and identifies the particular actions when there is uncertainty; then he comes to a decision by choosing on the basis both of its correctness and its attractiveness, and carries out the action under the guidance of both intellect and will. Because circumstances may change the validity of a particular means–end structuring, both intellect and will are constantly involved in the formulation, choice, and execution of all our actions.

Thomas was understood in his own time to be an intellectualist, and opposed as such by the Franciscans. In the voluntarist climate which succeeded, Cajetan found he could interpret Thomistic practical reason largely in terms of the will. Since both intellectualists and voluntarists are able to cite texts from Thomas in support of their position, the interpretation offered here, that Thomas conceived of the agent as using, at each stage, both cognitive and appetitive potencies together, gains in force. This complementary understanding (1) seems to be harmonious and consistent with the general position of Thomas, and gives the most coherent account of this section of the *Summa Theologiae*; (2) makes Thomas much closer to Aristotle, showing him to be a penetrating commentator but not unwilling to accept helpful innovations; and (3) shows that Thomas transcended the limitations of faculty psychology and anticipated the insights of modern philosophy in seeing the psychological unity of the agent.

PART IV
Rectifying Practical Reason

13
Prudence and the Integration of Human Action

PRUDENCE is the developed habit of the cognitive element in the process of action to make and execute good choices, and is summed up as *recta ratio agibilium*. It represents the agent's ability to deliberate, to decide, and properly to order the process of his practical reasoning to action. This disposition is quite different from moral science or conscience (as the knowledge of moral principles), or casuistic ability. Ethical knowledge and skill in analyzing difficult cases do not necessarily result in the actual good choices made by a person of moral virtue.

Action is a product of both intellect and appetite. In Thomistic psychology, the appetite is divided into rational and sensitive, with the latter category further subdivided into the 'concupiscible' and 'irascible' (*ST* 1-II qq. 22 and 23). It follows then that four distinct virtues are required: *prudentia* is the correct disposition of practical reasoning, *recta ratio agibilium* (1-II 57. 4), and its subject—or the psychological power to be perfected—is the practical intellect; the three other moral virtues deal with appetite: justice, temperance, and fortitude for the rational, concupiscible, and irascible appetites respectively (1-II 61. 2). Because an act is virtuous in so far as it is conformed to right reason, the perfecting of reason or prudence makes it the principal of the cardinal virtues, as it is rational in essence while the others are rational by participation.[1]

PRUDENCE AND PRACTICAL KNOWLEDGE

Thomas clearly distinguishes prudence from moral or practical knowledge. Unlike Albert the Great and others, he did not define *prudentia* as a *scientia*, but as *recta ratio*: not right 'knowledge' but

[1] *ST* 1-II 61. 4: Solum autem hoc quod est discretionem habere, quod attribuebatur prudentiae, videtur distingui ab aliis tribus, inquantum hoc est ipsius rationis per essentiam; alia vero tria important quandam participationem rationis, per modum applicationis cuiusdam ad passiones vel operationes.

right 'reasoning'. The avoidance of what had become the traditional way of describing prudence clearly shows that Thomas was
developing a view of prudence along genuinely Aristotelian lines,
in which there is a difference between practical knowledge and
practical wisdom.

Aristotle himself had identified both intellect and desire as principles of action, and had distinguished the man who knows how to
reason from the man of action who is able to make effective
decisions. For him the model for the *phronimos* was not the
philosopher but a political leader such as Pericles.[2] Much of the
current scholarship on Aristotle's doctrine of practical reason shows
the character of *phronēsis* to be a virtue which applies insight of
ends and means to particular actions, but which cannot be
described as mere knowledge, since it operates in conjunction with
orexis, desire, and therefore with other virtues.[3]

Thomas makes it clear that *prudentia*, though it involves *scientia*,
is not to be identified with the knowledge of moral principles,
because that would equate moral virtue with knowledge, and
Aquinas was keen to mark the separation between knowledge of
moral principles and actually having the habit of deciding and
acting correctly. He repeatedly describes the operation of prudence
as the choice of appropriate means to an end, with the end fixed by
moral virtue (see especially *ST* 2-II 47. 6). Prudence is the
developed ability to choose the right means, the disposition of
mind—dependent on right appetite—to make decisions, to consider other possibilities when necessary, and to put the decision
correctly into action.

Thomas made this division even clearer by stating that the
fundamental principles belong to *synderesis*, a kind of natural
reason; he made it a separate *habitus*, made up of these principles,
distinct from prudence (2-II 47. 6 ad 1).[4] *Synderesis*, or being able
to use first principles, is what 'moves' prudence (ad 3); so the
function of prudence is to apply general moral principles of *synderesis*, and practical knowledge dependent on it, to particular
actions. The prudent person is therefore cognizant of both univer-

---

[2] *EN* VI. 2–5, esp. 1140[b]5–15.

[3] See N. Sherman, *The Fabric of Character: Aristotle's Theory of Virtue* (Oxford, 1989).

[4] Cf. *ST* I 79. 12; *De veritate*, 16. 1–3; 17. 1, 2; *In II Sent.* 24. 2. 2; 39. 3. 2.

sal and particular.[5] This surely indicates that the essence of prudence is the effective linking between universal principle and particular situation, not (merely) the actual knowledge of either.

This teaching seems to be fairly consistent through the works of Thomas. In *De veritate* 5. 1, prudence is described in a consideration of providence. There are two aspects of actions to be considered, the end and the means, and prudence focuses on the means. Now the end of an action exists in us in two ways: (1) through a natural cognition which pertains to the intellect; and (2) in relation to affection; and in this way the ends of actions are in us through the moral virtues. In regard to the means, likewise, we are perfected in two ways: cognitively, through counsel, and appetitively through choice, and in these we are directed through prudence.[6]

This teaching is expanded on in the *Summa Theologiae*. The discussion of the difference between a moral and intellectual virtue in 1-II q. 58 is illuminating. Aquinas considers whether it is possible for one to have a moral virtue without intellectual ones (58. 4). Yes, he says, one may have moral virtue without *sapientia, scientia,* or *ars,* but not without *intellectus* and *prudentia.*[7] For good choice to occur, first one's moral virtue must correctly include the appetitive power; secondly, one then correctly accepts (*recte accipiat*) the means through the reason, which rightly counsels, judges, and commands. Thus correct action requires prudence and understanding; but this is *recta ratio,* not *scientia.*

In the following article (58. 5) prudence is even more carefully delineated. *Recta ratio* deals with the universal level, but also the particular, because actions are particular; reason needs to proceed not only from universal principles but also from particular principles.[8] The general principles are known through a natural under-

---

[5] *ST* 2-II 47. 3: necesse est quod prudens et cognoscat universalia principia rationis, et cognoscat singularia, circa quae sunt operationes.

[6] *De veritate,* 5. 1: et quantum ad cognitionem per consilium et quantum ad appetitum per electionem, et in his per prudentiam dirigimur. Thomas had not yet formulated *consilium* in relation to the stages of practical reasoning; but he clearly understood the importance of the combination of intellect and appetite.

[7] *ST* 1-II 58. 4: Dicendum quod virtus moralis potest quidem esse sine quibusdam intellectualibus virtutibus, sicut sine sapientia, scientia et arte: non autem potest esse sine intellectu et prudentia.

[8] 1-II 58. 5: non solum ex principiis universalibus, sed etiam ex principiis particularibus.

standing (which for the most fundamental ones would be *synderesis*) or through some body of practical knowledge (*per aliquam scientiam practicam*). This is not sufficient for right reasoning (*ad recte ratiocinandum*), that is for prudence, which requires moral virtue to keep the known principle from being corrupted or destroyed (*corrumpitur*) in the particular. Prudence is not the knowledge of general principles, nor of the more particular principles which belong to *scientia practica*: it is the outlook or disposition which enables the agent to arrive at the right application in the particular situation and to perform it.

Further, in 2-II 47. 16, Aquinas asks whether prudence can be lost through forgetfulness. One can indeed lose an art or a body of knowledge (*scientia*) in this way, since they are a matter of reason. But prudence is not in cognition alone but also in the appetite ('non consistit in sola cognitione, sed etiam in appetitu'), because its main act (*praecipere*) is the connection between cognition and the thing to be desired and done.[9] It follows, therefore, that prudence is not directly removed ('non directe tollitur') by forgetting; that prudence is not a *scientia*, which is in the reason alone (ad 1); and that prudence is not acquired by memory alone, but by experience (ad 2). A clear definition is given (in the response to the third objection): prudence mainly consists not in knowledge of general truths, but in the application of general truth to action ('sed in applicatione ad opera').

Prudence is the application of moral knowledge, dependent on principles, but oriented to action. The application of general principle to particular situation depends on, and expresses, the attitudes and desires of the agent. This makes the crucial difference in allowing the judgement of reasoning, guided by prudence in relation to correct appetite, to be the agent's 'real' or genuine choice, and not just the voice of his reason or conscience.

The difference between prudence as virtue and as knowledge was well expressed by St Thomas in his treatise on the virtues:

Prudence means something more than practical knowledge, which relates to making a general judgement about what to do, such as that fornication is evil, and one must not steal. It can happen that even having this knowledge, the judgement of reason can be impeded in a particular

---

[9] 2-II 47. 16: principalis eius actus est praecipere, quod est applicare cognitionem habitam ad appetendum, et operandum.

action so that it does not judge rightly; therefore prudence is equally a matter of virtue, since with mere knowledge, an agent may still sin against virtue.[10]

This is the rationale for making prudence at the stage of judgement (in choice) dependent on moral virtue, and this mutual relationship will be explained below. It follows that the most crucial stage in action is execution, and that even good judgement alone is not indicative of prudence without the corresponding action it is meant to produce; hence the *imperium* or *praeceptum* (these are equivalent terms),[11] the last cognitive element in the process of action, is the defining characteristic (*proprium*) of prudence, the final test of the prudent agent.

PRUDENCE AND THE PROCESS OF ACTION

Prudence refers to the good operation of the practical intellect, responsible for the cognitive element in the process of action. Since prudence is not responsible for setting the goal (*finis*) in an action but only the means (2-II 47. 6), its role should not be in intention, but in the stages of deliberation, decision, and execution. This is precisely how Thomas conceives it: there are three operations of reason in action, he says—*consiliare, iudicare, praecipere* (1-II 57. 6); these are distinct aspects and correspond to the cognitive elements of the process of action developed by Aquinas in 1-II qq. 13–17, namely *consilium, iudicium,* and *imperium* (see Fig. 2, p. 131). The threefold division of deliberation, choosing, and putting into operation a particular action is not arbitrary but integral to a coherent Thomistic philosophy of action, and the division is no less important in the analysis of prudence, the disposition of right

---

[10] *De virt. in comm.* q. un., a. 6, ad 1: prudentia plus importat quam scientia practica: nam ad scientiam practicam pertinet universale iudicium de agendis; sicut fornicationem esse malam, furtum non esse faciendum, et huiusmodi. Qua quidem scientia existente in particulari actu contingit iudicium rationis intercipi, ut non recte diiudicet; et propter hoc dicitur parum valere ad virtutem, quia ea existente contingit hominem contra virtutem peccare.

[11] In describing the process of action, Thomas used *imperium* for the executive stage (*ST* 1-II q. 17); in his treatment of the virtues and of prudence he used *praecipere* or *praeceptum* (e.g. 1-II 57. 6, 2-II 47. 8). Some have tried to argue from this that there is some inconsistency or confusion in Thomas, but the teaching is quite clear; see 1-II 61. 3, where *prudentia* is both *praeceptiva* and connected to *imperium*.

reasoning about actions. In the context of the general treatment of virtues, Thomas explains (1-II 58. 4) the rationale for the three stages: moral virtue requires good choice; this in turn requires the agent to accept the right means; and this is not possible unless reason is rightly deliberating, judging, and commanding.[12]

In a voluntarist view of human action which exaggerates the function of the will in choice and execution, the role of reason is reduced to *consilium* and perhaps a provisional *iudicium* providing an analysis of the options, and considering their advantages and disadvantages. In such a conception of action, prudence would be largely a matter of developing a disposition of good *inquisitio* or reasoning about possibilities, deliberating well about them, and discerning between them. But, says Thomas, *prudentia* is not only *bene consiliativa*, but also *bene iudicativa* and *bene praeceptiva* (1-II 58. 5 ad 3).[13]

The three-stage division of the operation of practical reason is developed more explicitly in the section specially devoted to the virtue of prudence. According to *ST* 2-II 47. 8, there are three operations of reason in *agibilibus*, the range of possible actions: *consiliari*, *iudicare*, and *praecipere*. Thomas provides some further description here: (1) the first regards discovery (*inventio*), because to take counsel is to search or investigate (*quaerere*); (2) the second is to judge what has been discovered (*iudicare de inventis*); (3) finally, practical reason goes further, and its operation consists in the application of what has been deliberated and judged to the matter to be done.[14] It is clear that Thomas is using as a model his analysis of action offered in 1-II qq. 13–17, with intention followed by three stages, and that prudence is meant to be seen as the virtue of the practical intellect corresponding to the cognitive side of that schema.

The distinctiveness of the aspects of prudence is consistent with the different operations of reason as described in the account of the basic psychological process of action. The distinction between the

---

[12] 1-II 58. 4: ut homo recte accipiat ea quae sunt ad finem: et hoc non potest esse nisi per rationem recte consiliantem, iudicantem et praecipientem.

[13] In 1-II 65. 1 Thomas focuses on the proper characteristic of moral virtue as making a right choice ('facere electionem rectam'); but also emphasizes that prudence is 'consiliativa, et iudicativa et praeceptiva'.

[14] 2-II 47. 8: qui quidem actus consistit in applicatione consiliatorum et iudicatorum ad operandum.

process of discursive reasoning in the stage of *consilium* and of the understanding of the intellect in *iudicium* is maintained. It occurs in the general discussion of virtue at 1-II 57. 6 ad 3, and is further explained in the particular discussion of prudence, where the roles of *ratio* and *intellectus* are clearly distinguished. The intellect, treated first (2-II 49. 2), performs an estimation of principles, but here there is a double involvement (49. 2 ad 1): it is *cognoscitivus universalium*, informed of general principles, and it is also aware of the singular (*cognoscitivus extremi*); thus it understands both. In other words, in the stage of decision, the act of judgement is the result of the mind bringing together the universal and the particular, and seeing the correct relationship between the two.

Ratio (2-II 49. 5), on the other hand, is needed to make up a defect in the understanding (ad 2). Thus judgement by the intellect is central to human action, and *consilium* is an aid or recourse for the human agent, who does not have intellectual power in full measure. When the particular action to be done is not clear or intelligible to the agent, he needs to conduct an *inquisitio* through discursive reasoning. Therefore, though *consilium* is not required for many actions, it is in precisely those difficult and uncertain situations requiring deliberation when it is essential for the prudent agent to be a good reasoner (*bene ratiocinativus*) so that he may then rightly apply (in the act of judgement) universal principles to particular situations which are various and uncertain.[15]

The distinctions between the stages of cognition in the process of action are given further definition by Thomas in the assignment of special terms for their perfection. The *habitus* of good counsel, though an aspect of prudence, has its own name, *eubulia*; and the ability to make sound decisions is *synesis*.[16] These distinctions may seem artifical or forced, but there are real purposes to be served by this incorporation of Aristotelian terms. The differentiation of the perfective dispositions for each stage (the 'parts' of prudence) shows that one may be able to arrive at decisions quickly and confidently, though they are sometimes not very sound because one has little skill or patience in analyzing possible courses of action

---

[15] 2-II 49. 5 ad 2: tamen ad prudentiam maxime requiritur quod sit homo bene ratiocinativus, ut possit bene applicare universalia principia ad particularia, quae sunt varia et incerta.

[16] See 1-II 57. 6, 2-II 48. 1, and 2-II 51. 1–3.

in complex or difficult situations; or on the other hand one may deliberate well but, perhaps because of immersion in the details, be poor at coming to a decision and fixing on one option with certainty and correctness. Here there is a value in distinguishing the virtues of *eubulia* and *synesis*.

Note that the virtue for *praeceptum*, the cognitive part of the final stage of execution, is not given a separate name, but is assigned simply to prudence. Since prudence includes all three stages, why did Thomas not make a virtue connected to *imperium* along the same lines as *eubulia* and *synesis*? To execute well necessarily implies good judgement and good counsel. *Praeceptum* or *imperium* is defined as an act of reason directing, with a certain motion, something to act;[17] and *imperium* belongs to the reason because it involves seeing and establishing a relation of one thing to another. If this ordering function is to be perfected, under the guidance of prudence, it requires right ordering to have been observed in the previous stages, namely the right ordering of particular action to circumstances involved in the process of counsel, and the right ordering of particular action to universal principle in the act of judgement. If the prudent agent is the one who has the *habitus* of making right *praecepta* in executing actions, his practical reasoning has necessarily been 'supervising' the allied virtues of *eubulia* and *synesis*.

THE PRINCIPAL ACT OF PRUDENCE

One would expect the chief act of prudence to be concerned with the agent's choice, or rather the cognitive part of choice, *iudicium*, especially in light of the crucial function of decision explained in previous chapters. In the general description of the necessity of prudence (1-II 57. 5) we find that prudence is necessary for *bene operari*, which in turn requires *recta electio*. In 58. 4 Thomas says that a moral virtue is a *habitus electivus*, because making a good choice is its essential characteristic, which is why prudence is so important. The same point is made in 1-II 65. 1, where the *proprium* or chief characteristic of a moral virtue is said to be making the right choice (*facere electionem rectam*), and prudence is therefore needed to enable the right choice to be made.

---

[17] 1-II 17. 5: imperium nihil aliud est quam actus rationis ordinantis, cum quadam motione, aliquid ad agendum.

Though choice or decision seems to be the central aspect of moral virtue, Aquinas says that the chief act of prudence is commanding: 'principalis actus est praecipere' (1-II 57. 6). This is maintained consistently in the section on prudence, e.g. in 2-II 47. 8 where *praecipere* is the principal act of the practical reason; and in 2-II 51. 3 ad 3, where we are told that the agent requires a final, principal virtue which is *bene praeceptiva*, and this is prudence itself.

The logical reason for this establishment of *praeceptum* or *imperium* as the principal act, and of the virtue which perfects this as the chief virtue, is the necessary inclusion of the other two stages in the final one. *Praeceptum* is the final stage, what the process of action leads to, so that the perfection of that stage necessarily implies the perfecting of the steps preceding. This is indicated by the reasoning of St. Thomas in 2-II 51. 2 ad 2: in explaining why *eubulia* is a virtue distinct from prudence he admits that there is one final end for all the different stages of the process of action, namely to live well overall ('bene vivere totum'); but the three aspects of *consilium*, *iudicium*, and *praeceptum* are ordered in steps towards this end, and *praeceptum* relates directly to the final end ('immediate se habet ad finem ultimum'), while counsel and judgement relate at a distance ('remote se habent'), and have their own secondary ends. Thus it is by virtue of its proximate relationship to the *finis* of the entire process that *praeceptum* is principal, not because it is more difficult, or requires more use of the intellect.

In 2-II 47. 8, Aquinas makes an important distinction between theoretical and practical reason. Taken in isolation, *consilium* and *iudicium* can be seen as functions also of speculative reason, in the sense that theoretical reasoning too has stages of *inventio* and *iudicium*[18] (see Fig. 1, p. 68). If the process ended there, however, no action would take place; so what is distinctive about practical reason is that it is related to action: it goes further and issues the *praeceptum*, which is the application of the results of deliberation

---

[18] 2-II 47. 8: primus est consiliari: quod pertinet ad inventionem, nam consiliari est quaerere . . . Secundus actus est iudicare de inventis: et hic sistit speculativa ratio. The misunderstanding of practical reasoning as moral knowledge followed by choice by the will has been reinforced by faulty texts in this passage. In place of *hic sistit* the Piana edn. has *hoc facit* (with other MSS reading *hoc finit* or *hic fiat*), which gives the impression that counsel and judgement are theoretical stages, and practical reasoning becomes really practical only in the third stage. The correct (Leonine) reading shows that Thomas was making a comparison to *ratio speculativa*, which has only two stages and stops after judgement.

and decision to the action to be done.[19] This act is closer to the end or purpose of practical reason, because action is what practical reason is all about, and hence it is the principal act of prudence.

A passage from St Thomas's treatment of the cardinal virtues makes the doctrine clearer:

Three things are required in practical cognition, of which the first is counsel, and the second a judgement about the results of that—just as there is also found in theoretical reasoning discovery or inquiry and judgement. But because the practical intellect issues an order to avoid or to pursue, which the speculative intellect does not do (as III *De Anima* tells us), there is a third stage belonging to practical reasoning, which is to be clear about what to do, and this is the 'command' to which the other two stages are set in relation.[20]

While this relationship of the incomplete to the complete, or midddle stage to final stage, is sufficient, I believe, to explain why Thomas assigned this prominence to *praecipere*, there is a further dimension, hinted at in the difference between speculative and practical reason, which gets at the moral character of prudence. In 1-II 57. 6, Thomas puts forth in the second argument the possibility that in terms of inferior and superior the act of judgement should be supreme, and that therefore *synesis* is not just an adjunct of prudence, but is the principal virtue itself. Thomas's reply to this is important: sometimes a person may make a good judgement about what to do and nevertheless not carry it out properly ('non recte exequi'); thus there is need for a final completion in which reason gives the right executive order.[21]

Thomas attached great importance to this final stage of practical reasoning. It is possible to judge well, to make a good decision, but nevertheless fail to do it. This is a failure not in deliberation or in decision (which may happen too, of course), but in execution. It is this last stage of execution, 'seeing' or making sure that the right action is performed, that is the primary responsibility of prudence. Thus the doctrine of prudence as principally the virtue of right *praeceptum* reveals the special insight of Thomas into prudence as

[19] 2-II 47. 8: Sed practica ratio, quae ordinatur ad opus, procedit ulterius, et est tertius actus eius praecipere: qui quidem actus consistit in applicatione consiliatorum et iudicatorum ad operandum.

[20] *De virt. card.* q. un., a. 1.

[21] *ST* 1-II 57. 6 ad 2: Sed ultimum complementum est, quando ratio iam bene praecipit de agendis.

both a moral and an intellectual virtue: the habits of good deliberation and sound judgement are not enough. Good execution, the
proper application *ad opus* of the good decision the agent has made,
is absolutely essential.

14

Error, Sin, and Defective Action

THE practical intellect differs from the theoretic in the way it relates to reality. Because practical reason relates to action, appetite is involved, and reality is considered under the aspect of a good, as the purpose of action. Practical intellect *qua* intellect, however, seeks not good (as that is formally the object of the will) but truth—truth related to action.[1] Thus the general operation of the intellect involves relation to truth, with the possibility of good and bad understanding. The explanation of the origin of error in the intellect in general forms the basis for a preliminary account of error and sin in action as well.

TRUTH AND ERROR IN JUDGEMENT

Thomas adapted the Aristotelian theory of cognition involving apprehension and judgement, by furnishing a complicated account of the translation from sense cognition to intellectual knowledge (see Ch. 5). The complexities involved in the account offer the advantages of basing knowledge in the realities of the world through sensation, and accounting for the possibilities of error in knowledge in the separate stage of judgement. Thomas affirmed that at the basic level simple apprehension is not false (therefore reliable), but that error can occur in the judgements made about reality.

Thomas's definition of truth as the proper relationship between mind and reality is well known.[2] Though in a secondary sense truth is said to be in all things which exist, in the context of cognition truth is to be located in the understanding, when it perceives correctly the proper relationship between reality and its own cognition. Simple apprehension is not enough to establish truth; the mind must affirm that it knows. Thus it is not in simple apprehension but in affirmations, composite statements, and judge-

---

[1] *De veritate* 22. 10 ad 4: obiectum intellectus practici non est bonum sed verum relatum ad opus.

[2] Veritas est adaequatio rei et intellectus. See *ST* I 16. 1 and *De veritate*, 1. 1.

ments that both truth and error occur. That a person's judgements can be erroneous or false might seem to cast too much scepticism on the process of cognition and undermine the basis for certitude. Thomas affirmed, however, that there is no error in the essential act of the intellect (operating with first principles); but error can arise in the process used by the mind to build up knowledge by the judgements it makes.[3]

Walking through a park one might be aware in a general way of flowers, trees, benches. Things which catch the eye, or which one notices especially, are the things which become objects of the second intention or the judgement. 'There are crocuses;' 'That park bench has just been painted—it was brown two days ago, and now it is green.' With this type of judgement about reality there is ordinarily little problem, although special knowledge may be required to prevent error: for example, there may be a very similar but different species of flower; or the old park bench might have been moved and replaced rather than repainted.

Error and ignorance differ. It is possible to be ignorant about things (which is part of the human condition), and yet not be in error; it is when a confident judgement or pronouncement (*sententia*) is made which is false because complete information is lacking, that error is added to ignorance.[4] The history of science (for instance, genetics or astronomy) shows the difference between erroneous opinions and true judgements that are made on the way towards a true knowledge.

There is much more scope for error in judgements about complex things such as human personalities and economic systems. 'You say that only because you are jealous' is probably a false judgement. The statement that 'the economy is slowing down because taxes are still too high' is in principle virtually impossible to verify because of the extraordinary number of facts which would have to be included to demonstrate positively that no other alternate explanation was possible.

---

[3] In *ST* I 85. 6 Aquinas states that the intellect is reliable in its apprehension of the quiddity of the thing, and the propositions directly related to it, just as there is no error regarding prime principles. But in the process of composition and division and in ratiocination itself the intellect may be mistaken.

[4] *De malo*, 3. 7: Error autem est approbare falsa pro veris; unde addit actum quemdam super ignorantiam: potest enim esse ignorantia sine hoc quod aliquis de ignotis sententiam ferat, et tunc est ignorans, et non errans; sed quando iam falsam sententiam fert de his quae nescit, tunc proprie dicitur errare.

In the case of opinions and beliefs an extra influence is required to affirm the truth of something for which complete evidence may be lacking. In either case a judgement is elicited under the influence of the will, which chooses to assent. The belief can never be based on sheer desire to believe, however, as a judgement about reality must always be based on some evidence. In every false judgement, therefore, there is some element of truth. According to Thomas, even in erroneous opinions and beliefs there must be intellectual motives, which may not be able to determine assent, but which must at least present an appearance of truth.[5]

This basis of truth and opinion in reality and its representation applies also to desire and appetite. The act of an appetitive power is an inclination towards some actual thing,[6] though it is directed according to a representation of the thing, which may be more or less true.

Thus assent to some explanation or description presupposes some correct apprehension of the object; but in error something else is illegitimately added, and assent is extended beyond apprehension in an unwarranted fashion. Assent in Aquinas can be summarized as: (1) an act of the intellect under the influence of the will; (2) belonging to the second act, the judgement which deals with what is true or false; and (3) varying in strength independently of the known evidence for the truth of the proposition.[7]

For Aquinas the ultimate reason for erroneous judgement is the weakness of man's intelligence before the complexity of nature. His account of the possibility of error shows his realism, and also how the theory of cognition can furnish both an explanation for knowledge and certitude and also for the real possibility of error.

Discussion before and after St Thomas was hampered by an inability to explain intellectual error without sacrificing certitude. St Augustine did not provide a study of judgement or of false judgement in relation to the operation of the intellect. Thus it was natural for the theological tradition to stress the infallibility of reason and turn to sensation or to the will as the chief factors for

---

[5] *In Boeth. de Trin.* 3. 1 ad 4.

[6] *ST* 1-II 15. 1: actus appetitivae virtutis est quaedam inclinatio ad rem ipsam, secundum quandam similitudinem.

[7] F. M. Tyrrell, *The Role of Assent in Judgment: A Thomistic Study* (Washington, DC, 1948), 125.

error.[8] In the centuries following Thomas the situation did not improve. Descartes, for example, tended to stress the luminosity of knowledge, and the direct apprehension of ideas by the intellect; but in Cartesian theory the act of judgement was an act of will, not of the intellect.[9]

The great difference in Thomas's account of truth is indicated for us in his treatment of wisdom, *sapientia*. Wisdom is essentially in the intellect, because its act is to judge rightly, but it has its cause in the will and thus is treated under the framework of charity (in *ST* 2-II 45. 2). Its opposing vice, *stultitia*, is regarded as a sin when it is not capable of judging spiritual things. Dullness of spirit, caused by preoccupation with pleasure, for example, results in an inability to judge. Thus it is not only in actions but in awareness of reality itself that a person can have erroneous judgements that are sinful.

ERROR IN PRACTICAL REASONING

The central place given by Aristotle to deliberation and choice in his account of human action was changed by the Stoics. Though they borrowed much from Aristotle's ethics, the word *prohairesis*, as well as the concept, 'almost disappeared from Stoic writings of the pre-Christian era'.[10] When the term was revived by Plotinus, 'the concept of choosing and of a character formed by choices is relegated to a subordinate position'.[11] When he talks of the freedom of the soul it is associated with wishing and not with *prohairesis*. Sin is thus given an explanation in the context of wishing, so that the soul does not choose to sin, but wishes to sin. In the words of Rist 'the Plotinian fall of the soul is essentially a non-rational, that is counter-rational act'.[12] The soul allows itself to be seduced by pleasure so that it does not use its rational powers or abide by previous decisions. For Plotinus, then, immorality has no reason for it, because one does not decide to do something wrong: one is

[8] L. W. Keeler, *The Problem of Error from Plato to Kant* (Rome, 1934), 70–1.

[9] See J. L. Evans, 'Error and the Will', *Philosophy*, 38 (1963), 136–48, for a discussion of Descartes and Spinoza.

[10] J. M. Rist, 'Prohairesis: Proclus, Plotinus et alii', in *De Jamblique à Proclus* (Geneva, 1974), 103–17, at 105.

[11] Ibid. 109.

[12] Ibid. 111.

misled to it. This type of explanation will find expression in the Christian tradition as well,[13] but St Thomas proceeded in a fundamentally different fashion.

For Aquinas there can be error in practical reason because of error in moral knowledge. The practical syllogism allows Thomas to explain how there can be truth in first principles but error in conscience (the application of knowledge to action). The example used in the commentary on the *Sentences* is that of a 'heretic' who believes that taking an oath is prohibited by God. When he uses the operative syllogism with the premiss 'do nothing prohibited' and the minor premiss 'swearing is prohibited', his conclusion will be 'do not take an oath'. Thus the agent's conscience may be mistaken, not in his good intention, but in his own specific principles. He is not mistaken in the principle that 'nothing illicit should be done', but errs in believing that 'all oath-taking is illicit', which he takes as a principle.[14]

In the *Summa Theologiae*, with its more comprehensive account of action and virtue, erroneous action is given a very wide and compelling description. There can be error at all stages of action, whether intention, deliberation, decision, or execution. And at each stage all potencies (intellect, will, and sensitive appetite) are part of the explanation of error and sin. In 2-II 53. 2, Aquinas lists the different parts of 'imprudence' which correspond to the stages of practical reason: at the stage of deliberation there may be rashness or temerity; in decision there may be inconsideration; and in the stage of execution inconstancy or negligence. Though these are faults in practical reason, they have their explanation in the relation of intellect to will and emotion.

In faulty deliberation the main problem is rashness—not taking care to go through the steps that are needed to see the

---

[13] For the influence of Stoic and Neoplatonic ideas on Christian theology of human action see B. Switalski, *Neoplatonism and the Ethics of St Augustine* (Chicago, 1946). These conclusions may be drawn: (1) the explanation of error and sin in terms of an opposition of reason and desire was a ready option and not only for Christians; (2) without a convincing account of the operation of reason in action, the pressure to account for error in terms of will or affection is very difficult to resist.

[14] *In II Sent.* 39. 3. 2: . . . non quia decipiatur in hoc communi principio, quod est, nullum illicitum esse faciendum; sed quia decipitur in hoc quod credit omne iuramentum esse illicitum, quod quasi pro principio accipit. Cf. *In II Sent.* 24. 2. 4 for a similar example.

situation properly. These steps involve memory, considering past experience; understanding the present circumstances; and skill in considering consequences or possible outcomes. It is also important for the agent to be able to reason well and make the proper inferences, and be able to accept the opinions or judgements of those who are more experienced, which is at the heart of taking counsel.

An agent may move too quickly into action by rushing through this process and arriving at a conclusion too quickly. This may happen if the agent is affected by an impulse of will or of passion ('ex impetu voluntatis vel passionis'); or it may occur if there is contempt for a rule which should govern the situation. This contempt would appear to be derived from the pride which refuses to submit to the rule of someone else (53. 3 ad 2).

At the stage of decision it is the person's ability to judge that may be affected. Judgement is the ability to discern properly the nature of the specific action in the light of relevant principles and of the circumstances. The need to be able to discern the relevant circumstances in order to form good judgements is even more important in practical matters than in theoretical.[15] Thomas describes the aspect of imprudence at this stage as *inconsideratio* or lack of thought or insight. The lack of sound judgement pertains to the vice of inconsideration to the extent that not judging rightly stems from scorning or neglecting to attend to the things from which right judgement proceeds;[16] in this case it becomes a sin.

The problem of lust also affects practical reason. Thomas cites Aristotle: 'pleasure corrupts the estimate of prudence.'[17] An intellectual virtue needs to be free from preoccupation with objects of sensation; and the pursuit of pleasure, especially sexual, drags the entire mind to sensual delight. Thus while other emotions can also deflect reason, lust causes inconstancy by extinguishing reason's judgement.[18]

The relation between intellect and passion is often set up as one

[15] *ST* 2-II 53. 4 ad 3.

[16] 2-II 53. 4: Unde et defectus recti iudicii ad vitium inconsiderationis pertinet: prout scilicet aliquis in recte iudicando deficit ex hoc quod contemnit vel negligit attendere ea ex quibus rectum iudicium procedit.

[17] *EN* VI. 5, 1140^{b}13–15.

[18] *ST* 2-II 53. 6 ad 1: sed luxuria causat inconstantiam totaliter extinguendo iudicium rationis.

of inherent opposition, with will as the arbiter. This is not the model used by St Thomas. His description of the operation of the different potencies does not rely on this kind of separation, and while he accepts the fact that passion can subvert reason, the way it does so is indirect, so that reason is not subverted into operating irrationally. Thomas accomplished this by a refined use of the syllogistic structure of practical reason.

EXPLAINING AKRASIA

The situation where the agent has correct principles, knows what he should do (and has demonstrated this in past behaviour), and yet chooses to do something contrary to this, is the real test of the adequacy of a model of practical reason. The Greek term *akrasia* has become much more familiar owing to the many treatments of Aristotle's account, and will be used here in preference to 'weakness of will' and other terms.[19]

The operative syllogism is used as an explanation for *akrasia* in the *ST* only at 1-II 77. 2 in the section dealing with sin. Thomas sees the problem, as posed by Socrates, in the conflict between knowledge and passion. To act correctly, a person needs a 'double knowledge', that is, of both general principle and particular situation, and a defect in either is sufficient to impede right action and will.[20] Someone may have general knowledge that a class of action is wrong (e.g. fornication) but not recognize (*cognoscat*) in the particular instance that this act (which is fornication) is not to be

---

[19] There is no ready term in English: 'incontinence' is not a happy equivalent for the Latin *incontinentia* (Thomas's term); we will use 'self-control' for *continentia* and *enkrateia*. The term 'weakness of will', though common enough even in studies of *akrasia* in Aristotle (e.g. N. O. Dahl, *Practical Reason, Aristotle, and Weakness of the Will* Minneapolis, 1984), begs the question because it reads into the description of the problem the solution, namely will, that many think is required for a Christian view, and which they use in interpreting St Thomas; e.g. T. D. Stegman, 'Saint Thomas Aquinas and the Problem of *Akrasia*', *Modern Schoolman*, 66 (1989), 117–28, at 128: 'the advance in Saint Thomas Aquinas' account of *akrasia* lies in his emphasis on the role of the will'; and R. P. Reilly, 'Weakness of Will: The Thomistic Advance', *PACPA* 48 (1974), 198–207.

[20] *ST* 1-II 77. 2: Cum enim ad recte agendum homo dirigatur duplici scientia, scilicet universali et particulari; utriusque defectus sufficit ad hoc quod impediatur rectitudo operis et voluntatis.

done. And this explains how the will might not follow the general knowledge of reason.[21]

A person might have right knowledge both on the general and particular level, but he does not consider it *in actu* and thus acts against his principles. There are three ways in which an agent can be impeded from making his disposition to knowledge actual: first, by a distraction; second, by a contrary influence of passion; and third, through a bodily change. Thomas summarizes what happens in the case of the akratic who 'yields' to temptation: he has knowledge on the general level, but because of the impediment of passion is not able to subsume the particular case under that general premiss and arrive at a conclusion (decision); but rather he uses another general premiss suggested by the inclination of passion, and reaches a conclusion in accordance with that premiss.[22] He refers to Aristotle's scheme of four propositions with two universal premisses: 'one of these is of reason, e.g. "no fornication should be committed", the other is of passion, e.g. that "pleasure is to be pursued". Passion therefore binds the reason so that it does not assume and conclude under the first, whence, while the passion remains, the agent assumes and concludes under the second.'[23]

This treatment is intelligible and coherent. But because the syllogisms are not spelled out, the nature of decision as the choice between syllogisms or lines of reasoning remains ambiguous for most readers, who are likely to encounter the discussion here in the *ST* rather than in *De malo* or the commentary on *EN*. It is thus not surprising that there has been a general lack of clarity in understanding Thomas's account of practical reasoning, his interpretation of Aristotle, and his explanation of the possibility of

---

[21] *ST* I-II 77. 2: Contingit igitur quod aliquis habeat scientiam in universali, puta nullam fornicationem esse faciendam; sed tamen non cognoscat in particulari hunc actum qui est fornicatio, non esse faciendum. Et hoc sufficit ad hoc quod voluntas non sequatur universalem scientiam rationis.

[22] I-II 77. 2 ad 4: Dicendum quod ille qui habet scientiam in universali, propter passionem impeditur ne possit sub illa universali sumere, et ad conclusionem pervenire: sed assumit sub alia universali, quam suggerit inclinatio passionis, et sub ea concludit.

[23] Ibid.: syllogismus incontinentis habet quatuor propositiones, duas universales: quarum una est rationis, puta nullam fornicationem esse committendam; alia est passionis, puta delectationem esse sectandam. Passio igitur ligat rationem ne assumat et concludat sub prima; unde, ea durante, assumit et concludit sub secunda.

error. This lack of understanding is shown in various translations of this reply in the *Summa*.[24]

There is a benefit in considering the more expanded explanations provided elsewhere. In his commentary on the *Sentences* Thomas uses the familiar test case of sexual sin (from the male point of view), presented as a choice between two syllogisms. The contrast between the two is not the simple opposition of reason and passion, but 'right reason' and reason influenced by passion:[25]

	I	2
Major:	I must not commit fornication.	All fornication is enjoyable.
Minor:	To lie with this woman is fornication.	
Conclusion:	I must not lie with this woman.	Enjoy this fornication.[26]

Though passion is the influence on the second line of reasoning, it does not subvert reason into irrationality, or prevent the mind from proceeding from general principle to conclusion. Note also that the minor premiss is the same for both; so passion affects the choice of general principle used for judging the situation. In other

---

[24] 1-II 77. 2 ad 4; in the English Dominican (1915) trans.: 'He that has knowledge in universal, is hindered, on account of a passion, from reasoning about that universal . . . but he reasons about another universal proposition suggested by the inclination of the passion'; cf. J. Fearon, Blackfriars edn. (1969), xxv. 167, who also misses the syllogistic structure of decision, clearly indicated by Thomas in *sumere sub universali* and *assumit sub alia universali*.

[25] *In II Sent.* 24. 3. 3: Verbi gratia, si dicatur: Nulla fornicatio est committenda, in hoc iudicium rationis perfectum est. Item proponatur alia: omnis fornicatio est delectabilis. Sub quibus duabus assumatur una particularis, haec scilicet: accedere ad hanc mulierem est fornicatio. Si ratio sit fortis ut nec etiam in particulari passione vincatur, inducet conclusionem negativam eligens fornicationem non committere. Si autem passione vincatur, eliciet conclusionem affirmativam, eligens in fornicatione delectari, et sic sumitur hic esse peccatum in ratione; qua scilicet post rationis deliberationem, eo quod ratio in particulari corrumpitur per passionem, sequitur prava electio.

[26] Ambiguity in the formulation of the operative syllogisms in the commentary on the *Sentences* and in the *De veritate* (noted in Ch. 11), resulting from the confusion of deductive reasoning, seems to apply here. The first syllogism, with the premiss 'Fornication must not be committed', is formulated properly as a syllogism of action. The second, however, with the premiss 'All fornication is enjoyable', carries the motive force 'pursue pleasure' only implicitly; as it stands, therefore, it seems more descriptive than a principle for action. Nor is the premiss a convincing contrast to the premiss of chastity; because, although the sex act is enjoyable, even a Don Juan will not consider all possible occasions for fornication as enjoyable.

words, the agent influenced by passion is not simply 'disobeying' the voice of reason; he chooses to see the action in terms of pleasure. The conclusion reached is a 'reasonable' conclusion even when wrong.[27]

Deciding to act on the basis of pleasure is not an irrational decision, and even when the decision is to commit fornication, it is still a decision made with the use of a plausible general principle, the perception of the particular situation, and a conclusion which follows. Even though the influence of passion accounts for the wrong action, the error lies also in the reason, not only in the will or in the passion; or, more precisely, error and sin do not result from the will or the passions themselves, but result from the incorrect operation of all the powers of the agent working together.

This appears clearly in the problem set up by the argument that sin is a matter of the affection and therefore not in the reason.[28] Thomas replies: reason, though cognitive, is directive of the will; thus there can be no error in the will unless it be in some way in the mind, especially since the will can only be for a good or apparent good.[29] The error, then, is the error of the agent, with all his faculties sharing the responsibility.

In his commentary on Aristotle's example of tasting sweet things (1147^a30 ff.), Thomas first states that reason is not so totally removed by concupiscence that the agent does not have true knowledge on the general level.[30] There is one general proposition prohibiting the inordinate eating of sweets, e.g. 'don't taste anything sweet between meals'. On the part of concupiscence, however, a general proposition is suggested, e.g. 'everything sweet is

---

[27] In describing the place of reason in action, it is helpful to distinguish between the reasons which are involved in a purposeful action (i.e. 'practical reasons') and reasons of the sort which underlie a person's better judgement; thus a person can be acting *for* a reason (directive sense), while acting *against* reason (in the evaluative sense); see A. F. Walker, 'The Problem of Weakness of Will', *Nous*, 23 (1989), 653–76, at 670–1.

[28] *In II Sent.* 24. 3. 3 arg. 1: Videtur quod in ratione non possit esse peccatum. Ratio enim potentiam cognitivam nominat. Sed peccatum ad affectum pertinet. Ergo in ratione peccatum non est.

[29] Ibid. ad 1: ratio quamvis sit cognitiva potentia, tamen est directiva voluntatis; unde non potest esse peccatum in voluntate nisi sit aliquo modo in ratione, praecipue cum voluntas non sit nisi boni, vel apparentis boni.

[30] *In VII Ethic.* (1147^a31), lect. 1347: quod in incontinente ratio non totaliter obruitur a concupiscentia quin in universali habeat veram scientiam.

enjoyable' and therefore to be sought.[31] The particular perception 'this is sweet' could be subsumed under either major premiss. Which premiss is selected depends on the way the agent perceives the situation and the universal he selects. As Thomas puts it, if in the particular circumstances the agent's desire binds (*ligat*) his reason, then he uses the major proposition suggested by desire, i.e. 'everything sweet is enjoyable and to be pursued'; with the perception 'this is sweet', the conclusion of action follows.

Thomas is concerned to emphasize that reason is not being opposed to sense desire, with the will poised to choose between them, making in one case a 'rational' decision, and in the other an 'irrational' one. In either case, whether the agent follows the line of reasoning suggested by his self-control or the line of reasoning suggested by his desire, he is still using a line of reasoning, a syllogism. In order to act, the human agent uses this structure of a general proposition, plus the perception of a particular instance of that proposition, and then the conclusion and action follow. Thus all human action follows a pattern of reasoning, syllogistic in structure, which may be called the operative syllogism or syllogism of action. What makes the conclusion wrong, or against the agent's real interest, or in conflict with principles that he holds, is not that he fails to use the syllogism (he could not make a voluntary choice without it), or even, in many instances, that his premisses are wrong, but that he has used the wrong line of reasoning in the circumstances.

Expanding on Aristotle's example, after a large dinner one might well accept and enjoy a chocolate or two with coffee, and do so correctly on the basis of the syllogism of pleasure. Sweet things are enjoyable; this is a sweet; take and enjoy. But after two or three such chocolates, that line of reasoning is no longer the best one to use, under the circumstances (i.e. having just enjoyed a sufficient amount). It is time to judge the situation under the other general principle, 'Don't take sweets at the improper time.' Thus, the general principles do not change or become invalid; but as most rules cannot be framed so as to cover all situations, what is required

---

[31] *In VII Ethic.* (1147ᵃ31), lect. 1347: sit ergo ita quod ex parte rationis proponatur una universalis prohibens gustare dulce inordinate, puta si dicatur: 'nullum dulce oportet gustare extra horam', sed ex parte concupiscentiae proponitur quod omne dulce est delectabile, quod est per se quaesitum a concupiscentia.

for responsible action is the correct perception by the agent of which principle to use in making his decision.[32]

De malo 3 deals with the various possible causes of sin and error, including the devil, ignorance, weakness, and malice. The ninth article is relevant here: whether one may have the right knowledge and yet sin from weakness ('utrum sciens ex infirmitate peccet'). St Thomas uses two Aristotelian distinctions, the difference between knowing in general and in particular, and between act and habit, and offers three answers. First, even without direct interference, the emphasis on one power of the soul may diminish the use of another: when one potency is intent on its act, another may be impeded in its act, as when a person who concentrates hard on hearing something may not perceive as readily with his other senses.[33] This unitary view of human psychology applies also to agency: when concupiscence and anger, for example, strongly affect a person, he is hampered in his ability to make use of his knowledge.[34]

Thomas next makes use of the universal/particular distinction: the passions of the soul, based in the sensitive appetite, are directed to particulars (this is the level on which non-rational animals entirely operate); for example, a man may desire the pleasure, when he perceives something sweet.[35] Knowledge, however, is on the general or universal level, and is not the principle of action unless applied to the particular, because actions are always particular.[36] This process of translating the general to the particular, clearly taught by Aristotle in the *De Anima*, is the heart of the

---

[32] That Thomas perceived this is indicated by his change of Aristotle's general principle of self-control 'Not to taste sweets' (so stated it would not be a general principle for the average person, for whom a bit of sugar or something sweet would not be an indulgence); thus Thomas qualified the principle with the phrase *extra horam* to indicate the need for the agent to perceive the appropriate occasion.

[33] *De malo*, 3. 9: Manifestum est enim quod quandocumque una potentia intenditur in suo actu, alia potentia vel impeditur vel totaliter avertitur a suo actu: sicut cum aliquis intentus est ad aliquem audiendum, non percipit hominem pertranseuntem.

[34] Ibid.: Sic igitur, cum fuerit concupiscentia fortis, aut ira aut aliquid huiusmodi, impeditur homo a consideratione scientiae.

[35] Ibid.: passiones animae cum sint in appetitu sensitivo, sunt circa particularia: concupiscit enim homo hanc delectationem, sicut et sentit hoc dulce.

[36] Ibid.: Scientia autem est in universali; et tamen universalis scientia non est principium alicuius actus, nisi secundum quod applicatur ad particulare: quia actus circa particularia sunt.

syllogism of action. Now what occurs sometimes, according to
Thomas, is that a strong passion for some particular thing can
'repel' the contrary movement of knowledge concerning the same
particular; this occurs not only by distracting the agent from the
consideration of his knowledge, but also by the corrupting influence of the contrary. Thus a strongly passionate person,
although he may have, in a fashion, correct consideration in
general, nevertheless is impeded in his consideration of the particular.[37]

The third explanation is probably easiest to grasp. The agent
may not be able to use his reason, or use it freely, because of a
physical condition, and this is obvious in the case of people who
are asleep or insane.[38] But physical changes can occur from passions
such as anger or concupiscence, and when they are strong, they
may in some way bind the reason ('ligant quodammodo
rationem'), so that the agent does not have free judgement about
particular actions. Thus sinning by weakness is not incompatible
with a person's having the disposition to right knowledge on the
general level.

This is the body of Aquinas's reply; it is clear, Aristotelian, and
concise. It may fall short, however, of a convincing explanation of
akrasia, how an agent may act against his better judgement. If he
really knows what he should do, then he should be able to follow
that; and this problem lies at the root of the suspicion, still voiced
by modern scholars, that Aristotle did not ultimately solve the
Socratic problem of knowledge and action, and that error in action
is the result of a faulty will, or of some irrational factor preventing
the agent from following his reason.[39]

Thomas appreciated the force of this difficulty and expressed it
clearly in the seventh counterargument set forth at *De malo* 3. 9:

[36] *De malo*, 3. 9: Quando igitur passio est fortis circa aliquod particulare,
repellit contrarium motum scientiae circa idem particulare, non solum distra-
hendo a consideratione scientiae, ut supra dictum est, sed etiam corrumpendo per
viam contrarietatis. Et sic ille qui in forti passione est constitutus, etsi consideret
aliquod modo in universali, in particulari tamen impeditur eius consideratio.
[38] Ibid.: ex aliqua corporali transmutatione ligatur usus rationis, ut vel totaliter
nihil consideret, vel quod non libere considerare possit, sicut patet in dormien-
tibus et phreneticis.
[39] Gauthier and Jolif, *L'Éthique à Nicomaque*, ii. 603, thought that Aristotle
really did not advance on the Socratic problem of ignorance in action: 'il ne peut
en définitive montrer que l'incontinence est autre chose qu'une ignorance.'

Whoever knows the universal, and also knows the singular is contained under the universal, then he should know by deduction the singular at the same time, as it says in I *Posterior Analytics*. For example, if he knows that all mules are sterile, and this animal is a mule, he knows that this animal is sterile. But he who knows that no fornication should be committed, unless he knows this act to be fornication, he ought not to be considered as sinning knowingly but in ignorance. Therefore, if he does not sin through ignorance, he does know, both in the universal and the particular.[40]

The force of this argument is that it is impossible to sin knowingly and not wilfully. In other words, either one does not know that it is sinful to act in such a way, or one simply decides to ignore what one knows and act anyway.

Thomas's reply uses the choice of parallel syllogisms available to the agent. He makes it very clear that a line of reasoning, the operative syllogism, is essential to all voluntary human action: 'every act, whether virtuous or sinful, requires a certain deduction, syllogistic in nature.'[41] He then applies the operative syllogism to all four character types identified by Aristotle: temperate, intemperate, self-controlled, and akratic. The temperate person uses this line of reasoning: no fornication is to be committed; this act is fornication; therefore it is not to be done.[42] Even the intemperate, who follows the path of indulgence, uses a syllogism of three propositions: everything pleasurable should be enjoyed; this act is pleasurable; therefore this is to be enjoyed.[43]

[40] *De malo*, 3. 9 arg. 7: Praeterea. Quicumque scit universale et scit singulare contineri sub universali, simul inducens cognoscit singulare, ut dicitur in I *Posteriorum*; sicut qui scit omnem mulam esse sterilem, simul dum scit hoc animal esse mulam, scit illud esse sterile. Sed ille qui scit nullam fornicationem esse faciendam, nisi etiam sciret hunc actum esse fornicationem, non reputaretur scienter sed ignoranter peccare. Ergo si non per ignorantiam peccat, non solum scit in universali, sed etiam scit in particulari.

[41] Ibid.: necesse est in quolibet actu virtutis vel peccati sit quaedam deductio quasi syllogistica.

[42] Ibid.: Temperatus enim movetur tantum secundum iudicium rationis; unde utitur syllogismo trium propositionum, et sic deducens: Nulla fornicatio est committenda; hic actus est fornicatio, ergo non est faciendum.

[43] Ibid.: Intemperatus vero totaliter sequitur concupiscentiam, et ideo etiam ipse utitur syllogismo trium propositionum, quasi sic deducens: omni delectabili est fruendum, hic actus est delectabilis, ergo hoc est faciendum. The will of the completely intemperate person is not sufficiently aligned with the principle of avoiding sin to be able to use that as a principle for judging his actions; or he may not be convinced that his sexual indulgence comes under that category.

The self-controlled and akratic waver between the two ways of looking at the situation. The two general premisses they may use are 'no sin is to be committed' and 'everything enjoyable should be pursued'. If the agent inclines to the judgement of reason involving the perception that this action is a sin, then he follows the line of reasoning of self-control, and deduces 'therefore this is not to be done'. The akratic agent, however, in whom the movement of desire dominates, assumes and concludes under the second premiss, with the perception that this action is pleasurable, concluding 'therefore it should be pursued'.[44] The syllogisms run like this:

	Self-controlled	*Akratic*
Major:	No sin is to be committed.	What is enjoyable should be pursued.
Minor:	This is sin.	This is enjoyable.
Conclusion:	This must not be done.	This should be pursued.

Note that the general premiss for self-control is 'no sin is to be committed', and not the premiss of temperance, i.e. 'no fornication is to be committed'. Precisely because there is an openness to the possibility of fornication (which is why there is a question of self-control here), the proposition forbidding it is not an operating premiss for these agents. Only the temperate, who has decided (as a fixed resolution) that he will not commit fornication, can have that specific rule as his premiss for action. Thus the practical reasoning of the self-controlled and of the akratic hinges on their perception of the nature of the action. If the perception 'this is sin' prevails, then it is subsumed under the premiss 'no sin should be committed', which is an operating premiss for both of them, and the conclusion not to do it follows. But if the character of the action as an instance of pleasure is the dominant perception (under the influence of desire) then it will be subsumed under the premiss of pursuing what is pleasurable. In either case there is a line of reasoning, following an operating premiss which the agent accepts.

The difference between the two lines of reasoning is not the

---

[44] *De malo*, 3. 9: Continens enim sic syllogizat: nullum peccatum est faciendum. Et hoc proponit secundum iudicium rationis, secundum vero motum concupiscentiae versatur in corde eius quod omne delectabile est prosequendum; sed quia iudicium rationis in eo vincit, assumit et concludit sub primo: hoc est peccatum, ergo non est faciendum. Incontinens vero, in quo vincit motus concupiscentiae, assumit et concludit sub secundo: hoc est delectabile, ergo est prosequendum.

perception of whether the proper description of the action is fornication (or adultery), but whether it is taken as an instance of sin or an instance of pleasure. The reminder that fornication is a sin will help the one agent to use the first syllogism of action and retain control. For the other, the thought that fornication is sin is submerged under the more dominant desire to judge the action under the syllogism of pleasure. The akratic (not the intemperate) is one who is capable of right action—of avoiding, in the example, sexual temptation—and does so on some other occasions; but there are times when the force of desire affects his vision, and the attractiveness of the other line of reasoning dominates.

To summarize error in choice, the operative syllogism is a model to explain the way an agent sees a situation and makes his decision to act. It allowed Thomas to explain wrong action in several ways. The incorrect way of seeing a situation might involve using the wrong general premiss (pleasure instead of avoiding sin), or wrong principles about what God's law requires. Also, it is possible to indicate how an agent is able to hold to a correct general principle and yet act in opposition to it, for instance when inadvertence or passion results in faulty perception of the situation. Since the conclusion of the operative syllogism which generates action is the product of the combined application of general to particular, the subtle and complementary relation of knowledge and perception yields a flexible and realistic account.

Contemporaries and successors of Thomas, without benefit of the operative syllogism (or suspicious of it because of its Aristotelian origins), resorted to an explanation of sin on the lines of the opposition between desire and reason. This simplistic but dominant view of the decision-making process split the functions of reason and will, with sin explained by the will's decision either to follow the voice of reason or to go along with passion.[45]

DEFECTIVE EXECUTION

Even when the right decision has been made, failure to act properly can occur. This failure in execution involves more than mere omission of the decision; it can be undue slowness to act, or a

[45] Cf. the commentary on *EN* VII in Johannes Versor, *Quaestiones super libros ethicorum Aristotelis* (Cologne, 1494; reprint, Frankfurt, 1967), fo. 59ʳ: Allicitur igitur voluntas appetitu sensitivo tanquam vehementer moto ex pulsu passionis; et sic ei consentit; et avertit se a iudicio rationis nec vult audire rationem.

certain kind of carelessness in execution, as Thomas explains in discussing the opposition of negligence to prudence.[46]

This is another dimension of *akrasia*—failure in execution—which is not present in Aristotle's account and is a significant contribution to the philosophy of human action for two reasons: (1) it offers a basis for a richer and more realistic account of the possibility and nature of *akrasia*, error, and sin; and (2) it assigns a share of responsibility for execution to the intellect. Not carrying a decision through, or doing it at the wrong time or hastily, is to a large extent a failure to see the situation properly (which is a cognitive function), and this results in poor application or total lack of application of the decision to the *operandum*.

The common tendency to misunderstand Thomas's account must be resisted: the explanation for failure in action is *not* attributed by Thomas to weakness of will, or to a failure of the will to carry out the decision. Failure in execution results from lack of proper application of decision to action, which Thomas consistently described as guided by reason in the principal act of prudence. One simply cannot make will the all-important link between decision and action without fundamentally destroying the structure of the Thomistic account.

Thomas treats defective execution under two headings, inconstancy and negligence. Inconstancy is 'a kind of drawing back from the good as definitely proposed' (by the agent's decision).[47] This is prompted, in the first instance, by the appetitive power, and Thomas cites (2-II 53. 5 ad 2) the possibility of envy and anger producing this inconstancy; but this wavering does not affect action unless there is a real failure in reason. The fault of the intellect is that it repudiates what it had already accepted.[48] Thus inconstancy is to be regarded as a defect of reason (not a lack of 'will-power'), showing its weakness in not holding firmly to the proposed good.

Negligence is more of an internally generated weakness. Thomas has in mind the lazy or sluggish execution of a decision which makes it defective. Lying behind this is spiritual apathy

---

[46] *ST* 2-II 54. 2 ad 1: pigritia autem et torpor magis pertinent ad executionem: ita tamen quod pigritia importat tarditatem ad exequendum; torpor remissionem quandam importat in ipsa executione.

[47] 2-II 53. 5: recessum quendam a bono proposito definito.

[48] Ibid.: quae fallitur in hoc quod repudiat id quod recte acceptaverat.

(*acedia*), which hinders the mind from operating.[49] This is a defect in the reason (responsible for the *praeceptum*), but it occurs from a certain *remissio* in the will so that the reason is not as careful in the executive direction of actions as it should be.[50]

The stage of execution (*imperium+usus*) was largely absent in Aristotle's account. The transition from decision to action was more directly addressed by Stoic theory, then modified and developed by Thomas in his doctrine of the preceptive function of practical reason which, under the guidance of prudence, applies the agent's decision correctly to the situation. This is a genuine improvement on Aristotelian theory, because to the extent that Aristotle's philosophy of action lacks a stage of execution, it fails fully to overcome the Socratic problem. Thomas's general description of the sin of imprudence summarizes these points. Even though the account of the defects possible at the various stages involves passion and will, the explanation of sin is not of a bad will against correct reason. Aquinas maintains that if there is sin and vice, then there is imprudence in the intellect: 'for no sin can occur unless there is a defect in some act of reason's direction, and this is a matter of imprudence.'[51] This is not a Thomistic version of the Socratic view of moral weakness, because to say that sin represents a defect in understanding is by no means to say that all sins are sins of ignorance.[52] Sin is essentially a disorder in action resulting from lack of the harmony which the act should have with the rule of reason and the law of God,[53] and the disorder can occur in intention for the wrong goods, faulty deliberation, erroneous judgement, and poor execution. Intellect, will, and emotion all mutually affect each other, and share in the order of virtue and the disorder of vice.

---

[49] 2-II 54. 2 ad 1: torpor ex acedia nascitur: quia acedia est tristia aggravans, idest impediens animum ab operando.

[50] 2-II 54. 3: negligentia provenit ex quadam remissione voluntatis, per quam contingit quod ratio non sollicitatur ut praecipiat ea quae debet, vel eo modo quo debet.

[51] 2-II 53. 2: nullum enim peccatum accidere potest nisi sit defectus in aliquo actu rationis dirigentis, quod pertinet ad imprudentiam.

[52] Cf. V. Cathrein, 'Utrum in omni peccato occurrat error vel ignorantia', *Gregorianum*, 11 (1930), 553–67, at 564.

[53] *De malo*, 2. 2: Deformitas autem actus est per hoc quod discordat a debita regula rationis vel legis Dei.

15

Prudence as a Virtue

ONE of the reasons for the growing emphasis on the will in medieval theology was its usefulness in explaining the possibility of sin: if the agent knows what he should or should not do, but acts contrary to this knowledge, the readiest explanation is lack of will-power, disobedience, or some other defect in the will.

The continued resort to 'weakness of will' in explaining both Aristotle and Aquinas on defective practical reason stems from restricting prudence to good deliberation, and not extending it to decision and execution where St Thomas centred it. A truncated prudence implies that the will is finally decisive in action, and that the perfection of the will is the true 'hinge' on which good human action turns. When the will is made the crucial factor, then its disposition is the heart of human action, and there is no longer a need to emphasize prudence and the other moral virtues for right action; obeying one's conscience becomes the focal point for ethics. The Thomistic psychology of action offers a much more comprehensive account of sin, involving cognition and appetite at all stages in the process of action, and this implies a much richer account of the virtues needed for improving the actions and character of the agent.

MUTUAL DEPENDENCE OF PRUDENCE AND THE MORAL VIRTUES

Prudence is a virtue of the practical intellect. It is included among the intellectual virtues, and three of the articles in *ST* 1-II q. 57 (on the intellectual virtues) are devoted to prudence.

The line of argument for prudence is presented in 1-II 57. 5: acting well requires right choice; choice concerns means to an end; thus right choice requires the right end and the right means; counsel and choice of means (*consiliari* and *eligere*) are acts of reason;[1] therefore it is necessary to have an intellectual virtue in the

---

[1] Note the apparent contradiction here if one restricts *electio* to will alone.

reason, through which it may be perfected towards what properly relates to the means. This virtue is prudence.[2]

Prudence may thus be distinguished from the other intellectual virtues of *sapientia*, *scientia*, and *intellectus*. The scope of prudence is action, its purpose being to enable the agent to act well (*bene operari*); thus the aim of the intellect is action, not knowledge. Thomas makes this distinction between the theoretic and practical in I-II 57. 1: one may have the *habitus* of theoretical knowledge and not be inclined to use it. The theoretical virtue is directed inwards to truth, while the practical is directed outwards to the exterior action.[3]

One could make the mistake of thinking that in I-II 57. 6 Thomas divides practical reasoning into theoretical and practical phases, because in speaking of the relation of *eubulia* and *synesis* to prudence he describes the results of the first two stages (*consiliari*, *iudicare*) as referring to the speculative intellect;[4] however, this means not that 'counsel' and 'judgement' are theoretical but that they correspond to similar stages in theoretical reasoning, and that *praecipere* or *imperium* (the rational part of execution) is what gives special distinctiveness to practical reasoning. Each stage, seen in the context of the whole process, is part of practical reason, just as *prudentia* as a whole (which includes *eubulia* and *synesis*) is *recta ratio agibilium*.

The separation of cognition and volition and the concomitant identification of decision with the will alone further encourages the separation of speculative and practical. By making *consilium* and *iudicium* cognitive processes which are prior to volitional ones, the tendency to see these as moral knowledge is irresistible. This separation between reason and will in action was cemented by the late scholastic conception of 'indifference': the attitude of the will towards the object presented by the intellect was thought not to be disposed one way or the other.

[2] *ST* I-II 57. 5: Et ideo necesse est in ratione esse aliquam virtutem intellectualem, per quam perficiatur ratio ad hoc quod convenienter se habeat ad ea quae sunt ad finem. Et haec virtus est prudentia.

[3] I-II 57. 1 ad 1: Practicum ergo, vel operativum, quod dividitur contra speculativum, sumitur ab opere exteriori, ad quod non habet ordinem habitus speculativus.

[4] I-II 57. 6: Circa agibilia autem humana tres actus rationis inveniuntur: quorum primus est consiliari, secundus iudicare, tertius est praecipere. Primi autem duo respondent actibus intellectus speculativi qui sunt inquirere et iudicare.

This explanation of the will's freedom is not only psychologically faulty but is manifestly false to Thomas's entire account of moral virtues and prudence. If the distinction between speculative and practical is between orientation to truth and to action, then the entire psychological process of action is part of practical reasoning. When an end has been intended, practical reasoning begins and one enters the realm of prudence. If because of circumstances or of weakness in the agent, for example, the process of action ends at the stage of deliberation, or of decision, we should not say that the reasoning was only theoretical (unless there never was a plan to act). Though in one sense the process is fully 'practical' only when it reaches the stage of execution, in the basic sense the process is practical as long as it is oriented to action guided by intention.

The critical difference between theoretical and practical and between moral and intellectual virtue is the relation to the will. It is not because one is thinking about an action that one is thinking 'practically'; it is because one is planning to do or achieve something, which requires appetite, that one is thinking practically. The virtues of the theoretical intellect do not perfect the appetitive part; only the intellective (I-II 57. 1); it is for the moral virtues to be perfective of appetite.

The distinction between art and prudence helps here. Both involve the intellect, both result in exterior production, so art can be called an operative or practical disposition (*habitus operativus*, I-II 57. 3). Yet, though art is like prudence in this general practical respect, it resembles more the virtues of the speculative intellect in that it is not directly related to the quality of the agent's appetite.[5] Thus art (as skill, craft, or technique), though concerned with practical matters, is basically an affair of the intellect. The difference between *facere* and *agere*, between *recta ratio factibilium* (*ars*) and *recta ratio agibilium* (*prudentia*), is the involvement of the appetitive part of the agent.

The distinctive quality of prudence, then, is its relationship between the practical intellect and appetite, or the will in particular. The subject of prudence is the intellect; but Thomas also maintains that prudence, unlike any other intellectual virtue, depends on right appetite, and therefore requires moral virtue

[5] I-II 57. 3: Et tamen in aliquo convenit cum habitibus speculativis: quia etiam ad ipsos habitus speculativos pertinet qualiter se habeat res quam considerant, non autem qualiter se habeat appetitus humanus ad illas.

which perfects the appetite (1-II 57. 4).[6] Throughout his exposition of virtue in general and of the virtue of prudence in particular, Thomas emphasizes that prudence depends on the desires of the agent being right, on his appetite being well disposed.[7]

This is partly explained by the relation of means to ends: the area of concern to prudence is the area of responsibility for the correct choice of means, while the ends are set by the desires of the agent. Since prudent reasoning deals with the stages of deliberation, decision, and execution, it is obvious that if intention is wrong, the subsequent reasoning will also be wrong; therefore prudence, correct practical reasoning, logically presupposes that the desires for ends have been made right by moral virtue.

Thomas wants to say more than this, however: *recta ratio* does not just function theoretically after an intention has been formed, that is, deliberate and judge, and then wait for the will to decide to carry this out or not; this would be more or less the process in the model of divided cognition and volition. No, the operation of the practical intellect is moved by the appetite toward action; and the appetite of the agent for action is guided all along by the practical intellect. The perfecting of the whole process by virtues involves right reason depending on the right disposition of appetite, and right appetite depending on prudence.

Truth for the practical intellect is achieved by conformity to right appetite (1-II 57. 5 ad 3),[8] and prudence is said to have the role of moral virtue because it is the application of right reason to action, which cannot be without right appetite.[9] If this means only that the ends must be right, then the actual function of practical reason is still speculative, a rational process to calculate best means. Full intelligibility of Thomas's position can be reached only by combining cognition and volition at each stage. Thus correct

---

[6] 1-II 57. 4: Et ideo ad prudentiam requiritur moralis virtus, per quam fit appetitus rectus.

[7] 1-II 58. 2: Sic igitur ad hoc quod homo bene agat, requiritur quod non solum ratio sit bene disposita per habitum virtutis intellectualis; sed etiam quod vis appetitiva sit bene disposita per habitum virtutis moralis; cf. 1-II 58. 3 ad 2; 1-II 65. 1; 2-II 47. 4.

[8] 1-II 57. 5 ad 3: Verum autem intellectus practici accipitur per conformitatem ad appetitum rectum.

[9] 2-II 47. 4: Ad prudentiam autem pertinet . . . applicatio rectae rationis ad opus, quod non fit sine appetitu recto.

deliberation depends on prudent counsel and good appetite; correct decision on sound judgement and right desire for it; and
effective execution on right 'command' and right appetitive application. So the principle of mutual interdependence between cognition and appetite, and between prudence and moral virtues, is
not just dependence on the rightness of the preceding stage, but
the rightness of the corresponding potency operating at the same
time.

The relationship between cognitive evaluation and appetitive
response as essential for moral virtue has been brought out in
studies of Aristotle.[10] The relationship is not only at the point
of *prohairesis*, but includes orientation to the end (one must desire
an end and judge that it is correct to pursue); the recognition of
means (one judges that certain means will serve the purpose,
and also desires these); and seeing opportunities for action
(by recognizing appropriate circumstances and desiring to act
accordingly).[11]

This model of joint cognition and volition helps to clarify what
Thomas teaches about moral and intellectual virtue in 1-II 58. 3:
that there are two principles of human action, *intellectus* (or *ratio*)
and *appetitus*; that the appetite relates to reason by participation (1-
II 60. 1); how the cardinal virtues are related and why prudence is
ranked amongst the moral virtues (61. 1); and how the virtues of
justice, temperance, and fortitude can be rational by participation
(61. 2). The model is especially helpful for the connection of the
moral virtues (65. 1): the inclination to the right end is not enough
for virtue without the direction of prudence; and prudence is not
possible without the moral virtues. Against the argument (1-II 65.
1 arg. 3) that the moral virtues are independent like the intellectual
ones, Thomas replies: the moral virtues depend on prudence (the
first principles of the speculative intellect do not depend on the
intellectual virtues in the same way), because appetite moves
reason in a way, and reason the appetite.[12] This mutual influence is
intimate, and therefore the complementary and unitary model
rather than the split and sequential model of cognition and volition

[10] M. F. Burnyeat, 'Aristotle on Learning to be Good', in A. O. Rorty (ed.),
Essays on Aristotle's Ethics (Berkeley, Calif., 1980), 69–92.

[11] Cooper, *Reason and Human Good*, 63.

[12] *ST* 1-II 65. 1 ad 3: sicut morales dependent a prudentia, eo quod appetitus
movet quodammodo rationem, et ratio appetitum.

does much more justice to Thomas's entire doctrine of prudence and moral virtue.

THE VIRTUES AND THE PERFECTING OF DECISION AND EXECUTION

In *ST* 1-II 58. 5 Thomas explains why prudence cannot exist without moral virtue. It is not only knowledge of general principles which one needs for right reasoning about particular actions, because this knowledge may be corrupted in the application to a particular action by some passion.[13] What happens is that the wrong conclusion is reached by a reasoning process gone astray, and not that the will has refused to obey the voice of reason. Thus the agent needs not only a disposition to good ends and a knowledge of principles, but also a perfecting, through certain dispositions, of the ability to judge rightly about the end.[14]

In view of the many ways that decisions and executions may be deformed, moral virtues (right dispositions to certain ends) are required so that the agent will be able to select and use the appropriate principles. Avoiding sin and enjoying pleasurable things are both valid principles; prudence and moral virtue are required to be able to use the right principles in appropriate situations. One may know that fornication is wrong, and 'in the abstract' be able to judge correctly about such an action; but if one's appetite is not rightly disposed to sensual pleasures, then the influence will be strong to let the passion of the moment affect one's judgement, to see the situation differently (in the context of pleasure rather than of sin, for example), use a wrong line of operative reasoning, and come to the wrong conclusion. Thus one might have excellent moral knowledge, but without temperance fail to make the right decisions at certain times.

There are two basic ways in which passion can affect reason (1-II 61. 2): there is the passion which is an impulse contrary to reason, and the passion which draws one away from what reason prescribes. The former is positive, the latter negative. To counter-

[13] 1-II 58. 5: Contingit enim quandoque quod huiusmodi universale principium cognitum per intellectum vel scientiam, corrumpitur in particulari per aliquam passionem.

[14] 1-II 58. 5: oportet quod perficiatur per aliquos habitus secundum quos fiat quodammodo homini connaturale recte iudicare de fine.

act these two passions, we require the virtues of temperance and fortitude, the former to control contrary desires, the latter to keep fear, sloth, and the like, from preventing good execution.

Thomas says that the passions can affect both the *iudicium* and the *praeceptum* (I-II 58. 5 ad 3), or both decision and execution. Though one might suspect that passional desire is more of a threat to decision, and fear to execution, it seems clear that both stages can be affected by the different passions. Thus temperance and fortitude are both needed in order to make the right decision and to carry it out (especially if difficult or unattractive) in the right way at the right time. The virtues of temperance and fortitude should be seen as dealing with the ensemble of emotional reactions to daily life and not just with the more obvious situations of desires for food and sex, or with fears of dangers.

Jane Austen's *Sense and Sensibility* depicts many of the dimensions of prudence in the contrast between Elinor and Marianne. Elinor represents good 'sense' (prudence) because she is able to pursue the right course of action in trying and baffling circumstances, while Marianne is thought to represent emotion or sentiment. It is not correct, however, to see Marianne as the 'emotional' figure, as if Elinor were herself cool and detached; the contrast between head and heart is not so simple. Elinor and Marianne are both capable of strong feeling; Elinor, no less than Marianne, has deep concerns, and experiences shock, disappointment, and joy. When she learns that Edward is not married to Lucy and is free (ch. 49), 'she was everything by turns but tranquil . . . it required several hours to give sedateness to her spirits, or any degree of tranquillity to her heart.'

Marianne, on the other hand, like her sister, did not lack instruction and training in moral principles and social conventions, so that her lack of prudence was not a deficiency in moral knowledge. The difference in their characters was in their judgement of situations and ability to act. Elinor was able to see how she should behave, with civility and concern for others, and hold firmly to this course, even though strongly affected otherwise. Marianne lacked the ability to be firm or balanced in either sorrow or joy (elation as well as disappointment or anger may lead to rash judgement), and in her times of self-absorption lacked the courage to face the annoying, depressing, or seemingly hopeless situations which Elinor was able to deal with.

Developing the affective virtues alone is not sufficient for moral virtue, because they must operate in harmony with right reason (which is in fact the definition of moral virtue).[15] No amount of benevolence or sensibility is capable of correct action without prudence. Thus the role of the moral virtues is to enable practical reason to operate properly, to enable choices of particular actions to be made in the light of what is truly good.[16]

There are some parallels between eighteenth-century moral theories of benevolence which Jane Austen was implicitly criticizing, and the medieval emphasis on the will and affection which Aquinas was opposing with his doctrine of practical reason. His combined cognitive-appetitive psychological model of agency here offers much to explain the agent's freedom, responsibility, and potential for error. Lack of knowledge, poor judgement of circumstances, use of wrong principles under the influence of passion, failure to abide by one's judgement, and fear or laziness at the moment of execution, are given much more scope in Thomistic theory.[17] The model shows how the virtues are truly interconnected: a prudent decision and action must be governed by justice (with due regard for relationships with others), temperance (desires for pleasure under control), and fortitude (being constant and firm in adversity).

THE DISTORTION OF PRUDENCE IN VOLUNTARISM

In spite of Aquinas's unambiguous teaching, there has been a constant tendency to misinterpret him, to make prudence into moral knowledge, to deny *imperium* as a cognitive function after choice, and to identify both decision and execution with the will. The pressure to take the view of prudence as knowledge of moral principles comes from a voluntarist view of choice which has been embedded in the common view of human action.

[15] *In III Ethic.* 1113ª29, lect. 494: Quia habitus virtutis moralis definitur ex hoc quod est secundum rationem rectam.

[16] Caldera, *Jugement par inclination*, 95, on the virtues: 'Par leur proximité à l'acte, ils facilitent le choix; par leur stabilité, ils aident à bien choisir, à choisir toujours et à chaque occasion selon l'*ordo amoris*.'

[17] That prudence involves not just good thinking but a larger scope of 'bodily apprehension of the world' is well brought out by McCabe, 'Aquinas on Good Sense', 429–30.

This is perhaps a surprising result of a view of action which is seen as the corrective to a Socratic or intellectualist account. Would not the view of prudence as correct knowledge in action be more characteristic of a Socratic account which explains wrong choice as a lack of information or ignorance of what is best? Yes, a Socratic view of human action does tend to a view of prudence as knowledge, that the practically wise person is one who sees the situation most clearly, who best understands what he should do; and as an account of human action it is defective because it ignores the affective aspect, explaining failure to do the right thing as lack of understanding, when the agent may well have correctly analyzed the situation, come to a conclusion about it, but wanted to do something else.

The voluntarist corrective to this, however, also restricts prudence to a matter of correct understanding. That is because it sees the choice or decision as an act made by the will *after* the intellect has reached its conclusion. When the operations of intellect and will are split, with the intellect preceding and the will following and deciding, then the role of prudence is primarily to perfect the intellectual operation before the actual choice. This makes the agent's decision (seen as an act of the will) a decision about the result of an intellectual operation already taken place. And no matter how 'practical' one makes the judgement of reason preceding choice, it is still reasoning leading 'up to' the decision, not part of the decision itself.

Within this voluntarist model of decision-making, prudence becomes the virtue of correctly specifying to the will a particular directive for action. Because the will's dynamic quality is to be attracted to something or to avoid it, it is not able to make finer distinctions or judgements; thus, if the will is to make a correct decision it requires the *eligendum* in a specified form: this is what I should do; will I do it or not? But when this specifying function of reason is split from the activity of will then it takes on a speculative character, remote from the decision itself, and becomes a refinement of reasoning from principles or a form of conscience as the source of specific guidance. Instead of being the judgement that a particular action is in correct relation to a general principle expressive of the agent's goal, it becomes the deduction of a particular command for the situation from more general rules, or an intuition of the particular action to take; either way, the choice of the will becomes a matter of whether to obey or disobey the particular judgement being offered.

With the model of human action splitting intellect from will, the perfection of the will by love becomes more important than prudence. Proper specification of action is assumed to be a rational matter; the real problem is in the agent's desire, whether to obey conscience or not. Thus for right action, the agent needs to obey the moral dictates; and the crucial link is right orientation of the will (the disposition to obey God comes through charity, supplied by grace, while in later naturalistic theories the emphasis was put on benevolence, good nature, and proper social training). The argument here that the emphasis on love at the expense of prudence is a direct corollary of a voluntarist account of human action is well supported by considering that the theologians known for their treatment of love are also key figures in the trend towards voluntarism: St Bernard, Henry of Ghent, the Franciscans in general, and Duns Scotus in particular. The doctrine of prudence in their hands was bound to be different from that of St Thomas.[18]

What Thomas Aquinas reflects is an attempt to be faithful to the balance between cognition and volition in the Augustinian view of love (this was also true of St Bonaventure, at least compared to many other Franciscans[19]). *Amor* for Augustine includes the operation of the intellect, and the notion of *ordo amoris* can be seen to correspond to prudence and love. When Thomas discusses (*ST* 2-II 23. 3) whether *caritas* is a virtue, he points out the characteristic of a virtue as the principle of human action, consisting in attaining to a double rule, namely human reason and God himself.[20] *Caritas* (and *amor* in general) operate in conformity to a standard, which involves *ordo*, correctly relating one thing to another; this automatically implies, in a properly Augustinian view of love, the

[18] For Duns Scotus, for instance, the need to guarantee freedom to the will led him to separate prudence from moral virtue, making prudence a correct operation of moral knowledge without corresponding virtue in the will; see S. Dumont, 'The Necessary Connection of Moral Virtue to Prudence according to John Duns Scotus—Revisited', *RTAM* 55 (1988), 184–206, at 187–8.

[19] R. P. Prentice, *The Psychology of Love according to St Bonaventure*[2] (Bonaventure, NY, 1957), 150–1, comments on the restraint of the treatment of love by Bonaventure compared to Bernard, Hugh of St Victor, and other theologians.

[20] *ST* 2-II 23. 3: humana virtus, quae est principium omnium bonorum actuum hominis, consistit in attingendo regulam humanorum actuum. Quae quidem est duplex . . . scilicet humana ratio, et ipse Deus.

operation of the intellect. Aquinas understood Augustine to be
teaching, in a non-Aristotelian psychological framework, the same
intimate combination of cognition and volition as the Aristotelian-
Thomist principle of action.

The only way of preserving the essential character of love is to
reunite cognition and volition in human action. Splitting reason
and will has two grave consequences: it emphasizes the affective
qualities of love at the expense of the intellective, which Augustine
did not do, tending toward a view of love which is often sentimen-
tal, emotional, or mystical; and, secondly, it removes the concept
of *ordo* from a principle of love itself to something exterior to it.
Thus instead of the *regula* of virtue being integral to it, it becomes
largely intellectual, prior to the movement of the will. If cognition
and volition are bifurcated, prudence perfects the conformity to
principles only in an intellectual way; when this conformity is seen
as alien to affection or appetite, then it takes on an exterior and
legalistic character.

The proper solution is to combine cognition and volition, so
that movement to the good and conformity to the rule of reason
occur together, each determining the other. Such an understanding makes the teaching of Thomas on the virtues much less
mechanical, more realistic, and also shows how he could use
Aristotle's psychology to explain the theology of Augustine.

INTEGRATION OF MORAL AND THEOLOGICAL VIRTUE

In one of the disputed questions Thomas distinguished the virtues
according to the intellective and appetitive parts of the human
psyche. He noted that the good of both the intellective and
appetitive aspects is twofold, namely the good which is the ultimate end, and the good pursued in things subordinate to that
end. This difference requires different sets of virtues: the moral
virtues for human life in general, and the theological virtues for the
true final end, which hold God not only as an end, but as their
object.[21]

---

[21] *De virt. in comm.* q. un., 12: Et ideo praeter omnes virtutes praedictas,
secundum quas homo bonum consequitur in his quae sunt ad finem, oportet esse
alias virtutes secundum quas homo bene se habet circa ultimum finem, qui Deus
est; unde et theologicae dicuntur, quia Deum habent non solum pro fine, sed
etiam pro obiecto.

This adds a new dimension to Thomistic prudence and virtue, but does not change its basis. Error, sin, and law are also major additions to the discussion of practical reasoning, but should be seen as Christian supplements and not as fundamental corrections (or 'distortions') of Aristotle, since Thomas maintained the basic metaphysical and psychological principles of Aristotelian action. This fundamental harmony can be seen consistently in his philosophical as well as theological and biblical treatises.

St Thomas in his biblical commentaries was consistent with the psychology of human action found in his expositions of Aristotle and in the *Summa Theologiae*. In his commentary on Romans he depicts the conflict between nature and grace in the mind of the Christian as the choice between two syllogisms or lines of reasoning: there is the one proposed by the flesh, which follows fleshly prudence (*prudentia carnis*), and the syllogism which comes from the Spirit.[22] Those who follow the carnal line of thought are brought towards death, while those who follow the Spirit are brought to life.

Reason is not identified with one side of the opposition, the spiritual, to create an opposition between rational spirit and irrational flesh, nor on the other hand with flesh to create an opposition between human reason and spiritual faith; both sides are reasonings (*syllogismi*), and both lines of thought have a kind of prudence. They have in common the virtue of prudence, *recta ratio agibilium*, which has three functions according to Thomas: to consider rightly, to judge rightly about the results of deliberation, and to execute the decision rightly and firmly.[23] The difference between prudence of the flesh and prudence of the Spirit is the difference in the overall end or goal. Worldly prudence (of nature

---

[22] Thomas interprets *caro* and *spiritus* not as different aspects of the human psyche (viz. body and soul), but as denoting the outlook, assumptions, values, and so on, of fallen human nature (the flesh) on the one hand, and of the person informed by grace (spirit) on the other. This is in line with the interpretation of C. E. B. Cranfield, *A Critical and Exegetical Commentary on the Epistle to the Romans* (Edinburgh, 1985), i. 386.

[23] *Super Rom.* 8. 1, lect. 617: prudentia est recta ratio agibilium, ut dicit Philosophus VI *Ethic.* Recta autem ratio agendorum unum praesupponit, et tria facit. Praesupponit enim finem qui est sicut principium in agendis, sicut et ratio speculativa praesupponit principia ex quibus demonstrat. Facit autem recta ratio agibilium tria. Nam primo, recte consiliatur; secundo, recte iudicat de consiliatis; tertio, recte et constanter praecipit quod consiliatum est.

without grace) counsels, judges, and executes actions for the end of
carnal enjoyment; the end of spiritual prudence, however, is life
and peace, so this prudence is the cause of grace and glory.[24]

Note that the conflict for the agent is not between reason and
desire, nor does Thomas say that the thinking of the 'flesh' is not
rational: there are two sets of thinking patterns, parallel ways of
looking at actions, and both have a kind of wisdom about them.
Yet there is a great difference between them in the ultimate end
adopted.

It is clear, then, that for correct decisions and choices the agent
requires the habit of using right operative syllogisms, i.e correct
patterns of deciding actions: not only having the right principles,
but being able to see when and how they apply, to use them
correctly as major premises for action, and to discern correctly the
nature of the particular action being judged by the principle in the
light of the overall values or ultimate end of the agent. This is the
rationale for the importance of the virtue of prudence, both natural
and informed by grace.

---

[24] *Super Rom.* 8. 1, lect. 617–18: Sic ergo ad prudentiam carnis requiritur quod
aliquis praesupponat pro fine delectabile carnis et quod consilietur et judicet et
praecipiat ea quae conveniunt ad hunc finem. Unde talis prudentia est mors, id
est, causa mortis aeternae . . . Dicitur autem secundum praedicta prudentia
spiritus, quando aliquis, praesupposito fine spiritualis boni, consiliatur et judicat et
praecipit quae ordinantur convenienter ad hunc finem. Unde talis prudentia est
vita, id est, causa vitae gratiae et gloriae.

16

Law and Prudence

THERE are many different reasons why Thomas has been misunderstood on the subject of law and ethics. This has something to do with the inherent difficulty of the subject, and the temptation to take parts of the *Summa* for the whole; but it has even more to do with developments in Western thought after Aquinas which have made proper understanding a problem.

There has been a recognition that the view of law stemming from the nominalist tradition and developed by Suarez has been defective at least, and in some respects positively inimical to a proper theological view of law. This has naturally led to distorted accounts of the function of law in Aquinas's thought. Until a faithful account of Thomistic practical reasoning is provided, the confusion about the place of natural law and law in general will remain.[1]

A discussion here of law might have been omitted entirely, to show that human moral action was based by Thomas on a metaphysics and psychology of agency removed from the notions of duty, obligation, and obedience. The account of human action in *ST* I-II qq. 12–17 goes from intention to execution with almost no reference to law or duty at all.

To say, however, that ethics for Thomas was based on right reason or virtue instead of law—and to leave it at that—would be to give the erroneous impression that there is an inherent contradiction between law and virtue, that Thomas had to choose between following Aristotle and Augustine, implying that the entire moral theology of the *ST* is flawed in some major way by a

---

[1] M. Rhonheimer, *Natur als Grundlage der Moral: Die personale Struktur des Naturgesetzes bei Thomas von Aquin* (Innsbruck, 1986), goes far towards relating practical reason and natural law; also cf. J. Owens, 'Human Reason and the Moral Order in Aquinas', *Studia Moralia*, 28 (1990), 155–73; but the integration with the actual process of practical reasoning is still needed.

lack of coherence. Thus a complete account of Thomistic prudence should show the harmony between Aristotelian practical reason and an Augustinian theology of law.[2]

The description of law takes its place in the *secunda pars* of the *Summa* (qq. 90–108) after the description of virtue in general and the nature and effects of sin, and before treatment of grace and the virtues in detail. In the prologue to the section on habits (which introduces virtues) Aquinas states that human actions have interior and exterior principles. The interior aspect of action is *potentia* (discussed in *ST* I) as well as dispositions and virtues discussed in *ST* II.

At the beginning of the section on law Thomas announces that he is now discussing the exterior principles of action. The exterior principle moving us toward good is God himself, who instructs us through law and helps us with grace. Note that this means that both law and grace (discussed here as *lex nova*) are external principles.

The fact that the psychological process of human action which begins the *secunda pars* is discussed with very little reference to law shows that human action can be fully described from the point of view of the agent, as Thomas did, in terms of inclination to apprehended good, the awareness of means to good by specific action, and the choice and execution of that action.

Law, then, from its context in the *Summa Theologiae* has to do with measuring the rightness and wrongness of action, with the standard for the development of virtue, and as a corrective for human weakness, error, and sin, which occur from misperception and ignorance and disordered affection. Thus law is an external standard of action, and it is discussed here in relation to providence and human action both natural and inspired by grace.

THE BASIS OF LAW IN PROVIDENCE

Prudence is closely related to providence, and is in fact etymologically related. At the beginning of his discussion in the *Summa Theologiae* of God's providence, Thomas makes explicit the link

---

[2] Note the change in Alasdair MacIntyre's view from *After Virtue*, where he stressed the conflict between Aristotle and Augustine, to his appreciation, in *Three Rival Versions of Moral Enquiry*, of the harmony achieved by St Thomas.

between prudence and the providence of God.³ The good of the order existing in created things was placed there by God, which implies that the *ratio* of the order of things towards an end pre-existed in God's mind. And this is how we are to define providence: the *ratio* of things to be ordered properly towards an end.⁴

Since the characteristic of prudence, according to Aristotle, is to order things towards an end—and this holds true whether we speak of a person who orders his own actions, or those of others, as in a household, city, or kingdom—it is therefore fitting to speak of prudence in connection with God.⁵ Although it is true that God does not need counsel, nor does he need to deliberate (which is not essential to right reason or to prudence), the commanding of things to be ordered towards an end, concerning which he has right reason, is fitting for God. God's 'counsel' spoken of in Ephesians 1: 11 does not refer to any enquiry he makes, but to the certainty of his knowledge of things.⁶

When Thomas later treated the virtue of prudence directly, he asked in article 2-II 49. 6 whether foresight (*providentia*) is an aspect of prudence. Against the (third) argument that commanding, judging, or deliberating (the three aspects of prudence) do not seem to be characteristic of foresight, Thomas replies that right ordering is included in the nature of foresight and implies rectitude of counsel, judgement, and command, without which correct ordering to an end is impossible.⁷

This helps us to understand that providence and law, like prudence, are not restricted to the intellect but include or presuppose the will. Providence is in understanding (as prudence is in the intellect), but it presupposes willing the end, because no one commands about things to be done for an end unless he wills the end. And so we can see that prudence presupposes the moral virtues, through which the appetite is related to the good.⁸

³ *ST* I 22, *prol.*: Nam et post morales virtutes, in scientia morali, consideratur de prudentia, ad quam providentia pertinere videtur.

⁴ I 22. 1: ratio autem ordinandorum in finem, proprie providentia est.

⁵ Ibid.

⁶ I 22. 1 ad 1.

⁷ 2-II 49. 6 ad 3: in recta ordinatione ad finem, quae includitur in ratione providentiae, importatur rectitudo consilii et iudicii et praecepti, sine quibus recta ordinatio ad finem esse non potest.

⁸ I 22. 1 ad 3: providentia est in intellectu, sed praesupponit voluntatem finis: nullus enim praecipit de agendis propter finem, nisi velit finem. Unde et prudentia praesupponit virtutes morales, per quas appetitus se habet ad bonum.

In the *Summa contra gentiles* there is even clearer teaching of the dual role of providence—the establishment of order and the execution of it, which require both cognitive and operative virtue.[9] Just as God's providence is an expression not only of his wisdom and his love but of his power and desire to carry out his plan, so prudence is not only proper understanding but *recta ratio* in the sense of seeing that actions are accomplished, thus presupposing the other virtues.

From this point of view the general definition of law which St Thomas provides can be appreciated in connection with both prudence and providence: law is nothing other than a certain rational ordering to the common good promulgated by the one who has the care of a community.[10] Since both prudence and providence are rational, but presuppose a will and disposition for the purpose to be achieved, it would be wrong to describe law as strictly a rational pattern without reference to the desire and will for the good to be achieved.

Since all of the created order comes under God's providence, all creatures share in the eternal law because all are governed by it. Thomas describes this participation in divine law as an 'imprint' by which all things have inclinations towards appropriate actions and ends.[11] Seedlings growing to be trees, animals caring for their young, chemicals reacting to other substances, all of the patterns of the created order are instances of sharing in providence. This is obviously the theological counterpart to the description of natural appetite and the metaphysics of agency discussed above in Chapter 4.

Human beings share in providence because they too have a natural inclination to due action and purpose. Observe, however, the distinction between 'natural appetite' and 'natural inclination'. Humans have a natural determined appetite only for *bonum*, good in general, which requires specification in a means–end structure for choice leading to action. Humans have a number of natural

[9] *SCG* III 77: ad providentiam duo requiruntur: ordinatio, et ordinis executio. Quorum primum fit per virtutem cognoscitivam . . . secundum vero fit per virtutem operativam.

[10] *ST* 1-II 90. 4: definitio legis, quae nihil est aliud quam quaedam rationis ordinatio ad bonum commune, ab eo qui curam communitatis habet, promulgata.

[11] 1-II 91. 2: omnia participant aliqualiter legem aeternam, inquantum scilicet ex impressione eius habent inclinationes in proprios actus et fines.

inclinations based on the nature they share in common with animals and other beings in the world, but these inclinations are not determinative of the will. They have a normative status in that there is an immediately obvious and attractive means–end structure to be recognized. In other words the requirements of being human such as nourishment, rest, understanding, friendship, education, and so on, are based on what a human being *is*; and making provision for these needs is in accordance with natural law (and Christians would add that this is part of God's providence). But each of these ends needs to be affirmed and chosen or denied and rejected by the agent's free choice in the light of the circumstances and of the agent's goals and vision of the good.

The connection of human beings and other creatures with the eternal law is on this same basis: being able to act in accordance with appropriate purposes; but the way in which a human being (or any rational creature) is subject to providence is 'by a more excellent mode', since he himself can be a participant in providence by proper care for himself and others.[12] And since the sharing in the eternal law is not just acting for appropriate purposes but sharing in God's mind by intellect and reason (thus understanding ends and choosing appropriate means), the sharing of rational creatures in the created order is more truly called law.[13]

A great many texts from St Thomas could be added on the subjects of the relationship between providence, prudence, and law, subjects which are at the heart of his synthesis of the Bible, Aristotle, and the Augustinian theological tradition. But in none of these places will we find Thomas expressing himself in this way: 'We may then be confident that the rules of prudence are a promulgation to our mind of God's law, a reflection in our mind of God's Providence.'[14] Setting aside the implicit Stoic assumption of the degree of intelligibility of God's law (about which St Thomas was much more agnostic than is often recognized), the

---

[12] 1-II 91. 2: Inter cetera autem, rationalis creatura excellentiori quodam modo divinae providentiae subiacet, inquantum et ipsa fit providentiae particeps, sibi ipsi et aliis providens.

[13] 1-II 91. 2 ad 3: Sed quia rationalis creatura participat eam intellectualiter et rationaliter, ideo participatio legis aeternae in creatura rationali proprie lex vocatur.

[14] P. Geach, *The Virtues* (Cambridge, 1977), 108.

heart of the problem we must examine is the notion that prudence operates by rules to generate commands for action.

THE FUNCTION OF LAW

The reading of the moral philosophy of Aquinas in deontological terms is a bad mistake, made even more serious by being repeated and asserted in the light of our better understanding of Aristotle's practical reasoning. Some continue to insist on interpreting Aquinas in terms of duty and obligation, and explicitly state that Aquinas should be read as anticipating the moral categories of Kant.[15] Though in appearance less extreme, the project of John Finnis and Germain Grisez is also a search for deontological norms. Finnis expresses regret that Thomas focused his ethical account on human action, and then treated moral questions in the context of virtues and vices instead of concentrating on the 'rational propositional principles' of action. This supposedly resulted in an omission and gap in his account.[16]

The problem Finnis and Grisez struggle with is needless (if they were to follow Aquinas), but inevitable, because they split intellect and will. The first principle of practical reason is inert in their view, and its specifications of the primary goods are descriptive; for the activation of the will, that is, for the motivation of the agent, a corresponding 'first principle of morality' and 'modes of responsibility' are required to direct the will.[17] A fundamental weakness of this entire enterprise is the lack of interest in Thomas's metaphysics and psychology of action, and a voluntarist view of free choice.[18]

There is much at stake in clarifying this problem, because of the extent to which nominalism and voluntarism have taken hold of Western thought. The trap of legalism is not avoided by affirming the rational (Thomistic) basis of law in opposition to a voluntarist

---

[15] See A. Donagan, *Human Ends and Human Actions* (Milwaukee, 1985), 17: 'early and late, St. Thomas thought of morality as a matter of law.'

[16] J. Finnis, 'Natural Inclinations and Natural Rights: Deriving "Ought" from "Is" according to Aquinas', in L. Elders and K. Hedwig (eds.), *Lex et Libertas* (Vatican, 1987), 50.

[17] Grisez, *Way of the Lord Jesus*, i. 205–28.

[18] Ibid. i. 42: 'The existential center of each human person is the will, insofar as it is the principle of free choices and of the self determined through choices.'

one (the Suarezian tradition), because this leaves untouched the error of a model of human agency based on splitting intellect and will.

Kant did combine intellect and will in his account of practical reason, but separated them from any teleological view of reality and provided the motivation for practical reason in the notion of duty in law. With natural appetite removed in the Kantian agent, intellect and will combine the functions of both internal and external principles of action. For St Thomas intellect and will are the internal principles of voluntary action; law and grace are external in providing the standard. In a Kantian view of human moral agency everything is internalized and subsumed under law: both the specification of action and its motivation ('exercise') are defined in terms of conformity to law, and the function of law as the standard of morality is provided by the universal character of rationality. This may not be inimical to freedom (defined in terms of autonomous agency), but it is in fundamental opposition to Thomistic practical reason.

In the Aristotelian-Thomist account of practical reason, especially in the practical syllogism, the decision of the agent 'Do this' has sufficient motivational force but is not in any motivational sense obedience to a command or law. It is the conclusion of the agent that in these circumstances this is what should be done as part of the process of fulfilment and the desire for the good which carries force for action. Intentions, whether generated by natural inclination or proposed by reasoning and imagination and specified by deliberation, need only to come under the judgement 'this is good' to be objects for choice and action.

All such voluntary actions are moral in the sense that they express the goals, attitudes, and dispositions of the agent; they can also be wrong, of course, even though they are moral. Thus there is need for a standard of right and wrong in action (where law is important), but this is different from a theory of duty; for Aquinas the moral structure and motivation for actions come from desiring certain ends, seeing the means to them, and choosing them. For good moral action clear understanding and properly channelled desires are both essential. The practical syllogism as a psychological account of decision shows that the agent uses as principles in practical reasoning those which he also accepts affectively.

The reason why Aquinas does not need an elaborate account of primary and secondary moral principles is that his psychology of action does not require it. The only principle needed to motivate intellect and will is 'Do good and avoid evil'. In this sense this first principle is unique, equivalent to the principle of identity for theoretic reasoning.

People can judge many of their actions to be right, and carry them out, on the basis of experience combined with proper perception of circumstances. There is no doubt that at a certain basic level human beings individually and collectively share in the ability to discern the right ordering of inclinations to purposes (which is what the notion of natural law conveys). They see that it is good to care for children, to work, to provide food and housing, to make provisions for cultural activity, and to treat people fairly. Thus the formal description of many actions (dealing with such basic goods) is: inclination or perception, plus the judgement 'this is to be done' based on experience and insight. Although there is a sense in which law functions as a standard (dealt with below) there is no need to invoke law for specification or motivation.

Some judgements of specific moral action are easy to make, even in difficult situations: for example, if a child has fallen into a river and no one else is there to help, we would decide to jump in and rescue her. This is not instinct but a clear decision made on the basis of perceiving what is good to do here and now. Such a decision to act would swiftly take into account alternative means of rescue, one's ability to swim in the conditions, and so on. There are those who might not help, and they make a decision which is not 'irrational' but one we might describe as fearful, or selfish (or 'prudent'!) depending on the circumstances.

When actions are not obvious, or involve conflicting inclinations and perceptions, rules are needed for discernment and right judgement. This is where the function of law, along with reason, as the standard of right and wrong in action should be handled.

St Thomas treated the standard of goodness and badness in the *ST* immediately after the psychology of action. The existence of anything depends on a formal and efficient cause; but the goodness of things, including human actions, is derived from the ends they relate to.[19] This sets up a fourfold quality of goodness: (1) generic,

---

[19] *ST* I-II 18. 4.

its quality as an action, sharing in being; (2) specific, its relation to its object; (3) the circumstances; (4) according to the end, in relation to the disposition of the agent to the cause of goodness. A donation of money, for example, is something good in itself. If given to relieve suffering, this will be good; but if given to raise money for a criminal's bail this may not be good. Depending on one's own resources and responsibilities, the circumstances could make the action bad (if a large donation prevented one from caring for one's own children, for example). Even when the first three conditions are met, it is easy to imagine improper motivation: desire for publicity, guilt, provoking envy, and so on.

From the standpoint of final cause, the goodness of the will depends on the end it intends. The ultimate end of the human will is the greatest good (which is part of the metaphysical definition of will as rational appetite), and the *summum bonum* is God. Thomas then draws this conclusion in 1-II 19. 9:

For an act of the will to be good, then, it must be ordered to this highest good. This good fundamentally and directly relates to the divine will as its proper object. Because each particular thing is right and good to the extent that it attains its proper measure, therefore the human will, if it is to be good, needs to be conformed to God's will.[20]

The standard for assessing the goodness of voluntary action is the human reason, and it has this quality (of being a standard) from the eternal law, the divine reason.[21] Thomas does not leave things unresolved as to which is to be final arbiter: the goodness of the human will depends much more on eternal law than its does on human reason; so where reason is lacking, we need to seek out the mind of God.[22]

Conforming to God's will refers to the scope of his will, namely the good of the whole universe. This is God's perspective. The

---

[20] 1-II 19. 9: Requiritur ergo ad bonitatem humanae voluntatis quod ordinetur ad summum bonum. Hoc autem bonum primo quidem et per se comparatur ad voluntatem divinam ut obiectum proprium eius. Unumquodque autem rectum et bonum est, inquantum attingit ad propriam mensuram. Ergo ad hoc quod voluntas hominis sit bona, requiritur quod conformetur voluntati divinae.

[21] 1-II 19. 4: Quod autem ratio humana sit regula voluntatis humanae, ex qua eius bonitas mensuretur, habet ex lege aeterna, quae est ratio divina.

[22] Ibid.: Unde manifestum est quod multo magis dependet bonitas voluntatis humanae a lege aeterna, quam a ratione humana: et ubi deficit humana ratio, oportet ad rationem aeternam recurrere.

human perspective, quite naturally, is for more particular goods, which are meant to be part of a vision for the common good. This explains how conflicts are generated by competing visions of what is good when they are not properly related to the common good.

Thus the will of a person directed to some particular good is not right unless he relates that good to the common good as an end. All the same, it is not necessary for every human action to be explicitly referred to God's will for it to be good. When someone wills some particular good, if it is part of the common good, then it has conformity to God's will in a formal way, because it conforms to the providential order.

When a parent prepares a meal for the family, this is good and right (providing the food is wholesome, the time is right, and so on). It serves not merely individual needs but the common good of society. In a very real way this action and the willing behind it (assuming it was not done in a grudging spirit) is in accordance with the divine will, even though not consciously articulated in those terms. Thomas explains it this way: when something follows an appropriate inclination in accordance with nature this comes from God as effective cause. Thus a person's will can be said to conform to God's will because the person wills that which God wants him to will.[23]

The goodness or badness of an act is measured by reason as a proximate rule, while the supreme rule is the eternal law.[24] Whenever an act proceeds towards an end according to the ordering of reason and the eternal law, then the action is right. Conversely, an act is bad when it departs from reason and the eternal law. Thus Thomas summarizes that every good act accords with reason and the eternal law.[25] Law functions as the rule and measure of all action; in every judgement of action ('this is to be done because it is good') a principle is used to judge the rightness of the act, and the intelligence of the agent has some share in God's law.

---

[23] 1-II 19. 10: quia hanc propriam inclinationem consequentem naturam, vel apprehensionem particularem huius rei, habet res a Deo sicut a causa effectiva. Unde consuevit dici quod conformatur, quantum ad hoc, voluntas hominis voluntati divinae, quia vult hoc quod Deus vult eum velle.

[24] 1-II 21. 1: regula proxima est ratio humana; regula autem suprema est lex aeterna.

[25] Ibid.: omnis actus bonus concordat rationi et legi aeternae.

LAW IN THE PROCESS OF ACTION

In a faulty but prevalent model of practical reason there are basically these stages: a deliberation (often from rules) about what to do, a conscience which translates this into obligation and motivation, then a decision by the will whether to carry it out or not. Specification becomes legalistic, choice voluntarist. The role of law for St Thomas is seriously misrepresented by such a model. A correct summary, however, of the relation of law to practical reasoning in Aquinas must be careful and provisional, because of the near absence of the mention of law in the section on human action.

Deliberation is the stage where applicable laws and principles are to be considered explicitly, although law is implicit in the other stages as well, inasmuch as all the stages are governed by right reason. Though intention is not the province of prudence, the inclinations provided by moral virtues are ones which have been regulated by reason, and therefore convey the benefit of past experience of virtuous action. Thus law is directly relevant to the stage of *consilium* or deliberation, but is implicit in all phases of action.

For example, a young man has an appointment to help a friend move furniture from his flat one evening (the end of the month). After supper he discovers his car won't start. There is not enough time to repair it and there is no public transportation and no other car to borrow. He notices that there is a bicycle at the neighbour's which is unlocked; he could take it, leave a note for the chap, and get to his friend's a little late, or else ring him up and say he can't make it.

The regulation of law operates at the different stages of action. The importance that he attaches to keeping promises and respect for property will influence the courses of action he considers or deliberates about. When he makes his decision he does so in accordance with moral principles (and perhaps civil laws) that he has applied to the situation; and he carries out his decision, aware of the changes that circumstances might make. For example, he may need his car for work the next day and may have to drop everything else and take it to a garage right away; or it may be in a part of the street where he cannot legally park.

It is in deliberation that the directives of law and reasoning from principles operate for clarification and regulation. In the context of the process of action Thomas states that when the agent is deliberating about what to do, then a law may provide direction for the agent because it becomes something which practical reason takes into account in the situation.[26] Laws provide a kind of filtering process for rejecting or approving certain courses of action.

There are times when ordinary rules do not apply, and when special discernment is required. Thomas gives in *ST* 2-II 51. 4 the time-honoured example of not returning a weapon to an enemy who plans harm to society, in which case the normal rule of returning property does not apply. If the agent, in making his decision, argued that he believed in following the rules as usual, he could well be making the wrong decision, perhaps fatal to himself and his friends. Hence another higher judicative virtue is needed, *gnome*, which implies a certain 'perspicacity of judgement'.[27]

If *gnome* is the developed disposition to be able to judge exceptional cases, there is a need for insight that the situation requires a different sort of judgement from that normally supplied by *synesis*, good judgment. To know when ordinary laws do not apply, and to recognize the factors creating such a situation, are important characteristics of the prudent person. That is another reason for understanding the function of law for Thomas not as a source of moral action but as the standard by which to judge the rightness and wrongness of actions.

Special insight for understanding difficult situations is one of the gifts of the Holy Spirit (*ST* 2-II 52. 2). Discernment and guidance by the Spirit become part of the wider resources available to the Christian in deliberation, and indicate the role of the 'new law' in the mind of the believer.

THE LEX EVANGELICA

If prudence is mainly a matter of seeing things in the right way so that proper judgements about good and bad can be made, then the concept of the new law is especially important, because it sets up a whole new relationship between the human mind and the mind of God through the Holy Spirit. That Thomas appreciated the richness and profundity of the new law in the life of the Christian, and

---

[26] 1-II 14. 3 ad 2; see the final section of Ch. 11, and n. 16 there.
[27] 2-II 51. 4: gnome, quae importat quandam perspicacitatem iudicii.

that the new law is addressed to the whole personality including intellect and will, is indicated by the many synonyms which he used in his description of the Gospel law in *ST* i-II qq. 106–8.[28] Though Thomas treats law in a comprehensive way in *ST* i-II, including natural law, positive law, and the laws of the Old Testament, much more attention should be paid, especially in understanding the relationship between prudence and love, to his teaching on the new law or *lex evangelica*. In his opening sentences of i-II 106. 1 he makes a fundamental equation between the new law, which is the principle of virtue in the life of the Christian, and the grace of the Holy Spirit given through faith in Christ.[29] This makes very little sense or appeal to us if understood in a legalistic fashion; but when prudence is understood as insight, and when grace is seen as the drawing of the mind and heart to share in the life of God, then a very rich doctrine of Christian prudence can be developed as the process of transforming the mind of the agent into the mind of Christ.

The new law, the power of the new covenant, comes from the Holy Spirit and can be described as principally 'the grace of the Holy Spirit itself '.[30] From this perspective the law of the Gospel as written is secondary to its character as formed in our hearts. The Gospel contains things relating to the life of Christ which further understanding through faith, enabling the reception of the grace of the Spirit; but the Gospel also works on the level of affections.

The new law has the same purpose as the old law, namely the obedience of people to God (107. 1); but there is a difference in the manner in which this is accomplished. The old law approaches us as a teacher of children, while the new law is the law of perfection, the law of love. Thomas explains in 107. 1 ad 2: a person without

---

[28] In addition to the equation of *lex evangelica* and *lex nova*, Aquinas used the following terms: *lex gratiae* (1-II 106. 3); *lex caritatis* and *lex amoris* (107. 1 and ad 2); *lex fidei* (107. 1 ad 3); *lex veritatis* (107. 2); and *lex libertatis* (108. 1).

[29] 1-II 106. 1: Id autem quod est potissimum in lege novi testamenti, et in quo tota virtus eius consistit, est gratia Spiritus Sancti, quae datur per fidem Christi. This teaching has received some attention: cf. P. Delhaye, 'La "loi nouvelle" dans l'enseignement de saint Thomas', in *San Tommaso e la filosofia del diritto oggi* (Vatican, 1975), 73–103; and Elders, 'Le Saint Esprit et la *lex nova* dans les commentaires bibliques de saint Thomas d'Aquin', *Autour de saint Thomas d'Aquin*, ii. 201–14; see also essays by U. Kühn, J.-M. Aubert, P. Rodriguez, and P. Delhaye in Elders and Hedwig, *Lex et Libertas*, 243–80.

[30] *ST* 1-II 106 aa. 1, 3: principaliter est ipsa gratia Spiritus Sancti.

virtue (one without the right *habitus* of intellect and will to discern and act) needs an extrinsic cause in order to be motivated to virtuous actions. This exterior cause comes in the form of rewards or punishments, which is why the old law is expressed in these terms. But those who have virtue are inclined to the works of virtue on account of the love of virtue and not because of punishment or reward. The power of the new law is the law of love embedded in the heart.

Truth is also expressed in the new law through Christ's teaching, since he showed the importance of the interior aspect of sin, the proper motivation in the observation of certain laws, and gave counsels to follow. This combination of understanding the truth of God's standard in a new way, plus the grace in the affective nature, can be summarized by describing the grace of the Holy Spirit as manifesting itself as faith working in love.[31]

It is true that in the new law some things are commanded and prohibited (this aspect of law is not contradictory to the essence of love), but many things are left open by Christ to each Christian to determine whether they should be done or avoided.[32] Thomas perceived this element of freedom in the new law, and that the principle of grace as interior habit required the provision of freedom for the believer. The things that are prohibited or commanded are basically things necessary to salvation, and there is freedom with respect to these as well, at least to the extent that Christians are able to fulfil them 'by the interior instinct of grace'.[33]

The link between the new law and the operation of practical reason is developed in 108. 3, where St Thomas describes how grace works in the interior movements. The proclamation of the Gospel puts in right order the inner human motivations relating both to oneself and to one's neighbour. The law speaks to the will for certain actions, by making clear the dimensions of actions— that not only the exterior actions themselves but the attitudes and motivations are important (as Jesus spoke about hate in relation to murder, and lust in relation to adultery); the new law also speaks to purposes and values in life, such as not seeking human glory or

---

[31] *ST* I-II 108. 1: principalitas legis novae est gratia Spiritus Sancti, quae manifestatur in fide per dilectionem operante.

[32] Ibid.

[33] 108. 1 ad 2: huiusmodi etiam praecepta vel prohibitiones facit nos libere implere, inquantum ex interiori instinctu gratiae ea implemus.

worldly wealth. After this the new law sets in order one's attitude to one's neighbour, not to judge him unjustly or presumptuously. The commands in the Sermon on the Mount to be generous and to give, hoping for nothing in return, speak to the formation of attitudes: to deal with covetousness and encourage generous treatment of the neighbour. Referring to the teaching of Augustine, Aquinas said these precepts are to be received as a preparation of the mind.[34]

The larger dimensions of Thomistic prudence emerge. It is a description combining Aristotle's practical reason with the wisdom of Scripture, not setting virtue against law, but showing how these elements function in the realms of both nature and grace. The teaching of Thomas on law, and especially his understanding of the connection between law, grace, and love, gains in profundity when read in the context of his psychology of action, and offers fruitful ground for ecumenical discussion.[35]

The terms most characteristic of Aquinas's description of prudence, which he employed to achieve this synthesis of the Bible, Aristotle, and St Augustine, are 'ordering' and 'judging'.[36] The ordering of means to end is the central Aristotelian feature, and at each stage of practical reason Thomas indicates the need for the *ordinatio* of agent to end, of means to end, and of decision to action.[37]

The correct functioning of reason is not enough, because prudence needs to be conformed with right appetite at each stage; thus all the powers of the soul involved in agency require ordering to each other and to reality. This correct ordering of powers is in fact the definition of virtue in general.[38] This involves not just the control of virtues by reason (the moderating role), but their structuring towards an overall purpose, because the essence of a virtue

---

[34] 108. 3 ad 2.

[35] See the appreciative treatment of Thomas's doctrine and its application to the Protestant concern for the relation of law and gospel by U. Kühn, *Via Caritatis: Theologie des Gesetzes bei Thomas von Aquin* (Göttingen, 1965).

[36] See B. Montagnes, 'Les Deux Fonctions de la sagesse: Ordonner et juger', *RSPT* 53 (1969), 675–86.

[37] For *ordinare* in intention: *ST* I-II 12. 1 ad 3; in choice: 13. 1; in deliberation: 14. 3 ad 3; in execution: 17. 1.

[38] I-II 55. 2 ad 1: Et ideo ipsa virtus est quaedam dispositio ordinata in anima: secundum scilicet quod potentiae animae ordinantur aliqualiter ad invicem, et ad id quod est extra.

implies a power that is perfected when it realizes its end, taking part in the greater ordering of an agent's whole life.[39]

The aspect of judgement (*krisis*) in Aristotle is present but slight, and this may be seen as the Augustinian element, expressing the need for a standard by which to judge the correctness of end and means, choice and execution of action. What St Thomas invests in judgement, which is not only the estimation of ends and means, of rule and situation, but also the decisive psychological link with action, joins prudence with the biblical view of wisdom and with the *discretio* of the earlier Christian tradition.[40] Right reason (using a standard for action on the natural level which can be described as natural law), and the wisdom of the Holy Spirit (the *lex evangelica* of grace), give the agent's mind the framework and orientation to judge correctly the various situations and actions of life in the light of his human life and his relationship to God.

[39] See F. J. Yartz, 'Virtue as an *Ordo* in Aquinas', *Modern Schoolman*, 47 (1970), 305–20, at 319.

[40] F. Dingjan, *Discretio: Les Origines patristiques et monastiques de la doctrine sur la prudence chez saint Thomas d'Aquin* (Assen, 1967), 218: *discretio* 'est un jugement sur le bien et le mal des actes particuliers'.

17
Prudence and Love

IN Thomistic philosophy it is the object which activates the powers of the mind. The object as something true (*verum*) is the object of the intellect, while the object as good (*bonum*) draws the will. The priority of cognition is a metaphysical one, since apprehension of form precedes inclination to it. In the process of free choice (*liberum arbitrium*) which is the principle of action, both intellect and will are active, with their functions designated as specification and exercise respectively.

THE ROLE OF LOVE

As a fundamental metaphysical principle, appetite is the inclination of being to perfection, and applies to all beings in their movement towards *bonum*, their perfection. Love (*amor*) relates to appetite, because they both share the same object, *bonum*[1], and at this very general level, appetite and love can be equated.[2] It would follow that there are various degrees of love corresponding to the various levels of appetite, namely natural, sensitive, and rational, and Thomas does speak of *amor naturalis*,[3] *amor sensitivus*, and *amor intellectivus* in *ST* I-II 26. 1. *Amor* is usually restricted, however, to what is in the will (26. 2).

On the natural human level, what is required for action is cognition (the object must be apprehended) and appetite. Where choice is required (where means to the end are to be specified for

---

[1] *ST* I-II 26. 1: amor est aliquid ad appetitum pertinens: cum utriusque obiectum sit bonum.

[2] See the text dealing with angelic *dilectio*, *ST* I 60. 1: Est autem hoc commune omni naturae, ut habeat aliquam inclinationem, quae est appetitus naturalis vel amor.

[3] Aquinas says, I-II 26. 2, that the force of gravity can be called, in a way, an *amor naturalis*; see J. Aumann, 'Thomistic Evaluation of Love and Charity', *Angelicum*, 55 (1978), 534–56.

decision), then reason should be perfected by prudence, the disposition for right judgement and execution. But for the corresponding appetitive movement, the agent already has a natural orientation towards the good, through both sensitive appetite and the will, which can be called *amor*.[4]

This is a crucial point in Thomist psychology, because it explains human dynamism in a way quite different from nominalism and the many modern philosophies deeply affected by it. For Thomas, *amor*, the tendency to the good, functions as a natural psychological force. The will does not require an added disposition to seek the good. The human agent needs training and instruction to understand what is good (hence prudence), but he has a natural motivation inclining him to it.

Justice is the special moral virtue of the will, but it is directed to those actions which involve relationship to another person, while the other moral virtues perfect the agent only in those things which pertain to himself.[5] There should be no rigid separation of individual and social: many actions would fall under responsibility to family or employer, or to the community, so that one's job, and the way one drives a car, and the activities pursued at home can be seen as expressing in some way the virtue of justice. Further, no personal actions can be excluded from the common good, so that in a way the good of all human action and virtue should be a matter of justice.[6] Justice governs human action, but in the area of relationships, not on the level of motivation.

According to the model of human action which Thomas used, all voluntary actions involving choice or decision are produced by a combination of the intellect and the appetite. For virtuous action, the appetite, and its dynamic motion, *amor*, need to be properly regulated by the reason, hence the need for right reason or prudence. The relationship between *orexis* and *phronēsis* in Aristotle

---

[4] *ST* 1-II 26. 1: Et similiter coaptatio appetitus sensitivi, vel voluntatis, ad aliquod bonum, idest ipsa complacentia boni, dicitur amor sensitivus, vel intellectivus seu rationalis.

[5] 2-II 57. 1: dicendum quod iustitiae proprium est inter alias virtutes ut ordinet hominem in his quae sunt ad alterum . . . Aliae autem virtutes perficiunt hominem solum in his quae ei conveniunt secundum seipsum.

[6] 2-II 58. 5: Secundum hoc igitur bonum cuiuslibet virtutis, sive ordinantis aliquem hominem ad seipsum sive ordinantis ipsum ad aliquas alias personas singulares, est referibile ad bonum commune, ad quod ordinat iustitia.

is comparable to that between *amor* and *prudentia* in Thomas Aquinas. For reason to be correct, the appetite needs to be properly ordered, seeking after proper goals, with contrary or excessive desires properly regulated, fear, anger, and so on under control, and proper regard for other persons' good held in the will. When reason and appetite are mutually regulated in this way, then the agent may be seen as virtuous.

There is a circularity in the Aristotelian model, because the standard for the *phronimos* is the one who is virtuous. *Phronēsis* is required for developing the other virtues, but to be prudent one must have the other virtues. Thomas, in his faithfulness to Aristotle, preserves this circularity: the moral virtues depend on *prudentia*; but prudence depends on having the moral virtues, which establish the proper *fines* for actions and control practical reasoning.

Although Aristotle did not escape the circle, Christian doctrine and especially the teaching of love provide for Aquinas the principle and standard for the true perfection of the agent. It is perhaps at this point, at the heart of the Christian doctrine of the relationship of love between God and man, that a gulf opens up between secular and Christian ethics, between Aristotle and Thomas. It is here, of course, that Thomas can be seen to be following the authority of St Augustine. Without denying the psychological basis that Aristotle provided, Thomas put the scheme of the virtues in the context of love, so that all the virtues can be comprehended in the Augustinian notion of *ordo amoris*, when the affections are properly ordered.[7] The essential character of virtue is one of 'ordered affection'. This means that virtue in general is primarily the order or ordering of love, in the sense that this is what virtue itself is directed toward.[8] It is important to elaborate the difference that the doctrine of Christian love (*caritas*) makes for Thomas's version of Aristotelian ethics.[9] The question 'can there be virtue without *caritas*?' pinpoints the problem. Looking at life from a

---

[7] 1-II 62. 2 ad 3: Si de amore communiter dicto, sic dicitur quaelibet virtus esse ordo amoris, inquantum ad quamlibet cardinalium virtutum requiritur ordinata affectio: omnis autem affectionis radix et principium est amor.

[8] 1-II 55. 1 ad 4: virtus dicitur ordo vel ordinatio amoris, sicut id ad quod est virtus: per virtutem enim ordinatur amor in nobis.

[9] See A. Wohlman, 'L'Élaboration des éléments aristotéliciens dans la doctrine thomiste de l'amour', *RT* 82 (1982), 247–69.

Christian point of view one is tempted to say 'no'. There is no true wisdom without grace, since even its beginning requires the fear of God. Man's righteousness, on his own, is as filthy rags, and to say that human nature is able to achieve what is good without grace is to deny those truths which St Augustine contended for against the Pelagians. Thus there was a strong tendency in the theological tradition, represented in Lombard's *Sentences*, to say that without *caritas* there could be no virtue, and no good could be accomplished without grace.[10]

Thomas most definitely wanted to affirm the importance of the grace of *caritas*, and also to say that virtue and good are possible without Christian grace. This is not just a case of Thomas wanting to have as well as to eat his Aristotelian cake; it is at the heart of his view of creation, of the possibility of the knowledge of things without illumination, of the relation between the natural and supernatural.

For the purpose of demonstrating the essential unity of all human moral life, and yet the difference between nature and grace, Thomas relied on the distinction between different kinds of love. All *caritas* is *amor*, but not all *amor* is *caritas*, since *caritas* depends on God's grace. Thus all moral virtues (Christian or otherwise) can be seen in general as an ordering of *amor*, but if one is speaking of the love in charity, then not all moral virtues are essentially to be seen as love.[11] By using the distinction between *amor* and *caritas*, Thomas was able to distinguish between levels of virtue, between nature and grace, and between a natural prudence and a supernatural prudence.

Thomas faced this challenge squarely in *ST* 1-II 65. 2 in the question whether there can be moral virtues without *caritas*. Thomas says that one may have natural moral virtues, which can be understood as dispositions for goods which do not exceed the natural faculty of man. In this sense, such virtues are found among many peoples, and so do not require the specifically Christian virtue of *caritas*, although these virtues are not possible without *prudentia*. Since they dispose the agent only for limited ends, however, or for an end in a particular area (*in aliquo genere*), they are not perfect, and so cannot be considered virtues *simpliciter*.

The notion of a partial sense of good possible within a limited

---

[10] *Sentences*, II. 25. 8.
[11] *ST* 1-II 62. 2 ad 3.

framework is helpful and important. Thomas discusses in *ST* 1-II 109. 2 what man is able to do, even granting the corrupted state of his nature; because he is not totally corrupt, he is able to perform some good (*aliquod bonum particulare*), such as to build homes, plant vines, and other such things.

In the treatise on the cardinal virtues, Thomas expands on the distinction between imperfect and perfect virtues, and establishes three levels:

(1) virtues which are imperfect, and may exist without prudence; these are more like inclinations which some people have to certain good deeds;

(2) virtues which attain right reason (they are governed by prudence); they are complete in a limited sense, i.e. in the natural order, by reference to a human good, but they do not attain the prime rule, God;

(3) virtues with *caritas*; these virtues make a person's actions good without qualification, in reference to the ultimate end.[12]

This notion of proper ordering explains the possibility of other senses of good, and of limited virtue, and also the relativity and imperfection of all actions without *caritas*. If all action receives its character from its relation to the end, then the question of the ultimate end becomes more important as the end to which all other ends are related.

One may have a proper end—such as care for one's family, or service to the community—and be a virtuous person (in an Aristotelian sense, or the second level above); but if the ultimate end is self-ambition, then the actions which, though considered within the limited sphere (responsible citizenship, for example) are good, are then vitiated by an improper relation to the higher end. That is why the agent needs charity, to be supplied by grace, to establish the overall *ordo*, or structure of ends, for his actions. On the level of natural virtues, prudence is required to direct human actions: it is the co-ordinator; it provides the *ordo* for *amor*. So, on the higher level, all the virtues, including prudence, depend on charity for proper ordering. Thus as prudence is to the moral virtues, so charity is to prudence and all the virtues (*ST* 2-II 23. 4 ad 1).

If charity is so all-important for true virtue, then the question of

---

[12] *De virt. card.* q. un., a. 2.

the relation of intellect and will thus recurs again in the area of the virtues. Prudence for Thomas was a moral virtue, intimately related to the will, but essentially the virtue of practical reason. It is to be expected that the Franciscans and others would have emphasized the will more; but an easy division of positions on this question cannot be made.[13]

It might well seem that the terms of reference change for the Christian who lives under grace, and that the diminution of prudence in moral theology reflects the realization of the more important position of charity. Aristotle obviously did not know the life of grace, the doctrine of *agapē*; and would this not change the whole structure of his ethics? We might say that Thomas could retain the doctrine of prudence for the purposes of describing natural human morality (and to recover this is of great value); but for the Christian does not the need for prudence yield to the dominical commands to love God and love one's neighbour?

It might even be argued that a proper doctrine of love includes the notion of prudence anyway. After all, the summary of the command is to love God with all one's heart, soul, mind, and strength, which undoubtedly indicates that all the potencies are to be an expression of love. The role of charity is nicely summed up by Thomas as the form of the virtues in *ST* 2-II 23. 8. That which sets for an action its ordering to an end gives it its form. Thus since all actions are given relation to the final end through charity, it is thus the form of the virtues. Since the moral virtues set the ends for prudence, charity can therefore be seen as the ultimate moral virtue.

The description of the relation between prudence and charity is important, because this is the point at which St Thomas must show how he combines the Augustinian tradition with Aristotelian practical reason. One way of putting the relation is to separate descriptions of actions from motivation, using the terms 'right' and 'good'. Thus ordinary human life can come under prudence and the moral virtues, so that one can be right (act correctly), but lack the motivation of charity for real goodness; but this view leads to

---

[13] Philip the Chancellor and Albert associated prudence with the will as well as with reason, while Bonaventure, a Franciscan who emphasized love, recognized the importance of prudence and placed it in the intellect; see M. Behnen, *De virtute prudentiae apud S. Bonaventuram* (Rome, 1965), 136.

some conclusions foreign to St Thomas.[14] Aquinas does not say that the Christian adds 'goodness' to an act which is basically right, but that the non-Christian is able to perform acts of particular or limited goodness.

CHARITY REQUIRES PRUDENCE

There is a strong temptation to say that prudence is necessary for a common natural morality, but that in a Christian view of the life of grace prudence is assimilated to love. The centrality of will and affection in Christian psychology and spirituality has led to the identification of both charity and the grace necessary for it with the will (rather than the whole mind) in much of the theological tradition.[15] St Thomas was not unaware of the reasoning behind such a move. In fact he made this question of the relation of prudence and love the starting point of his treatment of prudence in the *Summa Theologiae*. The very first argument in 2-II 47. 1 is the quotation from Augustine that 'prudentia est amor', love choosing wisely between things which help and those which hinder.[16]

Aquinas is also able to cite Augustine in the *sed contra* to the effect that prudence is the cognition concerning the things to pursue and to avoid.[17] So the important question was raised within the theological tradition (leaving Aristotle out of the picture for the time being) with the authority of Augustine on the importance of prudence, and that it can be described both in terms of love and of cognition.

Because of the many ways of expressing the nature of willing and knowing and their combination, and in view of the fact that we have been affected in one way or another by the theories of

---

[14] J. F. Keenan, 'Distinguishing Charity as Goodness and Prudence as Rightness: A Key to Thomas's *Secunda Pars*', *Thomist*, 56 (1992), 407–26, is misleading; since decisions are made under an action description involving ends and means discerned and affirmed by both intellect and will, if an act is right it also has its share of goodness.

[15] This reduction is characteristic of the Scotist tradition after Aquinas; see A. J. Falanga, *Charity the Form of the Virtues according to Saint Thomas* (Washington, DC, 1948), 59–76.

[16] Cf. Augustine, *De moribus eccl. cath.* i. 15 (PL xxxii. 1322): prudentia, amor ea quibus adjuvatur ab eis quibus impeditur, sagaciter seligens.

[17] *De diversis quaest.* 61. 4 (CCSL 44A, 127).

Scotus, Ockham, Descartes, and Kant, it is impossible to give a proper reply to the question 'is prudence really love for Aquinas?' without the kind of metaphysics and psychology of action he carefully described.[18]

Even when the metaphysical and psychological doctrines of Thomas are accepted, they might be understood as applying basically to the natural level of human action, and not to the supernatural. That is, the need for the will to work with the intellect is all very well for ordinary cognition and practical reasoning; but when entering the supernatural realm of grace and love for God, the intellect may be of little use, while the relationship to God is basically one of love, will, and affection. This will seem a natural step to take not only for theological fideists and mystics, but for the wider and more common group who have simply inherited the spectacles of Scotist voluntarism. It will also seem right if the problem of sin in human action is thought to be primarily a matter of the will.

Thomas himself seems to lend weight to this case. He has a discussion of the relation of charity to other virtues and argues for the superiority of *caritas* to faith and hope, based on the difference in the corresponding modes of being. In the case of cognition the object exists in the knower; but if one considers the relationship of the virtue to the object, then the object of love is higher than the person, and perfects the person because it draws him closer to the object.[19] Since the object of charity, God, exists above the human level, the virtue is nobler. It is on this basis that Thomas can be represented as saying that on the supernatural level the pre-eminence of love means the diminution of prudence.[20]

Thus it is important to note that Thomas did not leave a high theology of love to the Franciscan theologians; indeed he can be read and has been represented as emphasizing the will and elevat-

---

[18] This is why C. O'Neil's attempt to answer the question 'Is Prudence Love?', *Monist* 58 (1974), 119–39, is not very satisfactory, despite verve and insight.

[19] *ST* 1-II 66. 6 ad 1; cf. 2-II 23. 6.

[20] See R. Hittinger, 'When it is More Excellent to Love than to Know: The Other Side of Thomistic "Realism"', *PACPA* 57 (1983), 171–9, at 178: 'For a natural ethics, the issue of *verum* will have a certain priority to that of *bonum*. But when we consider conduct in reference to that which is superior, this concern moves in the other direction.' Thomas's metaphysics, however, makes both *verum* and *bonum* secondary to *esse*, which is the object of the intellect not the will (see Chapter 4).

ing love. It is true that there are plenty of passages with evidence for the importance of the intellect, and this has been impressive to some commentators;[21] but more have been impressed by the texts supporting the superiority of love in Thomas.[22]

The way to reply to this should be clear. First, from the metaphysical principles of Thomas and from his description of the function of the will, the activation of the will requires cognition. There can be no exception to this, even on the supernatural level. There is no object of the will unless apprehended by the intellect—and this applies also to love for God. The object of charity is of course no sensible good, but divine good; this is recognized by the intellect, and therefore becomes an object of the will or rational appetite.[23]

In the supernatural order love cannot simply attain God without corresponding activation of the intellect. This of course is not a question of normal cognition; since we are in the realm of grace, a perfection of the intellect by grace is also required, and this is faith. From this it also follows that love, though 'higher' than the other theological virtues, is not separable from faith and hope. From the point of view of the apprehension of God as ultimate end, faith indeed is primary, because this final end must be an object of the intellect (as faith) before it can be an object of the will (as charity).[24] Thus when Thomas speaks of love for God and the virtue of charity, we are not to understand this to be an elevation of the will, but as the will presupposing faith.

On Thomas's principles it is misleading to compare the relative importance of faith and love; though differing in function, they are both essential. One responds to the highest reality from the stand-

[21] e.g. P. Rousselot, *The Intellectualism of Saint Thomas*, trans. J. E. O'Mahony (London, 1935); for an even stronger intellectualist view see R. McGinnis, *The Wisdom of Love: A Study in the Psycho-Metaphysics of Love according to the Principles of St Thomas* (Rome, 1951).

[22] See H.-D. Simonin, 'La Primauté de l'amour dans la doctrine de saint Thomas d'Aquin', *La Vie spirituelle*, 53 (1937), suppl., 129–43; H. M. Christmann, *Thomas von Aquin als Theologe der Liebe* (Heidelberg, 1958); A. Ilien, *Wesen und Funktion der Liebe bei Thomas von Aquin* (Freiburg im Breisgau, 1975); and Wadell, *The Primacy of Love*.

[23] *ST* 2-II 24. 1: Caritatis autem obiectum non est aliquod bonum sensibile, sed bonum divinum, quod solo intellectu cognoscitur.

[24] 2-II 4. 7: Ipse autem ultimus finis oportet quod prius sit in intellectu quam in voluntate: quia voluntas non fertur in aliquid nisi prout est in intellectu apprehensum.

point of truth; the other responds from the standpoint of the attraction of the ultimate good. In relation to the object in the 'order of perfection' the will can be seen to be more central; in the 'order of generation', however, cognition has priority; but the description of 'higher' or 'lower', 'prior' or 'later' should not be taken to contain a valuation.[25] In the supernatural relationship to God faith and charity begin to unite their respective potencies, because of the unity of the object. Where ordinary intellection is based on observation of reasoning and judging, and bases its certitude on the correctness of the first principles (though not without an element of the will in the act of assent), faith in the supernatural realm has a closer affinity to the will and affection; certitude exists more in the area of the affection than in cognition.[26]

The discussion of the relationship of love to other virtues has often centred on the question of the beatific vision. The question of the relationship of the natural end of man to the ultimate end, God himself, is an important and fundamental one, and it is worth taking the trouble to get it right in order to clarify what Aquinas and Aristotle taught about human nature.[27] In relation to love in an ultimate sense, faith, prudence, and the other virtues are secondary, because these other virtues are for human life in pilgrimage. There is a difference between the degree of charity in this life, 'which follows the cognition of faith', and the charity of heaven which follows the open vision.[28]

[25] See E. Michel, *Nullus potest amare aliquid incognitum: Ein Beitrag zur Frage des Intellektualismus bei Thomas von Aquin* (Fribourg, 1979), 145: 'Amor und Cognitio sind als gleichwertige, aber andersartige Möglichkeiten zur Erfassung der Realität gesehen. Ihre Wertung als "nobilior", "altior", "melior", oder "potior" erfolgt nicht von ihrer Beschaffenheit her, sondern leitet sich aus der Art des Objekts ab, das sie erfassen.'

[26] *In III Sent.* 23. 2. 3 sol. 1 ad 2: Fides autem habet certitudinem ab eo quod est extra genus cognitionis, in genere affectionis existens; see B. Duroux, *La Psychologie de la foi chez saint Thomas d'Aquin* (Tournai, 1963), 220–1.

[27] See J. Laporta, *La Destinée de la nature humaine selon Thomas d'Aquin* (Paris, 1965); for a short summary, see G. Grisez, 'The Natural End of Man', *NCE* v. 132–8; much misunderstanding could have been avoided if it had been more clearly seen that *appetitus naturalis* in a rational nature is an appetite for general good.

[28] *ST* 2–II 24. 7 ad 3: Non est autem eadem ratio quantitatis caritatis viae, quae sequitur cognitionem fidei, et caritatis patriae, quae sequitur visionem apertam. See T. Horvath, *Caritas est in Ratione: Die Lehre des hl. Thomas über die Einheit der intellektiven und affektiven Begnadung des Menschen* (Münster, 1966), 152: 'darum ist die Erneuerung der Gottesliebe nur durch die Erneuerung des Glaubens möglich.'

Though it is true that prudence will not be needed when the vision of God is attained, when love will have reached its goal, yet in this life actions need to be guided by prudence. Whenever deliberation is required, where decisions must be made and actions undertaken, prudence is essential for living, even with the gift of charity. Having the right end, namely the attainment of God through love, does not guarantee good actions, because as Thomas so frequently states, right action is a matter of proper ends *and* right choice of means. Having the right ultimate end is necessary for complete virtue but not sufficient: one continues to need prudence to judge not only particular actions, but the secondary ends which now become means to the ultimate end.

Thus charity and prudence combine in the action of the Christian, who needs to be formed by each in his thinking and desiring. This is consistent with Aquinas's whole teaching, and can be described in terms of his metaphysics: prudence is a form in the order of formal cause, in constituting the proper object of virtue, while charity 'informs' in the order of efficient cause, by an 'effective motion'.[29] The relationship between intellect and will as specification and exercise still obtains, although on this supernatural level the grace of God must elevate both *amor* and *prudentia*.

The clearest teaching on this is, appropriately, in a passage in *De caritate* where Thomas wants to establish that charity is distinct from the other virtues. It is simply not true that 'all you need is love'; actions depend on many principles, says Thomas, and just as prudence depends on temperance and fortitude, charity requires prudence. 'For right action, one is required not only to be rightly related to the end, but also to the means.'[30] Although a person is given the right relation to his ultimate goal through charity, it is necessary that he have other virtues by which to be rightly related to the means. Charity, however, is more basic and 'architectonic'

---

[29] *De veritate*, 14. 5; see C. A. J. van Ouwerkerk, *Caritas et ratio: Étude sur le double principe de la vie morale chrétienne d'après s. Thomas d'Aquin* (Nijmegen, 1956), 49.

[30] *De caritate*, q. un., 5: Et ideo ad rectam operationem, aliquem non solum oportet bene dispositum esse ad finem, sed etiam bene dispositum ad ea quae sunt ad finem.

'since it is directed to the end' than those virtues which relate to the means.[31]

Regarding God as final end, new actions will be undertaken in the life of grace, specifically related to growing in love for God. Though varying in time and place, they will involve prayer, worship, and new ways of showing love to other people. The activities characteristic of ordinary human life will not change *per se*, because they have their own goodness and finality in the natural order, but they will change in relation to a firmly held conviction of God as the true final end of living. The importance of eating, friendship, acquiring knowledge, and so on will be retained, but will be seen from a different perspective. There may be a change in the time or attention given, but primarily there will be a difference in the attitude and the quality of intention brought to bear.

This relation of activities to God may in many cases result in an enrichment rather than a diminution of enjoyment. Eating and friendship, for example, when seen in relation to the love of God, take on a new purpose, a new awareness of God's presence and providence, and therefore a greater source of joy than when pursued as primary goods in themselves. It is in this way that Thomistic prudence, rather than being a narrower version of Aristotle's *phronēsis*, is actually broadened.

The basic human goods will remain normative in a way, founded as they are on the reality of human nature and on God's purposes in creation. But the Christian with prudence informed by grace, taking seriously the challenge to love God with all his soul above all things, can treat with some openness even the basic norms of natural human good, because earthly purposes can be seen as means to the chief purpose of life and therefore secondary. Physical life, careers, family, achievements and the development of talents, friendship, and so on, are meant to be means of human fulfilment; and because of the continuity of nature and grace they are the means used by God for growth in grace. Failure or loss of such goods (and especially the inevitable loss of physical health), however, is different in the Christian view (from the Aristotelian), because these are secondary to the ultimate purpose, life in union with God.

---

[31] *De caritate*, q. un., 5: Est ergo caritas alia ab his quae ordinantur ad ea quae sunt ad finem, licet illa quae ordinatur ad finem, sit principalior, et architectonica, respectu earum quae ordinantur in ea quae sunt ad finem.

THE ULTIMATE UNION OF PRUDENCE AND LOVE

In much post-Kantian moral philosophy prudence is given a self-referential definition ('doing what is in one's own interest'), often seen in opposition to moral obligation.[32] The split between prudence and morality would not be possible for Aquinas, since an agent who did not properly consider his obligations, or was not able to refer his actions to the common good, would not be prudent. Prudence as right practical reason by definition includes justice.

There may yet remain a deep theological suspicion of the self-referential aspect of prudence. If one starts from an interpretation of *agapē* in the New Testament as essentially self-sacrificial or self-giving, then an ethic of self-fulfilment or perfection of nature will seem incompatible with a truly Christian ethic. This criticism has been most prominently presented by the Lutheran theologian Anders Nygren, but the problem of reconciling charity and self-love has occupied Roman Catholic thought as well.[33]

This may seem to furnish ground for concluding that the attempt to combine a Christian doctrine of love and Aristotelian practical reasoning was doomed to failure, even in the subtle thought of Thomas Aquinas. Despite the exquisite refinements which Thomas gave it, prudence still seems to retain the self-referential character of a secular, human-centred ethic. A psychological and ethical teaching which makes use of the notion of desire, or seeking good for oneself, may not seem to be compatible with an ethic based on selfless love.

When St Thomas discusses love of self in *ST* 2-II 25. 4, he avoids any hint of egoism by putting it in the context of love for God, implying that self-love without *caritas* is not benign but disordered. But neither is love for self inherently contradictory to love for God, a point Aquinas is able to make by treating *caritas* as *amicitia*, a kind of friendship. Because we belong to God through

[32] R. M. Hare, *Moral Thinking: Its Levels, Method, and Point* (Oxford, 1981), 191: 'it is hard to see why anybody should ever have thought that it was the case that to do what we morally ought to do is always in our prudential interest.'

[33] A. Nygren, *Agape and Eros*, trans. P. S. Watson (London, 1932–9), asserted the failure of medieval theology, including Aquinas, to overcome the inherent opposition between self-love and love for God. There has been a parallel discussion among Catholics concerning 'disinterested' love in grace and charity; see L.-B. Geiger, *Le Problème de l'amour chez saint Thomas d'Aquin* (Paris, 1952).

union, when we love God we love the things which belong to him, including ourselves. Thus love for self has its place as an extension of love for God. In the history of interpretation, unfortunately, the teaching of St Thomas that charity is essentially friendship, a sharing in the life of God, has been just as obscured (and so in need of recovery) as his description of prudence.[34]

For a theological view of the problem of prudence and love, the metaphysical principles of being and love are not as important as Thomas's doctrine of God, based on Scripture and St Augustine, which enables him to explain this. In God there is unity of intellect and will, of truth and goodness, of providence and love. God is also the source and principle of the fundamental unity of prudence and love in the experience of grace in the Christian life.

There can also be no question of any fundamental contradiction between God's law as ultimate norm for human action and love for what is good and perfect as the purest form of motivation; rather rules, principles, and virtues combine in the truly prudent agent. Rules form the exterior standard for judging actions, virtues inform the agent's interior motivations: 'true moral rectitude is necessarily grounded in the orientation of the whole personality that charity creates; and yet, charity cannot be exercised, or even exist, unless the moral rules generated by right reason are observed.'[35]

The union should be expressed even more strongly than this, however, because the source of both direction and motivation (or of prudence and love) in the life of grace is the Holy Spirit. Thomas makes a bold equation between law and grace: the new law, the *lex evangelica*, is 'principally the grace of the Holy Spirit', because 'that which is most powerful in the law of the new covenant and in which its entire virtue consists is the grace of the Holy Spirit which is given through faith in Christ.'[36]

---

[34] F. Kerr, 'Charity as Friendship', in B. Davies (ed.), *Language, Meaning and God: Essays in Honour of Herbert McCabe, OP* (London, 1987), 22: Aquinas's rethinking of the nature of charity in the light of Aristotle's analysis 'was soon distorted out of all recognition or simply consigned to oblivion', replaced by a mystical merging of the individual with the absolute, or by the moralistic notion of 'doing good'.

[35] Porter, *'De Ordine Caritatis'*.

[36] *ST* I-II 106. 1: Id autem quod est potissimum in lege novi testamenti, et in quo tota virtutis eius consistit, est gratia Spiritus Sancti, quae datur per fidem Christi. Et ideo principaliter lex nova est ipsa gratia Spiritus Sancti.

The link between the grace of the Holy Spirit and prudence is made in 2-II q. 52, in the discussion of the gift of counsel. The gifts of the Spirit in general are dispositions of the soul, and the proper means of moving a rational creature is through means of counsel. In this way the Spirit aids by giving guidance.[37] Not only is human reasoning given this help; this grace of the Spirit is the way in which the virtue of prudence is developed and perfected in a way impossible naturally: 'Prudence, which is a matter of the rectitude of reason, is most perfected and aided according as it is regulated and moved by the Holy Spirit.'[38]

Charity, too, is defined in terms of the Holy Spirit: 'charity is not something which is in us naturally or acquired through natural powers, but through the infusion of the Holy Spirit who is the love between the Father and the Son, whose sharing in us is charity itself.'[39] Thus the quality of charity as directed towards the ultimate good is implied (and brought out by Thomas) in the doctrine of the relations of the Trinity. Union with God has been achieved by the work of Christ, and is actualized by the Holy Spirit, by whom Christians are able then to share in the divine life. Though the Holy Spirit is clearly the source of love, Thomas spoke of his work in the heart as a communication or sharing, and specifically denied the direct equation of love with the Holy Spirit.[40]

All human thinking, desiring, and doing, when it is right, is ultimately related to God by grace through the Holy Spirit. Not only prudence but the highest knowledge and wisdom possible are related to love:

Wisdom, which is an intellectual virtue, enables a person to judge things correctly in the light of God's principles; to judge these things rightly by a certain connaturality to them belongs to that wisdom which is a gift of the

[37] 2-II 52. 1, and ad 1.
[38] 2-II 52. 2: Et ideo prudentia, quae importat rectitudinem rationis, maxime perficitur et iuvatur secundum quod regulatur et movetur a Spiritu Sancto.
[39] 2-II 24. 2.
[40] Early in his treatment of charity, at 2-II 23. 2, Thomas explicitly disagrees with the statement from Lombard's *Sentences*: 'caritas non est aliquid creatum in anima, sed est ipse Spiritus Sanctus mentem inhabitans', because this would be contrary to the nature of the voluntary, and undermines the nature of love. On the way in which Thomas pursues a doctrine of love faithful to the intention of Augustine but founded on an Aristotelian view of nature see G. Hibbert, 'Created and Uncreated Charity: A Study of the Doctrinal and Historical Context of St. Thomas' Teaching on the Nature of Charity', *RTAM* 31 (1964), 63–84.

Spirit . . . and that affinity or connaturality for divine things is caused in us by that charity which unites us to God, because he who joins with God is one spirit with him (1 Cor. 6: 17). Thus the wisdom which is a gift has its cause in the will, namely love; but it has its essence in the intellect, whose function is to judge rightly.[41]

Participation in the divine life by the Holy Spirit is the principle of ultimate unity between intellect and will, and between wisdom, prudence, and charity.

It is not too much to claim that Thomas has provided an account of prudence which covers both the natural and supernatural orders, developed with a view to being consistent with principles drawn from Aristotle's metaphysics and psychology, but which is also profoundly biblical and theological. Thomas Aquinas has developed a teaching on practical reasoning and its perfecting in the virtue of prudence which is rooted in Aristotle yet able to be integrated with Christian theology in a profound way. It is a view of the human person, responsible in freedom for his actions, guided by the created order, and perfected in grace by sharing in the knowledge and love of God.

---

[41] *ST* 2-II 45. 2: Sic igitur circa res divinas ex rationis inquisitione rectum iudicium habere pertinet ad sapientiam quae est virtus intellectualis: sed rectum iudicium habere de eis secundum quamdam connaturalitatem ad ipsa pertinet ad sapientiam secundum quod donum est Spiritus Sancti . . . Huiusmodi autem compassio sive connaturalitas ad res divinas fit per caritatem, quae quidem unit nos Deo: secundum illud I *ad Cor.*, *Qui adhaeret Deo unus spiritus est.* Sic igitur sapientia quae est donum causam quidem habet in voluntate, scilicet caritatem: sed essentiam habet in intellectu, cuius actus est recte iudicare.

BIBLIOGRAPHY OF WORKS CITED

ARISTOTLE

Greek texts from the series of Oxford Classical Texts were consulted; for medieval Latin translations, *Aristoteles Latinus*, xxvi. 1–3, ed. R.-A. Gauthier (Leiden, 1972–4); for English translations, reference made mostly to J. Barnes (ed.), *The Complete Works of Aristotle: The Revised Oxford Translation* (Princeton, NJ, 1984).

Other translations used:

De Anima, Books II and III, trans. D. W. Hamlyn (Oxford, 1968).
Eudemian Ethics, *Books I, II, and VIII*, trans. with commentary by M. Woods (Oxford, 1982).

THOMAS AQUINAS

Texts are cited from the Leonine edition of *Opera Omnia* (Rome, 1882–) where available, though the orthography of the most recent editions has not always been followed.

Other editions used:

Expositio et lectura super Epistolas Pauli Apostoli, Marietti edn., 2 vols. (Rome, 1953).
Expositio super Dionysium De divinis nominibus, Marietti edn. (Rome, 1950).
Expositio super librum Boethii de Trinitate, ed. B. Decker (Leiden, 1955).
In Librum Beati Dionysii De divinis nominibus expositio, Marietti edn. (Rome, 1950).
Quaestiones de anima, ed. J. H. Robb (Toronto, 1968).
Quaestiones Disputatae, Marietti edn., 2 vols. (Rome, 1964–5).
Scriptum super libros Sententiarum, ed. Mandonnet and Moos, 4 vols. (Paris, 1929–47).
Summa Theologiae, Latin text with English trans., Blackfriars edn. (London, 1964–74).

OTHER PRIMARY SOURCES

Albertus Magnus, *Opera Omnia*, ed. A. Borgnet, 38 vols. (Paris, 1890–9).
—— *Opera Omnia*, ed. Albertus Magnus Institute (Cologne, 1951–).
Augustine, *De diversis quaestionibus octoginta tribus*, ed. A. Mutzenbecher (*Corpus Christianorum*, 44A; Turnholt, 1975).

—— *De Trinitate*, ed. W. J. Mountain (*Corpus Christianorum*, 50; Turnholt, 1968).

Bonaventure, *Opera Omnia*, 10 vols. (Quaracchi, 1882–1902).

Chartularium Universitatis Parisiensis, eds. H. Denifle and A. Chatelain (Paris, 1891–9).

John Damascene, *De fide orthodoxa*, trans. Burgundio of Pisa and Cerbanus, ed. E. M. Buytaert (Franciscan Inst. Publications, Text ser. no. 8; St Bonaventure, NY, 1955).

Nemesius, *De natura hominis*, trans. Burgundio of Pisa, ed. G. Verbeke and J. R. Moncho (*Corpus Latinum Commentariorum in Aristotelem Graecorum*, suppl. 1; Leiden, 1975).

Peter Lombard, *Sententiae in IV Libris Distinctae* (Grottaeferrata, 1971).

Pseudo-Dionysius, 'De divinis nominibus', *PG* iii, 585–996.

Suarez, F., *Opera Omnia*, 28 vols. (Paris, 1856–78).

Versor, Johannes, *Quaestiones super libros ethicorum Aristotelis* (Cologne, 1494; reprint, Frankfurt, 1967).

SECONDARY SOURCES

ABBA, G., *Lex et Virtus: Studi sull'evoluzione della dottrina morale di san Tommaso d'Aquino* (Biblioteca di scienze religiose, 56; Rome, 1983).

ACKRILL, J. L., 'Aristotle on "Good" and the Categories', in Barnes *et al.*, *Articles on Aristotle*, ii. 17–24.

AERTSEN, J., 'The Convertibility of Being and Good in St. Thomas Aquinas', *New Scholasticism*, 59 (1985), 449–70.

—— *Nature and Creature: Thomas Aquinas's Way of Thought* (Studien und Texte zur Geistesgeschichte des Mittelalters, 21; Leiden, 1988).

ALLAN, D. J., 'Aristotle's Account of the Origin of Moral Principles', in J. Barnes *et al.* (eds.), *Articles on Aristotle*, ii. 72–8.

—— 'A New Commentary on the Ethics' 'review of Gauthier and Jolif, *L'Éthique à Nicomaque*', *Classical Review*, 12 (1962), 135–9.

—— 'The Practical Syllogism', in *Autour d'Aristote: Recueil d'études de philosophie ancienne et médiévale offert à Msgr. A. Mansion* (Louvain, 1955), 325–40.

ANSCOMBE, G. E. M., 'Action, Intention, and "Double Effect"', *PACPA* 56 (1982), 12–25.

—— *Intention*[2] (Oxford, 1963).

—— 'Modern Moral Philsophy', *Philosophy*, 33 (1958), 1–19.

ARMSTRONG, A. H. (ed.), *The Cambridge History of Later Greek and Early Medieval Philosophy* (Cambridge, 1967).

AUBENQUE, P., 'La Prudence aristotélicienne, porte-t-elle sur la fin ou sur les moyens?', *Revue des études grecques*, 78 (1965), 40–51.

—— *La Prudence chez Aristote*[2] (Paris, 1976).

AUMANN, J., 'Thomistic Evaluation of Love and Charity', Angelicum, 55 (1978), 534–56.

BARNES, J., SCHOFIELD, M., and SORABJI, R. (eds.), Articles on Aristotle, ii. Ethics and Politics (London, 1977).

BEHA, H. M., 'Matthew of Aquasparta's Cognition Theory', Franciscan Studies, 20 (1960), 161–204; 21 (1961) 1–79, 383–465.

BEHNEN, M., De virtute prudentiae apud s. Bonaventuram (Studi e testi Francescani, 32; Rome, 1965).

BILLUART, C.-R., Summa Sancti Thomae Hodiernis Academiarum Moribus Accommodata (8 vols.; Paris, 1876).

BOURKE, V. J., 'Aquinas and Recent Theories of Right', PACPA 48 (1974), 187–95.

—— 'The Background of Aquinas' Synderesis Principle', in Gerson, Graceful Reason, 345–60.

—— Ethics: A Textbook in Moral Philosophy (New York, 1966).

—— 'Is Aquinas a Natural Law Ethicist?', Monist, 58 (1974), 52–66.

—— 'The Nicomachean Ethics and Thomas Aquinas', St Thomas Aquinas, 1274–1974: Commemorative Studies (Toronto, 1974), i. 239–59.

—— 'Right Reason in Contemporary Ethics', Thomist, 38 (1974), 106–24.

—— Will in Western Thought: An Historico-Critical Survey (New York, 1964).

BOYLE, J. M., Jr., 'Praeter Intentionem in Aquinas', Thomist, 42 (1978), 649–65.

BRENNAN, R. E. (ed.), Essays in Thomism (New York, 1942).

BROWN, O., Natural Rectitude and Divine Law in Aquinas (Toronto, 1981).

BUJO, B., Moralautonomie und Normenfindung bei Thomas von Aquin: Unter Einbeziehung der neutestamentlichen Kommentare (Paderborn, 1979).

BURNYEAT, M. F., 'Aristotle on Learning to be Good', in Rorty, Essays on Aristotle's Ethics, 69–92.

CALDERA, R.-T., Le Jugement par inclination chez saint Thomas d'Aquin (Paris, 1980).

CATHREIN, V., 'Quo sensu secundum S. Thomam ratio sit regula actuum humanorum?', Gregorianum, 5 (1924), 584–94.

—— 'Utrum in omni peccato occurrat error vel ignorantia', Gregorianum, 11 (1930), 553–67.

CHARLES, D., Aristotle's Philosophy of Action (London, 1984).

CHATILLON, J., 'L'Exercice du pouvoir doctrinal dans la chrétienté du XIIIe siècle: le cas d'Étienne Tempier', in Le Pouvoir (Institut Catholique de Paris, Faculté de philosophie, Philosophie, 3; Paris, 1978), 13–45.

CHILDRESS, M., 'The Prudential Judgment', PACPA 22 (1947), 141–51.

CHRISTMANN, H. M., Thomas von Aquin als Theologe der Liebe (Heidelberg, 1958).

CLARK, R. W., 'Aquinas on Intentions', *Thomist*, 40 (1976), 303–10.

COOPER, J. M., *Reason and Human Good in Aristotle* (Cambridge, Mass., 1975).

COPLESTON, F., *A History of Philosophy*, ii. *Medieval Philosophy: Augustine to Scotus*, (Westminster, Md., 1950).

COTTIER, G. M.-M., 'Intellectus et Ratio', *RT* 88 (1988), 215–28.

CRANFIELD, C. E. B., *A Critical and Exegetical Commentary on the Epistle to the Romans*, vol. i (Edinburgh, 1985).

CROSBY, J., 'Are Being and Good Really Convertible? A Phenomenological Inquiry', *New Scholasticism*, 57 (1983), 465–500.

CROWE, M. B., 'Synderesis and the Notion of Law in Saint Thomas', in *L'Homme et son destin d'après les penseurs du moyen âge: Actes du premier congrès international de philosophie médiévale* (Paris, 1960), 601–9.

—— 'The Term *Synderesis* and the Scholastics', *Irish Theol. Quart.* 23 (1956), 151–64, 228–45.

DAHL, N. O., *Practical Reason, Aristotle, and Weakness of the Will* (Minneapolis, 1984).

D'ARCY, E., *Conscience and its Right to Freedom* (London, 1961).

—— *Human Acts: An Essay in their Moral Evaluation* (Oxford, 1963).

DAVIDSON, D., *Essays on Actions and Events* (Oxford, 1980).

DAVITT, T. E., *The Nature of Law* (St Louis, 1951).

DELHAYE, P., 'La "loi nouvelle" dans l'enseignement de saint Thomas', in *San Tommaso e la filosofia del diritto oggi* (Studi Tomistici, 4; Vatican, 1975), 73–103.

DEMAN, T. H., 'Le "Liber de bona fortuna" dans la théologie de s. Thomas D'Aquin', *RSPT* 17 (1928), 38–58.

—— 'Pour une restauration de la vertu de prudence', in A.-M. Henry (ed.), *Prudence chrétienne* (Paris, 1948), 21–31.

—— 'Le "précepte" de la prudence chez saint Thomas d'Aquin', *RTAM* 20 (1953), 40–59.

—— *La Prudence: Somme théologique, 2a-2ae, questions 47–56*, with notes and appendices (Paris, 1949).

DEWAN, L., 'The Real Distinction between Intellect and Will', *Angelicum*, 57 (1980), 557–93.

—— 'St. Thomas and the Causality of God's Goodness', *Laval théologique et philosophique*, 34 (1978), 291–304.

—— 'St. Thomas and the Integration of Knowledge into Being', *International Philos. Quart.* 24 (1984), 383–93.

DINGJAN, F., *Discretio: Les Origines patristiques et monastiques de la doctrine sur la prudence chez saint Thomas d'Aquin* (Assen, 1967).

DOBLER, E., *Nemesius von Emesa und die Psychologie des menschlichen Aktes bei Thomas von Aquin (ST Ia IIae, qq. 6–17): Eine quellenanalytische Studie* (Lucerne, 1950)

DONAGAN, A., *Human Ends and Human Actions: An Exploration in St Thomas' Treatment* (Milwaukee, 1985).
—— 'Thomas Aquinas on Human Action', *CHLMP* 642–54.
DUMONT, S., 'The Necessary Connection of Moral Virtue to Prudence according to John Duns Scotus—Revisited', *RTAM* 55 (1988), 184–206.
DUROUX, B., *La Psychologie de la foi chez saint Thomas d'Aquin* (Tournai, 1963).
EFFLER, R., *John Duns Scotus and the Principle 'Omne quod movetur ab alio movetur'* (Franciscan Inst. Publications, Phil. Series, 15; St Bonaventure, NY, 1962).
ELDERS, L., *Autour de saint Thomas d'Aquin: Recueil d'études sur sa pensée philosophique et théologique* (Paris, 1987).
—— and HEDWIG K., (eds.), *Lex et Libertas: Freedom and Law According to St. Thomas Aquinas* (Studi Tomistici, 30; Vatican, 1987).
ENDRES, J., 'Anteil der Klugheit am Erkennen des konkret Wahren und am Wollen des wahrhaft Guten', *Studia Moralia*, 1 (1963), 221–63.
ESCHMANN, I. T., 'St. Thomas's Approach to Moral Philosophy', *PACPA* 31 (1957), 25–33.
ETHERIDGE, S., 'Aristotle's Practical Syllogism and Necessity', *Philologus*, 112 (1968), 20–42.
EVANS, J. L., 'Error and the Will', *Philosophy*, 38 (1963), 136–48.
FABRO, C., 'Le "Liber de Bona Fortuna" chez saint Thomas', *RT* 88 (1988), 556–72.
FALANGA, A. J., *Charity the Form of the Virtues according to Saint Thomas* (Washington, DC, 1948).
FINNIS, J., *Fundamentals of Ethics* (Oxford, 1983).
—— 'Natural Inclinations and Natural Rights: Deriving "Ought" from "Is" according to Aquinas', in Elders and Hedwig, *Lex et Libertas*, 43–55.
—— *Natural Law and Natural Rights* (Oxford, 1980).
—— 'Object and Intention in Moral Judgments according to Aquinas', *Thomist*, 55 (1991), 1–27.
FUCHS, J., *Personal Responsibility and Christian Morality* (Washington, DC, 1983).
FURGER, F., *Gewissen und Klugheit in der katholischen Moraltheologie der letzten Jahrzehnte* (Lucerne, 1965).
—— 'Prudence and Moral Change', trans. T. L. Westow, in F. Bockle (ed.), *The Social Message of the Gospels* (Concilium, 35; New York, 1968), 119–31.
GARCEAU, B., *Judicium: Vocabulaire, sources, doctrine de saint Thomas d'Aquin* (Montreal, 1968).

GARDEIL, A., 'Acte humain', *DTC* i. 339–46.

—— 'Élection, acte humain', *DTC* iv. 2242–3.

GARRIGOU-LAGRANGE, R., 'Du caractère métaphysique de la théologie morale de saint Thomas: En particulier dans les rapports de la prudence et de la conscience', *RT* 8 (1925), 341–55.

—— 'La Prudence: Sa place dans l'organisme des vertus', *RT* 9 (1926), 411–26.

GAUTHIER, R.-A., *La Morale d'Aristote*³ (Paris, 1973).

—— review of Jaffa, *Thomism and Aristotelianism*, *BT* 9 (1954–6), 157–9.

—— 'Saint Maxime le Confesseur et la psychologie de l'acte humain', *RTAM* 21 (1954), 51–100.

—— and JOLIF, J.Y., *Aristote: L'Éthique à Nicomaque*² (Louvain, 1970).

GEACH, P., *The Virtues* (Cambridge, 1977).

GEIGER, L.-B., *Le Problème de l'amour chez saint Thomas d'Aquin* (Paris, 1952).

GERHARD, W. A., 'The Intellectual Virtue of Prudence', *Thomist*, 8 (1945), 413–56.

GERSON, L. P. (ed.), *Graceful Reason: Essays in Ancient and Medieval Philosophy Presented to Joseph Owens, CSSR* (Toronto, 1983).

GILBY, T., 'Prudence', *NCE* xi. 925–8.

—— 'Thought, Volition and the Organism', *Thomist*, 2 (1940), 1–13.

GILLEMAN, G., *The Primacy of Charity in Moral Theology*, trans. W. F. Ryan and A. Vachon (Westminster, Md., 1961).

GILSON, E., *The Christian Philosophy of Saint Augustine*, trans. L. E. M. Lynch (New York, 1960).

—— *History of Christian Philosophy in the Middle Ages* (New York, 1955).

—— 'Pourquoi saint Thomas a critiqué saint Augustin', *AHDLMA* 1 (1926), 1–127.

—— *Saint Thomas moraliste*² (Paris, 1974).

GREDT, J., *Elementa Philosophiae Aristotelico-Thomisticae*⁶ (Freiburg im Breisgau, 1932).

GRISEZ, G., 'The First Principle of Practical Reason: A Commentary on the *Summa Theologiae* 1-2, Question 94, Article 2', *Natural Law Forum*, 10 (1965), 168–201.

—— 'The Natural End of Man', *NCE* v. 132–8.

—— *The Way of the Lord Jesus*, i. *Christian Moral Principles* (Chicago, 1983).

GUNDLACH, G., 'Klugheit als Prinzip des Handelns', *Gregorianum*, 23 (1942), 238–54.

GUTHRIE, W. K. C., *A History of Greek Philosophy*, vi. *Aristotle: An Encounter* (Cambridge, 1981).

HARDIE, W. F. R., *Aristotle's Ethical Theory*² (Oxford, 1980).

HARE, R. M., *Moral Thinking: Its Levels, Method, and Point* (Oxford, 1981).

HÄRING, B., *The Law of Christ*, i. *General Moral Theology*, trans. E. G. Kaiser (Westminster, Md., 1961).

HARTMANN, H. E., 'St. Thomas and Prudence', Ph.D. thesis (Univ. of Toronto, 1979).

HENRY, A.-M. (ed.), *Prudence chrétienne* (Cahiers de la vie spirituelle; Paris, 1948).

HERING, H. M., 'Quomodo solvendi sunt casus: recurrendo ad sola principia an etiam ad prudentiam?', *Angelicum*, 18 (1941), 311–35.

HESSEN, J., *Augustins metaphysik der Erkenntnis* (Leiden, 1960).

HIBBERT, G., 'Created and Uncreated Charity: A Study of the Doctrinal and Historical Context of St. Thomas' Teaching on the Nature of Charity', *RTAM* 31 (1964), 63–84.

HIBBS, T. S., 'Against a Cartesian Reading of *Intellectus* in Aquinas', *Modern Schoolman*, 66 (1988), 55–69.

HILDEBRAND, D. VON, 'The Role of Affectivity in Morality', *PACPA* 32 (1958), 85–95.

HISSETTE, R., 'Étienne Tempier et ses condamnations', *RTAM* 47 (1980), 231–70.

HITTINGER, R., 'When it is More Excellent to Love than to Know: The Other Side of Thomistic "Realism"', *PACPA* 57 (1983), 171–9.

HOENEN, P., *Reality and Judgment according to St. Thomas*, trans. H. F. Tiblier (Chicago, 1952).

HÖNES, M., *Ens et bonum convertuntur: Eine Deutung des scholastischen Axioms unter besonderer Berücksichtigung der Metaphysik und Ethik des hl. Thomas von Aquin*, Inaugural-Dissertation, Albert Ludwigs University (Freiburg im Breisgau, 1968).

HORVATH, T., *Caritas est in Ratione: Die Lehre des hl. Thomas über die Einheit der intellektiven und affektiven Begnadung des Menschen* (BGPTM 41. 3; Münster, 1966).

ILIEN, A., *Wesen und Funktion der Liebe bei Thomas von Aquin* (Freiburg im Breisgau, 1975).

INWOOD, B., *Ethics and Human Action in Early Stoicism* (Oxford, 1985).

IRWIN, T. H., 'The Scope of Deliberation: A Conflict in Aquinas', *Review of Metaphysics*, 44 (1990), 21–42.

ISAAC, J., 'La Notion de dialectique chez saint Thomas', *RSPT* 34 (1950), 481–506.

JACOB, J., *Passiones: Ihr Wesen und ihre Anteilnahme an der Vernunft nach dem hl. Thomas von Aquin* (Mödling, 1958).

JAFFA, H. V., *Thomism and Aristotelianism: A Study of the Commentary by Thomas Aquinas on the Nicomachean Ethics* (Chicago, 1952).

JOACHIM, H. H., *Aristotle: The Nicomachean Ethics* (Oxford, 1951).

JORDAN, M., 'Aquinas's Construction of a Moral Account of the Passions', *FZPT* 33 (1986), 71–97.

KEELER, L. W., *The Problem of Error from Plato to Kant* (Analecta Gregoriana, 6; Rome, 1934).

KEENAN, J. F., 'Distinguishing Charity as Goodness and Prudence as Rightness: A Key to Thomas's *Secunda Pars*', *Thomist*, 56 (1992), 407–26.

KELLY, M. J., 'Agency in Aquinas', *Laval théologique et philosophique*, 33 (1977), 33–7.

KENNEDY, L. A., 'The Nature of the Human Intellect according to St Albert the Great', *Modern Schoolman*, 37 (1960), 121–37.

KENNY, A., *The Anatomy of the Soul: Historical Essays in the Philosophy of Mind* (Oxford, 1973).

—— (ed.), *Aquinas: A Collection of Critical Essays* (London, 1969).

—— *The Aristotelian Ethics: A Study of the Relationship between the Eudemian and Nicomachean Ethics of Aristotle* (Oxford, 1978).

—— *Aristotle on the Perfect Life* (Oxford, 1992).

—— *Aristotle's Theory of the Will* (London, 1979).

—— 'Intellect and Imagination in Aquinas', in Kenny (ed.), *Aquinas*, 273–96.

—— 'Practical Inference', *Analysis*, 26 (1965–6), 65–75.

—— 'The Practical Syllogism and Incontinence', *Phronesis*, 11 (1966), 163–84.

—— *Will, Freedom, and Power* (Oxford, 1975).

KERR, F., 'Charity as Friendship', in B. Davies (ed.), *Language, Meaning and God: Essays in Honour of Herbert McCabe, OP* (London, 1987).

KLUBERTANZ, G., *The Philosophy of Human Nature* (New York, 1953).

KLUXEN, W., *Philosophische Ethik bei Thomas von Aquin* (Mainz, 1964).

KÜHN, U., *Via Caritatis: Theologie des Gesetzes bei Thomas von Aquin* (Göttingen, 1965).

KUKSEWICZ, Z., 'Criticisms of Aristotelian Psychology and the Augustinian-Aristotelian Synthesis', *CHLMP* 623–8.

LADRIÈRE, J. A., 'Reasoning', *NCE* xii. 119–21.

LAPORTA, J., *La Destinée de la nature humaine selon Thomas d'Aquin* (Études de philos. médiévale, 55; Paris, 1965).

—— 'Pour trouver le sens exact des termes *appetitus naturalis, desiderium naturale, amor naturalis*, etc. chez saint Thomas d'Aquin', *AHDLMA* 40 (1973), 37–95.

LEBACQZ, J., *Libre Arbitre et jugement* (Museum Lessianum, section philosophique, 47; Paris, 1960).

LECLERCQ, J., *La Philosophie morale de s. Thomas devant la pensée contemporaine* (Bibliothèque philosophique de Louvain, 15; Louvain, 1955).

LEHU, L., 'Si la "recta ratio" de s. Thomas signifie la conscience', *RT* 8 (1925), 159–66.

LITT, T., *Les Corps célestes dans l'univers de saint Thomas d'Aquin* (Philosophes médiévaux, 7; Louvain, 1963).

LONERGAN, B., *Verbum: Word and Idea in Aquinas*, ed. D. Burrell (Notre Dame, 1967).

LOTTIN, O., 'Liberté humaine et motion divine', *RTAM* 7 (1935), 52–69, 156–73.

—— 'Le Libre Arbitre chez saint Thomas', *RT* 12 (1929), 400–30.

—— 'La Preuve de la liberté humaine chez saint Thomas d'Aquin', *RTAM* 23 (1956), 323–30.

—— 'Psychologie de l'acte humain', *RTAM* 29 (1962), 250–67.

—— *Psychologie et morale aux XIIe et XIIIe siècles* (Gembloux, 1942–60).

—— 'Raison théorique, raison pratique et volonté chez les précurseurs de saint Thomas d'Aquin', *RTAM* 28 (1961), 242–50.

LUMBRERAS, P., 'Ethica situationis et doctrina Aquinatis', *Angelicum*, 35 (1958), 139–58.

LYONS, W., *Emotion* (Cambridge, 1980).

McANDREW, P. J., 'The Theory of Divine Illumination in St Bonaventura', *New Scholasticism*, 6 (1932), 32–50.

McCABE, H., 'Aquinas on Good Sense', *New Blackfriars*, 67 (1987), 419–31.

—— 'The Structure of the Judgment: A Reply to Fr. Wall, O.P.', *Thomist*, 19 (1956), 232–8.

McGINNIS, R., *The Wisdom of Love: A Study in the Psycho-Metaphysics of Love according to the Principles of St Thomas* (Rome, 1951).

McINERNY, R., 'Action Theory in St. Thomas Aquinas', in A. Zimmerman (ed.), *Thomas von Aquin*, 13–22.

—— 'Prudence and Conscience', *Thomist*, 38 (1974), 291–305.

MACINTYRE, A., *After Virtue: A Study in Moral Theory*² (Notre Dame, 1985).

—— *Three Rival Versions of Moral Enquiry* (Notre Dame, 1990).

MAGUIRE, D. C., '*Ratio Practica* and the Intellectualistic Fallacy', *Journal of Religious Ethics*, 10 (1982), 22–39.

MAHONEY, E. P., 'Sense, Intellect, and Imagination in Albert, Thomas, and Siger', *CHLMP* 602–22.

MAHONEY, J., *The Making of Moral Theology: A Study of the Roman Catholic Tradition* (Oxford, 1987).

—— *Seeking the Spirit: Essays in Moral and Pastoral Theology* (London, 1981).

MAKIN, S., 'Aquinas, Natural Tendencies, and Natural Kinds', *New Scholasticism*, 63 (1989), 253–74.

MARKUS, R. A., 'Marius Victorinus and Augustine', in Armstrong, *Cambridge History of Later Greek and Early Medieval Philosophy*, 331–419.

MAURER, A., *Medieval Philosophy*² (Toronto, 1982).

MERCKEN, P., 'Transformations of the Ethics of Aristotle in the Moral Philosophy of Thomas Aquinas', in *Tommaso d'Aquino nel suo settimo centenario: Atti del Congresso Internazionale* (Naples, 1974), v. *L'agire morale*, 151–62.

MERKELBACH, B.-H., *Summa theologiae moralis ad mentem sanctae Thomae*[3] (Paris, 1938).

MICHAUD-QUANTIN, P., 'La Classification des puissances de l'âme au XIIe siècle', *Revue du moyen âge latin*, 5 (1949), 15–34.

—— *La Psychologie de l'activité chez Albert le Grand* (Bibliothèque Thomiste, 36; Paris, 1966).

MICHEL, E., *Nullus potest amare aliquid incognitum: Ein Beitrag zur Frage des Intellektualismus bei Thomas von Aquin* (Studia Freiburgensia, 57; Fribourg, 1979).

MONTAGNES, B., 'Les Deux Fonctions de la sagesse: Ordonner et juger', *RSPT* 53 (1969), 675–86.

MORISSET, B., 'Le Syllogisme prudentiel', *Laval théologique et philosophique*, 19 (1963), 62–92.

MORISSET, P., 'Prudence et fin selon saint Thomas', *Sciences ecclésiastiques*, 15 (1963), 73–98; 439–58.

NAUS, J., *The Nature of the Practical Intellect according to St Thomas Aquinas* (Analecta Gregoriana, 108; Rome, 1959).

NELSON, D. M., *The Priority of Prudence: Virtue and Natural Law in Thomas Aquinas and the Implications for Modern Ethics* (University Park, Pa., 1992).

NIJENHUIS, J., *The Structure of the Judgment according to Aquinas* (Rome, 1971).

NOBLE, H. D., 'Prudence', *DTC* xiii. 1023–76.

NUSSBAUM, M. C., *Aristotle's De Motu Animalium*, ed. with trans. and interpretive essays (Princeton, 1978).

NYGREN, A., *Agape and Eros*, trans. P. S. Watson (London, 1932–9).

O'DONOVAN, O. M. T., '*Usus* and *Fruitio* in Augustine: *De Doctrina Christiana* I', *Journal of Theol. Studies*[2] 33 (1982), 361–97.

OESTERLE, J. A., *Ethics: The Introduction to Moral Science* (Englewood Cliffs, NJ, 1957).

—— 'Human Act', *NCE* vii. 206–9.

O'NEIL, C. J., *Imprudence in St Thomas Aquinas* (Milwaukee, 1955).

—— 'Is Prudence Love?', *Monist*, 58 (1974), 119–39.

—— 'Prudence, the Incommunicable Wisdom', in R. E. Brennan (ed.), *Essays in Thomism*, 187–204.

OUWERKERK, C. A. J. VAN, *Caritas et ratio: Étude sur le double principe de la vie morale chrétienne d'après s. Thomas d'Aquin* (Nijmegen, 1956).

OWENS, J., 'The Ethical Universal in Aristotle', *Studia Moralia*, 3 (1965), 27–47.

—— 'Human Reason and the Moral Order in Aquinas', *Studia Moralia*, 28 (1990), 155–73.

—— 'Judgment and Truth in Aquinas', *Mediaeval Studies*, 32 (1970), 138–58.

PAPADIS, D., *Die Rezeption der Nikomachischen Ethik des Aristoteles bei Thomas von Aquin: Eine vergleichende Untersuchung* (Frankfurt, 1980).

PAYER, P. J., 'Prudence and the Principles of Natural Law: A Medieval Development', *Speculum*, 54 (1979), 55–70.

PEGHAIRE, J., *Intellectus et ratio selon s. Thomas d'Aquin* (Paris, 1936).

PEGIS, A. C., *At the Origins of the Thomistic Notion of Man* (New York, 1963).

—— *St. Thomas and the Problem of the Soul* (Toronto, 1934).

PIEPER, J., *Traktat über die Klugheit* (Munich, 1949).

—— *Die Wirklichkeit und das Gute* (Munich, 1949).

PINCKAERS, S., 'Le Rôle de la fin dans l'action morale selon saint Thomas', *RSPT* 45 (1961), 393–421.

—— *Les Sources de la morale chrétienne: Sa méthode, son contenu, son histoire* (Études d'éthique chrétienne, 14; Paris, 1985).

—— 'La Structure de l'acte humain suivant s. Thomas', *RT* 55 (1955), 393–412.

PORTER, J., '*De Ordine Caritatis*: Charity, Friendship, and Justice in Thomas Aquinas' *Summa Theologiae*', *Thomist*, 53 (1989), 197–213.

—— *The Recovery of Virtue: The Relevance of Aquinas for Christian Ethics* (Louisville, Ky., 1990).

POTTS, T., *Conscience in Medieval Philosophy* (Cambridge, 1980).

PRENTICE, R. P., *The Psychology of Love according to St Bonaventure* (Franciscan Inst. Publications, phil. series, 6; Bonaventure, NY, 1957).

PREUS, A., 'Intention and Impulse in Aristotle and the Stoics', *Apeiron*, 15 (1981), 48–58.

PRÜMMER, M., *Manuale Theologiae Moralis secundum principia Sancti Thomae Aquinatis* (Freiburg im Breisgau, 1928).

PUNZO, V., 'Natural Law and the Normative Function of Reason', *PACPA* 54 (1980), 197–206.

QUINN, J. F., *The Historical Constitution of St. Bonaventure's Philosophy* (Toronto, 1973).

—— 'The Moral Philosophy of St. Bonaventure', in R. W. Shahan and F. J. Kovach (eds.), *Bonaventure and Aquinas: Enduring Philosophers* (Norman, Okla., 1976), 25–56.

RAZ, J. (ed.), *Practical Reasoning* (Oxford, 1978).

REILLY, G. C., *The Psychology of Saint Albert the Great Compared with that of Saint Thomas* (Washington, DC, 1934).

REILLY, R. P., 'Weakness of Will: The Thomistic Advance', *PACPA* 48 (1974), 198–207.

REILLY, R. P., 'Will and the Concept of a Person', *PACPA* 53 (1979), 71–7.

RHONHEIMER, M., *Natur als Grundlage der Moral: Die personale Struktur des Naturgesetzes bei Thomas von Aquin: Eine Auseinandersetzung mit autonomer und teleologischer Ethik* (Innsbruck, 1986).

RIESENHUBER, K., *Die Transzendenz der Freiheit zum Guten: Der Wille in der Anthropologie und Metaphysik des Thomas von Aquin* (Pullacher philosophische Forschungen, 8; Munich, 1971).

—— 'Der Wandel des Freiheitsverständnisses von Thomas von Aquin zur frühen Neuzeit', *Rivista di filosofia neo-scolastica*, 66 (1974), 946–74.

RIST, J. M., 'Prohairesis: Proclus, Plotinus, et alii', in *De Jamblique à Proclus* (Entretiens sur l'antiquité classique, 21; Geneva, 1974), 103–17.

ROHMER, J., 'Synderèse', *DTC* xiv. 2992–6.

ROMITI, J., *De processu evolutivo doctrinae de actu humano completo in operibus Sanctae Thomae Aquinatis* (Milan, 1949).

RORTY, A. O. (ed.), *Essays on Aristotle's Ethics* (Berkeley, Calif., 1980).

ROSS, W. D., *Aristotle*⁵ (London, 1949).

ROSSNER, W. L., 'An Inclination to an Intellectually Known God: The Question of the Existence of Intellectual Love', *Modern Schoolman*, 52 (1974), 65–92.

ROUSSELOT, P., *The Intellectualism of Saint Thomas*, trans. J. E. O'Mahony (London, 1935).

SANTAS, G., 'Aristotle on Practical Inference, the Explanation of Action, and Akrasia', *Phronesis*, 14 (1969), 162–89.

SCHLÜTER, D., 'Der Wille und das Gute bei Thomas von Aquin', *FZPT* 18 (1971), 88–136.

SCHOCKENHOFF, E., *Bonum Hominis: Die anthropologischen und theologischen Grundlagen der Tugendethik des Thomas von Aquin* (Tübinger Theologische Studien, 28; Mainz, 1987).

SEARLE, J. R., *Intentionality: An Essay in the Philosophy of Mind* (Cambridge, 1983).

SERTILLANGES, A.-D., *La Philosophie morale de saint Thomas d'Aquin*² (Paris, 1922).

SHERMAN, N., *The Fabric of Character: Aristotle's Theory of Virtue* (Oxford, 1989).

SIEDLER, D., *Intellektualismus und Voluntarismus bei Albertus Magnus* (BGPTM 36. 2; Munster, 1941).

SIMON, Y., *Freedom of Choice*, ed. P. Wolff (New York, 1969).

—— *Practical Knowledge*, ed. R. J. Mulvaney (New York, 1991).

SIMONIN, H.-D., 'La Primauté de l'amour dans la doctrine de saint Thomas d'Aquin', *La Vie spirituelle*, 53 (1937), suppl., 129–43.

STEENBERGHEN, F. VAN, *Introduction à l'étude de la philosophie médiévale* (Philosophes médiévaux, 18; Louvain, 1974).

—— *Maître Siger de Brabant* (Philosophes médiévaux, 21; Louvain, 1977).

—— *La Philosophie au XIIIe siècle* (Philosophes médiévaux, 9; Louvain, 1966).

STEGMAN, T. D., 'Saint Thomas Aquinas and the Problem of *Akrasia*', *Modern Schoolman*, 66 (1989), 117–28.

SWITALSKI, B., *Neoplatonism and the Ethics of St Augustine* (Chicago, 1946).

THIRY, A., 'Saint Thomas et la morale d'Aristote', in *Aristote et saint Thomas d'Aquin* (Louvain, 1957), 229–58.

TYRRELL, F. M., *The Role of Assent in Judgment: A Thomistic Study* (Washington, DC, 1948).

URDANOZ, T., 'Esencia y proceso psicólogico del acto libre según santo Tomás', *Estudios filosóficos*, 2 (1953), 291–318.

URMSON, J. O., *Aristotle's Ethics* (Oxford, 1988).

VANDERMARCK, W., 'Ethics as a Key to Aquinas's Theology', *Thomist*, 40 (1976), 535–54.

VERBEKE, G., 'Le Développement de la vie volitive d'après saint Thomas', *Revue philosophique de Louvain*, 56 (1958), 5–34.

—— 'The Meaning of Potency in Aristotle', in Gerson, *Graceful Reason*, 55–73.

VEUTHEY, L., 'Les Divers Courants de la philosophie augustino-franciscaine au moyen âge', in *Scholastica ratione historico-critica instauranda: Acta Congressus Scholastici Internationalis* (Rome, 1951), 627–52.

WADELL, P., *The Primacy of Love: An Introduction to the Ethics of Thomas Aquinas* (New York, 1992).

WALKER, A. F., 'The Problem of Weakness of Will', *Nous*, 23 (1989), 653–76.

WALSH, J. J., *Aristotle's Conception of Moral Weakness* (New York, 1963).

WÉBER, E.-H., *Dialogue et dissensions entre s. Bonaventure et s. Thomas d'Aquin à Paris (1252–1273)* (Bibliothèque thomiste, 41; Paris, 1974).

WEISHEIPL, J., *Friar Thomas d'Aquino: His Life, Thought and Works*² (Washington, DC, 1983).

—— 'Thomas' Evaluation of Plato and Aristotle', *New Scholasticism*, 48 (1974), 100–24.

WESTBERG, D., 'Did Aquinas Change his Mind about the Will?', *Thomist*, forthcoming.

—— 'Reason, Will, and Legalism', *New Blackfriars*, 68 (1987), 431–6.

WIELAND, G., *Ethica-scientia practica: Die Anfänge der philosophischen Ethik im 13. Jahrhundert* (BGPTM 21; Münster, 1981).

—— 'The Reception and Interpretation of Aristotle's Ethics', *CHLMP* 657–72.

WIGGINS, D., 'Deliberation and Practical Reason', *Proc. Arist. Soc.* 76 (1975–6), 29–51.

WIPPEL, J. F., 'The Condemnations of 1270 and 1277 at Paris', *Journal of Medieval and Renaissance Studies*, 7 (1977), 169–201.

WOHLMAN, A., 'L'Élaboration des éléments aristotéliciens dans la doctrine thomiste de l'amour', *RT* 82 (1982), 247–69.

WOODS, M., *Aristotle's Eudemian Ethics* (Oxford, 1982).

YARTZ, F. J., 'Virtue as an *Ordo* in Aquinas', *Modern Schoolman*, 47 (1970), 305–20.

ZIMMERMAN, A. (ed.), *Thomas von Aquin: Werk und Wirkung im Licht neuerer Forschungen* (Miscellanea Medievalia, 19; Berlin, 1988).

INDEX

Index

Augustine:
  amor 225–6, 247, 251
  cognition theory 95–7
  illumination 69, 96–7, 99
  judgement 64 n., 200, 244
  law 229–30
  and Plato 95–6
  prudence 11, 251
  rationes aeternae 69, 99
  uti and frui 132
  virtue 247
  will and error 200
Augustinians 90, 111
  cognition theory 95–9
  and Thomism 113–15, 233
Aumann, J. 245 n.
Austen, Jane 222–3
Averroes 69, 97, 111
Avicenna 71, 97, 111

beatitude 54–5, 93, 125, 171
Beha, H. M. 113 n.
Behnen, M. 250 n.
being:
  and good 45–6, 75
  and intellect 59
  verum and bonum 53, 58
Bernard, St 81, 225
Billuart, C.-R. 120 n., 125, 130, 132, 176
Boethius 81
Bonaventure:
  action, theory of 128
  and Aristotle 98–9, 111
  cognition 98–100
  conscience 101
  free choice 107–9
  intellect 99
  Plato 99, 101
  prudence 250 n.
  synderesis 101–2
bonum intellectum 56 n., 59, 92–3, 114, 174
Bourke, V. J. 9 n., 33, 35 n., 82 n., 105 n., 120 n., 155 nn.
Boyle, J. M., Jr. 145 n.
Brown, O. 103 n.
Bujo, B. 11 n.

bulisis 127
Burnyeat, M. F. 220 n.

Cajetan 55 n., 123–5, 129, 132, 176, 183
Caldera, R.-T. 78 n., 223 n.
caritas 12, 14, 225–6, 247–8
  and amor 248
  and faith 254
  and Holy Spirit 259
  and moral virtues 249–50, 254–6
  and prudence 250–60
Cathrein, V. 6 n., 215 n.
casuistry 7, 9
causality:
  efficient 46, 59–60, 255
  final 46, 58–60, 91, 142–3, 255
  formal 46, 58–60, 76, 91, 255
certainty (certitude):
  cognition 64, 70–1, 96, 106
  and error 200
  practical reasoning 160
choice:
  Albert the Great 129
  Aristotle 16–18
  belief and desire 37–8
  not will only 83–4, 86, 123–5
  in process of action 8, 176
  and prudence 194, 216–17
  see also decision; electio; free
    choice; prohairesis
Charles, D. 22, 37, 38 n.
Chatillon, J. 112 n.
Childress, M. 6 n.
chrēsis 178
Christmann, H. M. 253 n.
Cicero 43 n., 178
Clark, R. W. 64 n.
cognition:
  and error 200
  and intention 136
  and moral theory 95, 113–15
  perfect and imperfect 50
  process 62, 68 (fig.)
  in practical reasoning 14, 56, 61–8, 131
  and volition 220–1
command, see imperium